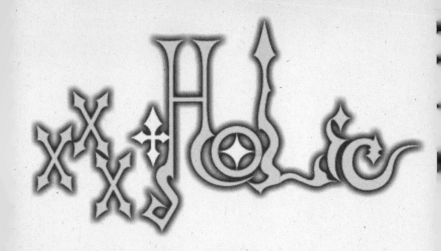

CLAMP

TRANSLATED AND ADAPTED BY
William Flanagan

LETTERED BY
Dana Hayward

BALLANTINE BOOKS · NEW YORK

xxxHOLiC crosses over with *Tsubasa*. Although it isn't necessary to read *Tsubasa* to understand the events in *xxxHOLiC*, you'll get to see the same events from different perspectives if you read both series!

xxxHOLiC, Volume 4 is a work of fiction. Names, characters, places, and incidents are the products of the author's imagination or are used fictitiously. Any resemblance to actual events, locales, or persons, living or dead, is entirely coincidental.

2005 Del Rey Books Trade Paperback Edition

Published in the United States by Del Rey Books, an imprint of The Random House Publishing Group, a division of Random House, Inc., New York.

Del Rey is a registered trademark and the Del Rey colophon is a trademark of Random House, Inc.

First published in serialization and subsequently published in book form by Kodansha Ltd. Tokyo in 2004.

ISBN 0-345-47788-X

Printed in the United States of America

Del Rey Books website address: www.delreymanga.com

6 7 8 9

Translator and Adaptor—William Flanagan
Lettering—Dana Hayward
Cover Design—David Stevenson

Contents

Honorifics Explained

Throughout the Del Rey Manga books, you will find Japanese honorifics left intact in the translations. For those not familiar with how the Japanese use honorifics, and more important, how they differ from American honorifics, we present this brief overview.

Politeness has always been a critical facet of Japanese culture. Ever since the feudal era, when Japan was a highly stratified society, use of honorifics—which can be defined as polite speech that indicates relationship or status—has played an essential role in the Japanese language. When addressing someone in Japanese, an honorific usually takes the form of a suffix attached to one's name (example: "Asuna-san"), or as a title at the end of one's name or in place of the name itself (example: "Negi-sensei," or simply "Sensei!").

Honorifics can be expressions of respect or endearment. In the context of manga and anime, honorifics give insight into the nature of the relationship between characters. Many translations into English leave out these important honorifics, and therefore distort the "feel" of the original Japanese. Because Japanese honorifics contain nuances that English honorifics lack, it is our policy at Del Rey not to translate them. Here, instead, is a guide to some of the honorifics you may encounter in Del Rey Manga.

-san: This is the most common honorific, and is equivalent to Mr., Miss, Ms., Mrs., etc. It is the all-purpose honorific and can be used in any situation where politeness is required.

-sama: This is one level higher than "-san." It is used to confer great respect.

-dono: This comes from the word "tono," which means "lord." It is an even higher level than "-sama," and confers utmost respect.

-kun: This suffix is used at the end of boys' names to express familiarity or endearment. It is also sometimes used by men among friends, or when addressing someone younger or of a lower station.

-chan: This is used to express endearment, mostly toward girls. It is also used for little boys, pets, and even among lovers. It gives a sense of childish cuteness.

Bozu: This is an informal way to refer to a boy, similar to the English term "kid" or "squirt."

Sempai: This title suggests that the addressee is one's "senior" in a group or organization. It is most often used in a school setting, where underclassmen refer to their upperclassmen as "sempai." It can also be used in the workplace, such as when a newer employee addresses an employee who has seniority in the company.

Kohai: This is the opposite of "-sempai," and is used toward underclassmen in school or newcomers in the workplace. It connotes that the addressee is of lower station.

Sensei: Literally meaning "one who has come before," this title is used for teachers, doctors, or masters of any profession or art.

[blank]: Usually forgotten in these lists, but perhaps the most significant difference between Japanese and English. The lack of honorific means that the speaker has permission to address the person in a very intimate way. Usually, only family, spouses, or very close friends have this kind of permission. Known as *yobisute*, it can be gratifying when someone who has earned the intimacy starts to call one by one's name without an honorific. But when that intimacy hasn't been earned, it can also be very insulting.

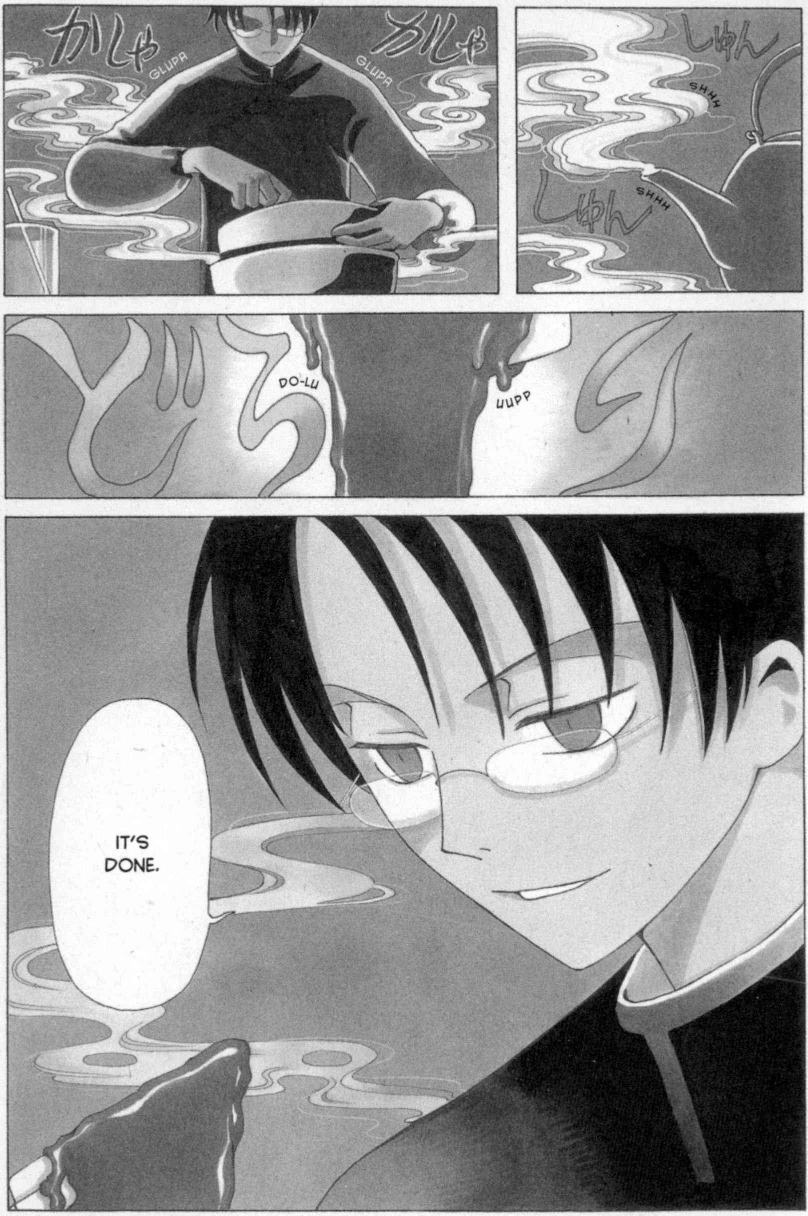
しゅん
SHHH
しゅん
SHHH
かしゃ
GLUPA
かしゃ
GLUPA
UUPP
どろ
DO-LU
IT'S DONE.

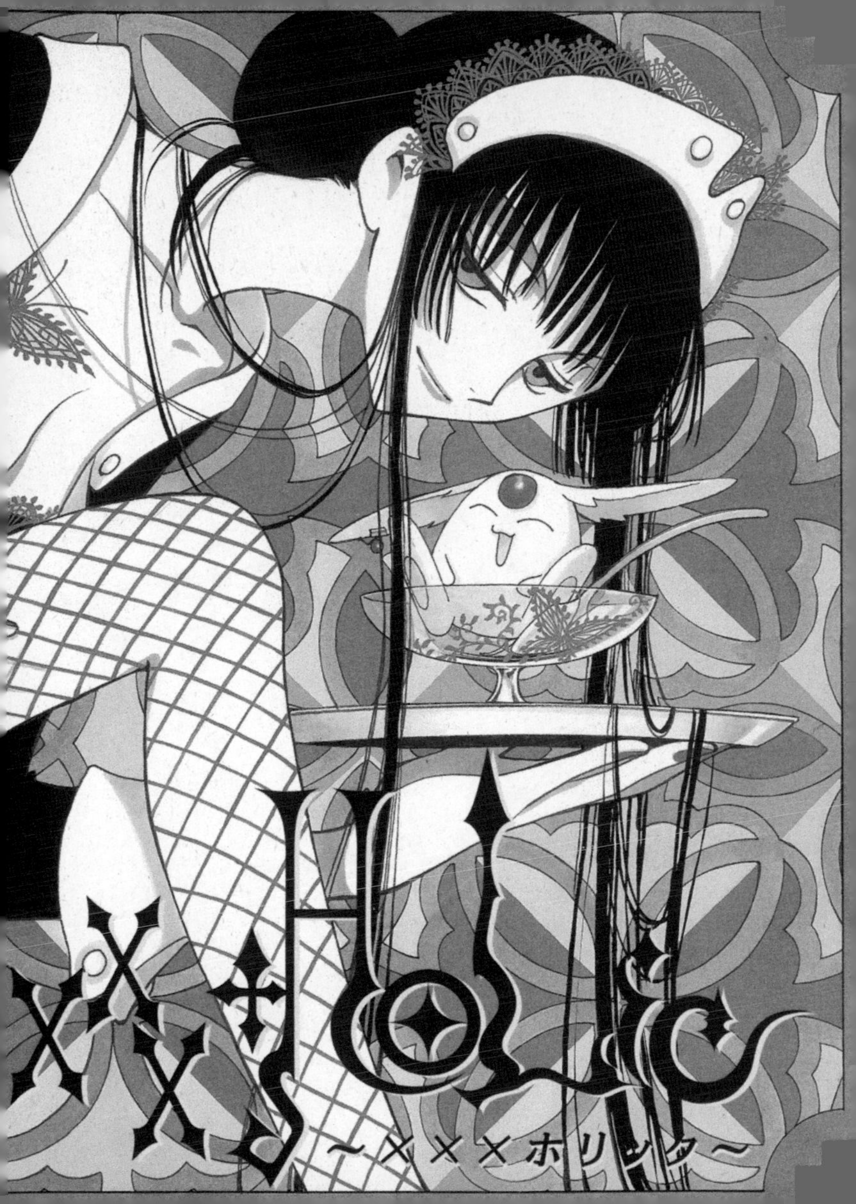
xxxHolic
〜×××ホリック〜

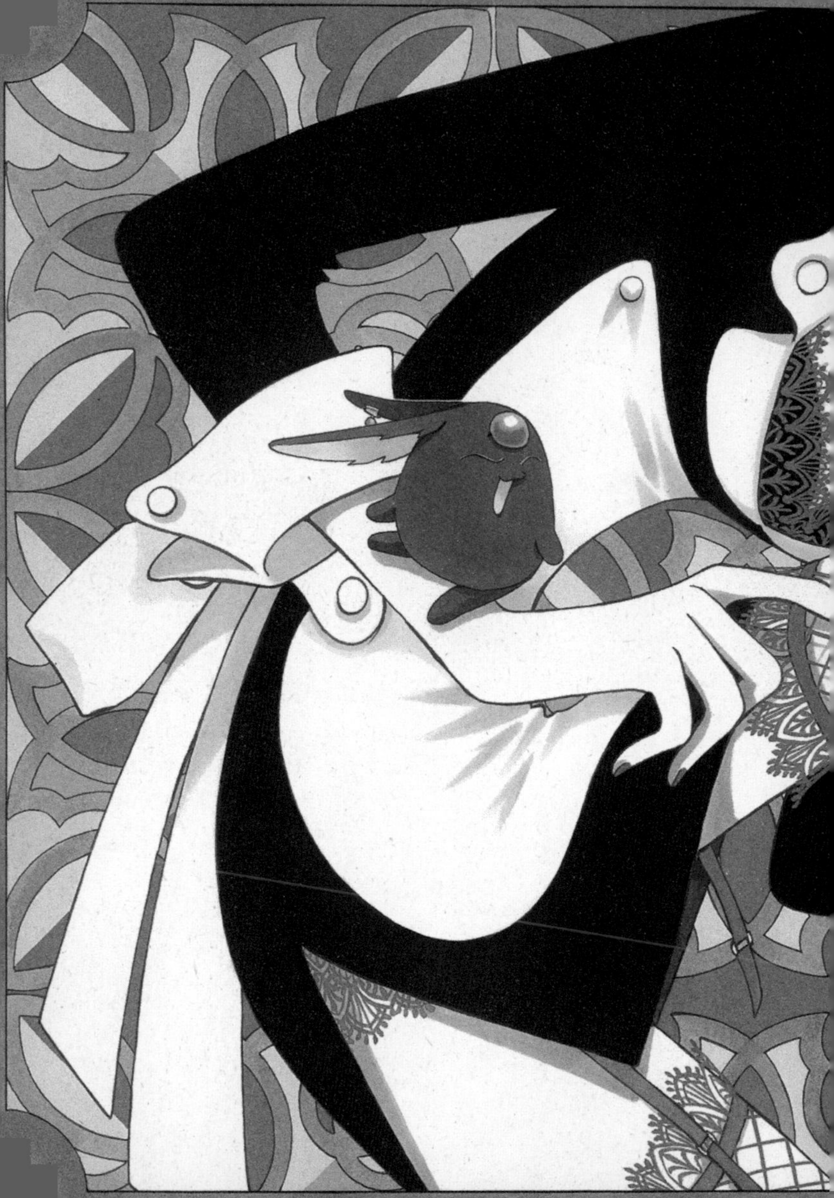

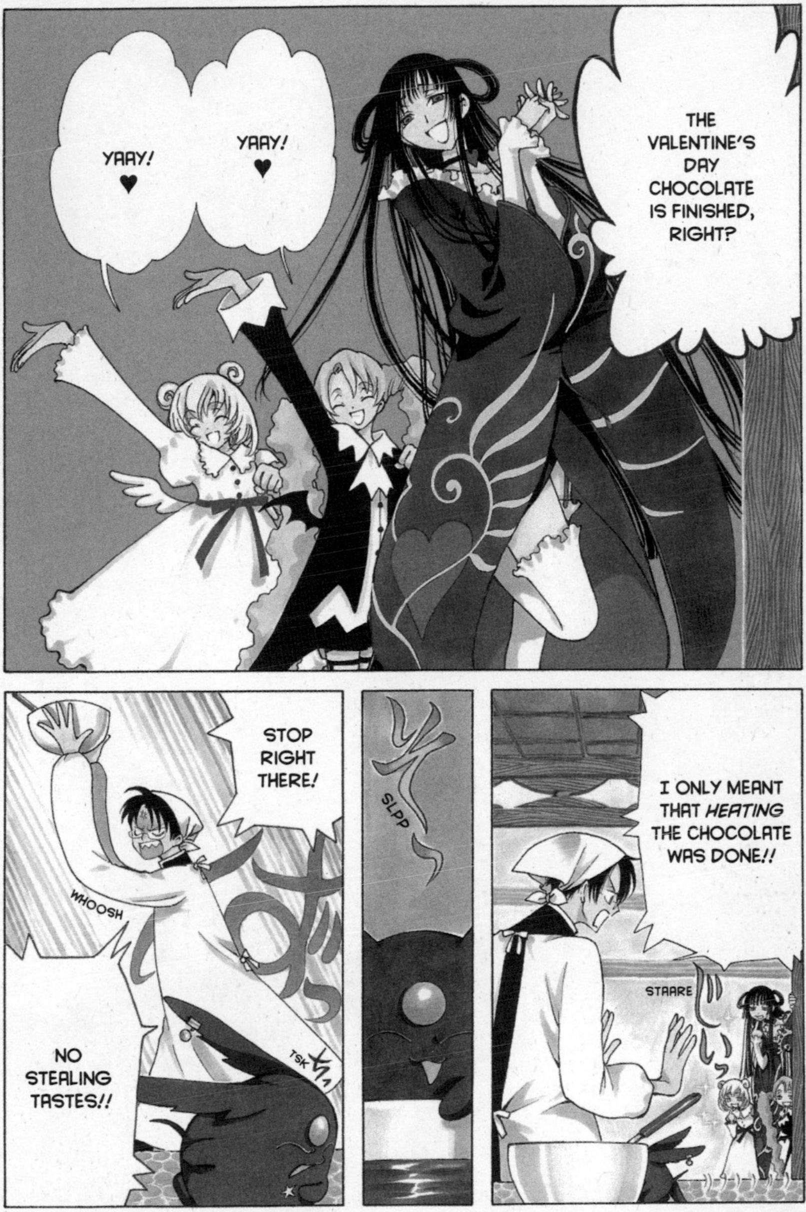
THE VALENTINE'S DAY CHOCOLATE IS FINISHED, RIGHT?
YAAY! ♥
YAAY! ♥
I ONLY MEANT THAT *HEATING* THE CHOCOLATE WAS DONE!!
STAARE
SLPP
STOP RIGHT THERE!
WHOOSH
TSK
NO STEALING TASTES!!

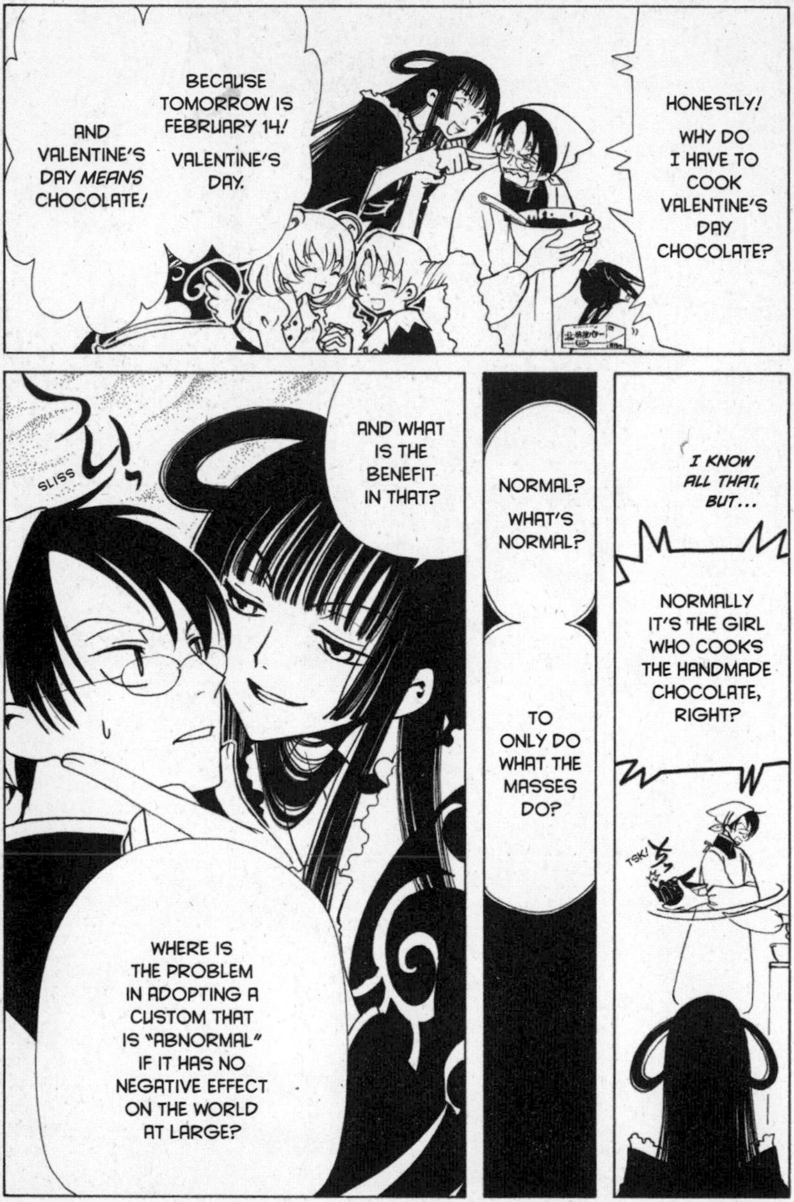
HONESTLY! WHY DO I HAVE TO COOK VALENTINE'S DAY CHOCOLATE?
BECAUSE TOMORROW IS FEBRUARY 14! VALENTINE'S DAY.
AND VALENTINE'S DAY *MEANS* CHOCOLATE!
I KNOW ALL THAT, BUT...
NORMALLY IT'S THE GIRL WHO COOKS THE HANDMADE CHOCOLATE, RIGHT?
TSK!
NORMAL? WHAT'S NORMAL?
TO ONLY DO WHAT THE MASSES DO?
AND WHAT IS THE BENEFIT IN THAT?
SLISS
WHERE IS THE PROBLEM IN ADOPTING A CUSTOM THAT IS "ABNORMAL" IF IT HAS NO NEGATIVE EFFECT ON THE WORLD AT LARGE?

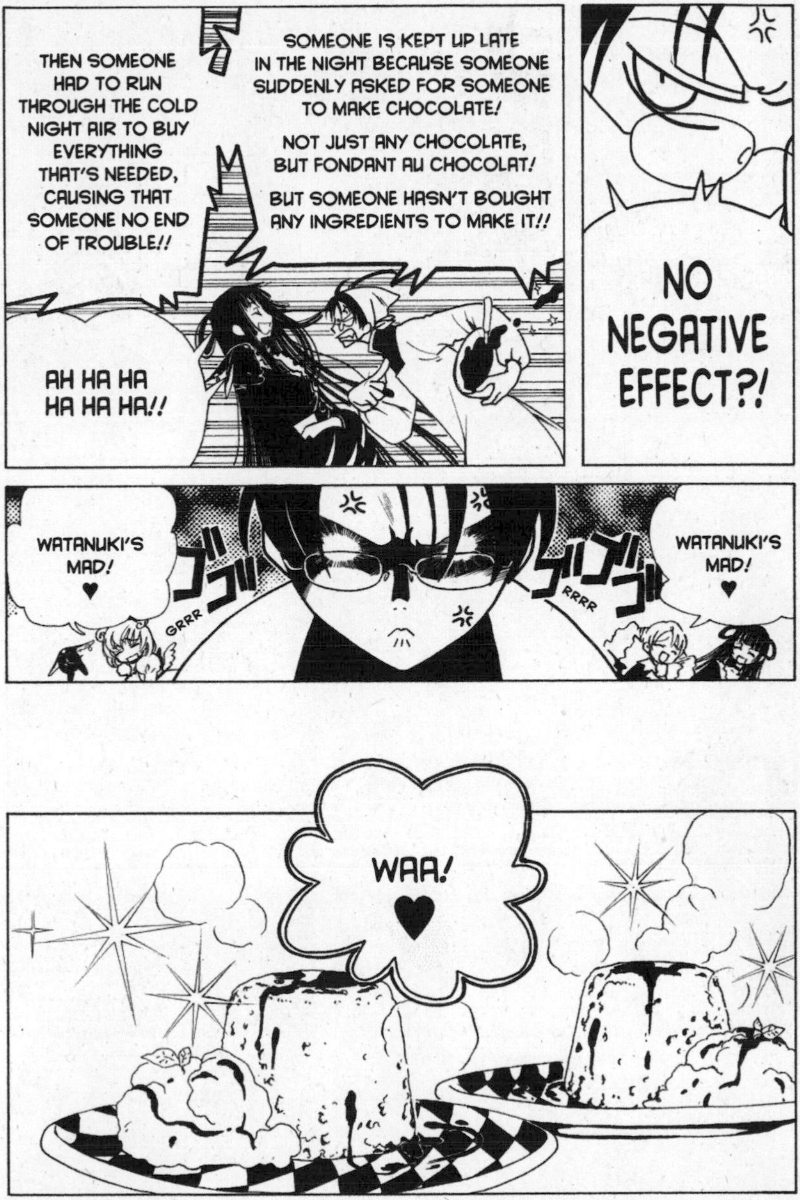
NO NEGATIVE EFFECT?!
SOMEONE IS KEPT UP LATE IN THE NIGHT BECAUSE SOMEONE SUDDENLY ASKED FOR SOMEONE TO MAKE CHOCOLATE!
NOT JUST ANY CHOCOLATE, BUT FONDANT AU CHOCOLAT!
BUT SOMEONE HASN'T BOUGHT ANY INGREDIENTS TO MAKE IT!!
THEN SOMEONE HAD TO RUN THROUGH THE COLD NIGHT AIR TO BUY EVERYTHING THAT'S NEEDED, CAUSING THAT SOMEONE NO END OF TROUBLE!!
AH HA HA HA HA HA!!
WATANUKI'S MAD! ♥
RRRR
GRRR
WATANUKI'S MAD! ♥
WAA! ♥

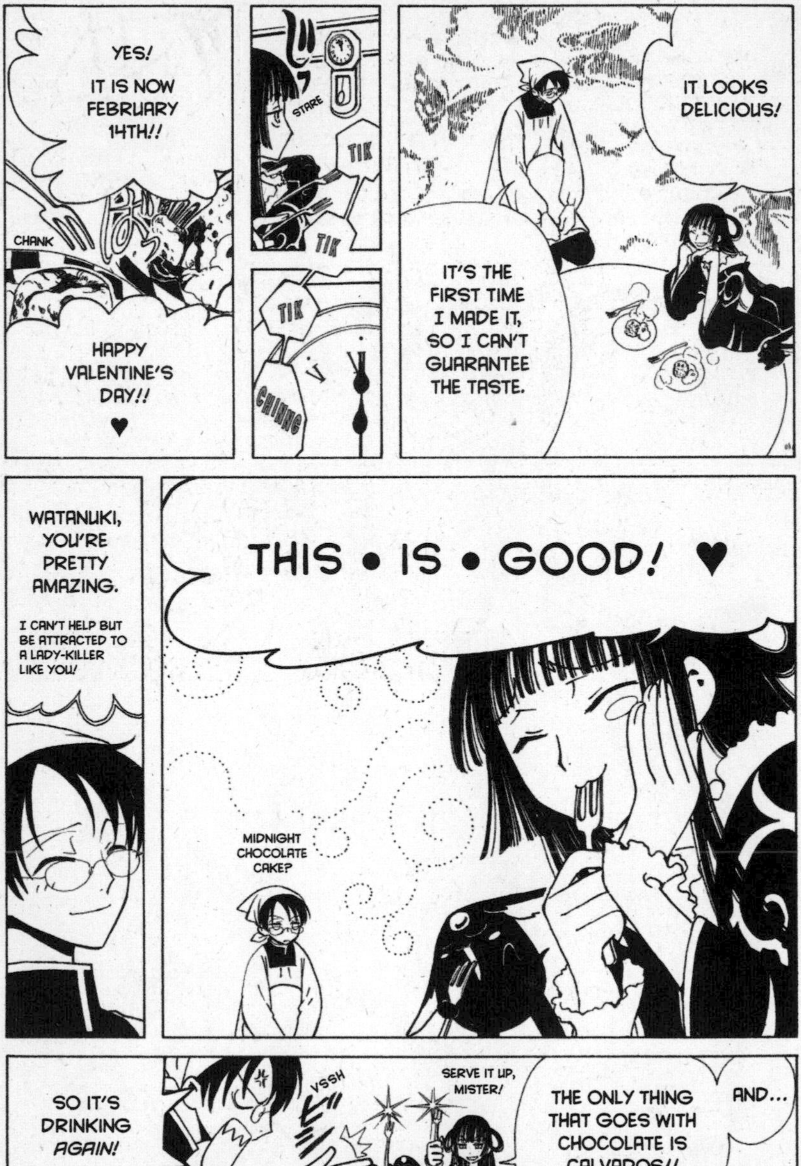
IT LOOKS DELICIOUS!
IT'S THE FIRST TIME I MADE IT, SO I CAN'T GUARANTEE THE TASTE.
STARE
TIK
TIK
TIK
CHINNG
YES! IT IS NOW FEBRUARY 14TH!!
CHANK
HAPPY VALENTINE'S DAY!! ♥
THIS • IS • GOOD! ♥
MIDNIGHT CHOCOLATE CAKE?
WATANUKI, YOU'RE PRETTY AMAZING.
I CAN'T HELP BUT BE ATTRACTED TO A LADY-KILLER LIKE YOU!
AND...
THE ONLY THING THAT GOES WITH CHOCOLATE IS CALVADOS!!
SERVE IT UP, MISTER!
VSSH
SO IT'S DRINKING AGAIN!

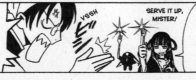

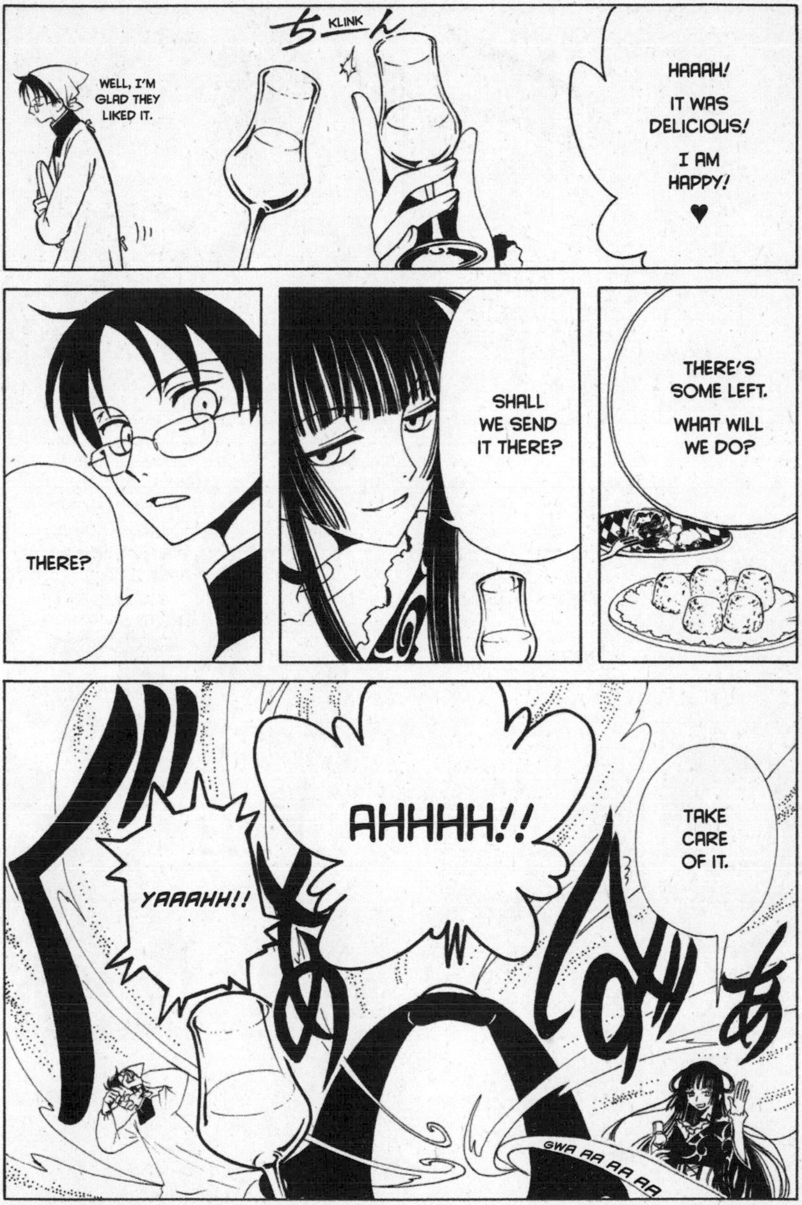
HAAAH!
IT WAS DELICIOUS!
I AM HAPPY!
♥
ちーん KLINK
WELL, I'M GLAD THEY LIKED IT.
THERE'S SOME LEFT.
WHAT WILL WE DO?
SHALL WE SEND IT THERE?
THERE?
TAKE CARE OF IT.
AHHHH!!
YAAAHH!!
GWA AA AA AA

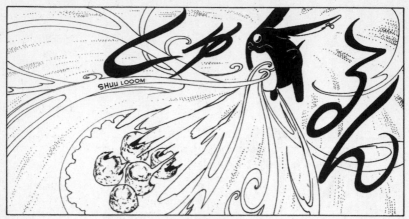

SHUU LOOOM
THAT WAY THE OTHER MOKONA CAN GIVE OUR BRAVE DIMENSION-TRAVELERS A TASTE OF FONDANT AU CHOCOLAT.
GULP
STARE
OH, TO SYAORAN AND THOSE GUYS?
THAT'S PRETTY NICE OF YOU, YÛKO-SAN.
HO HO HO HO HO!
THAT WAY, WE'RE ALL SET FOR WHITE DAY!
I EXPECT GREAT PRESENTS FROM THEM!!
HO HO HO!
YOU WILL BE GIVEN AN ENTIRE WORLD, YÛKO!
SO THAT WAS YOUR PLOT ALL ALONG!!

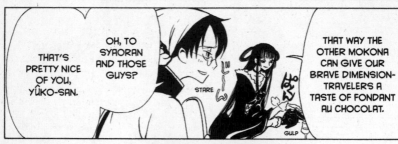

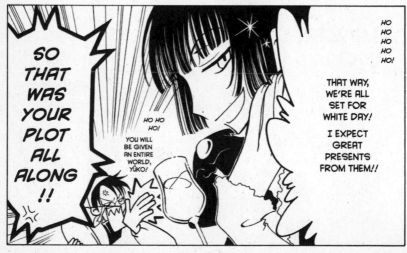

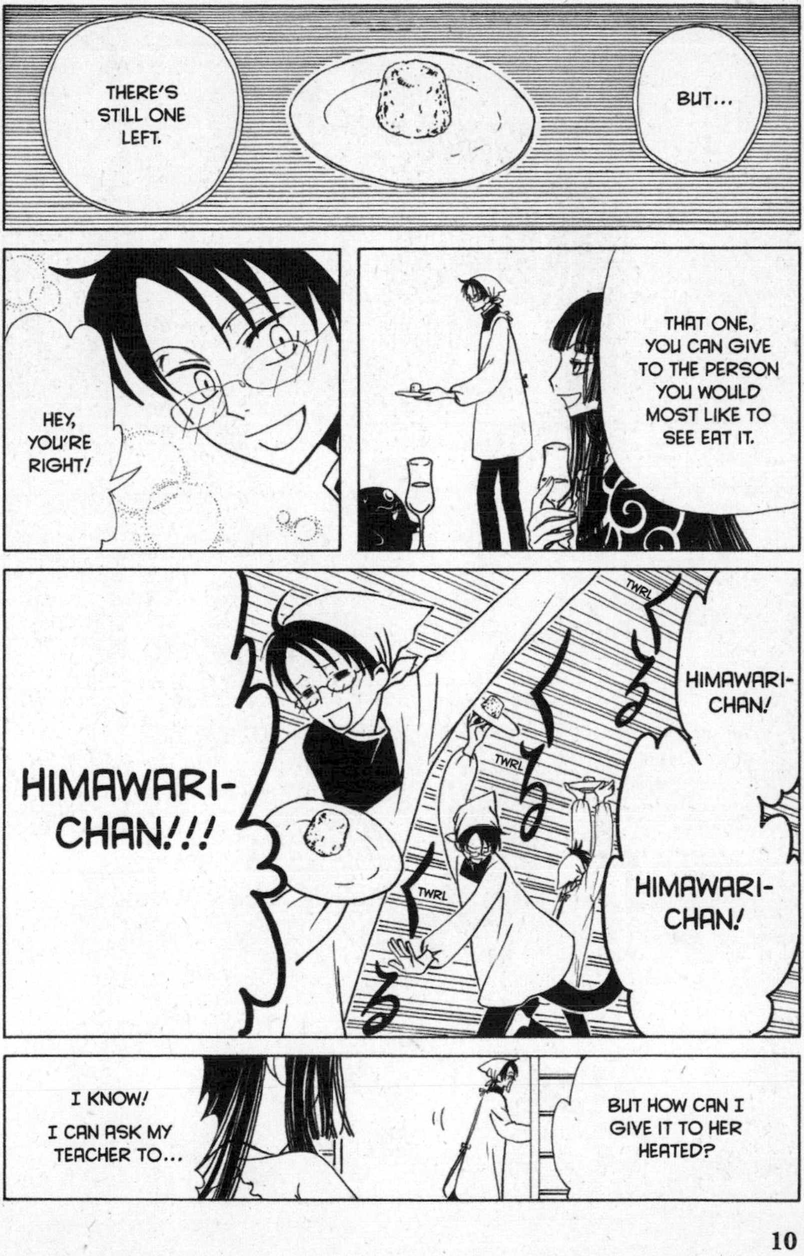
BUT...
THERE'S STILL ONE LEFT.
THAT ONE, YOU CAN GIVE TO THE PERSON YOU WOULD MOST LIKE TO SEE EAT IT.
HEY, YOU'RE RIGHT!
TWRL
HIMAWARI-CHAN!
HIMAWARI-CHAN!
TWRL
TWRL
HIMAWARI-CHAN!!!
BUT HOW CAN I GIVE IT TO HER HEATED?
I KNOW!
I CAN ASK MY TEACHER TO...

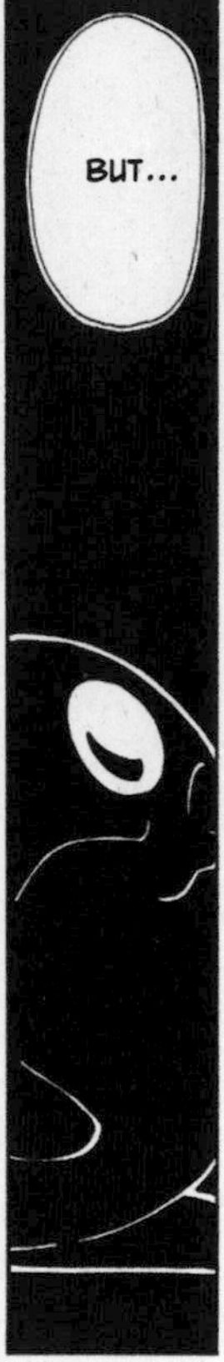
BUT...
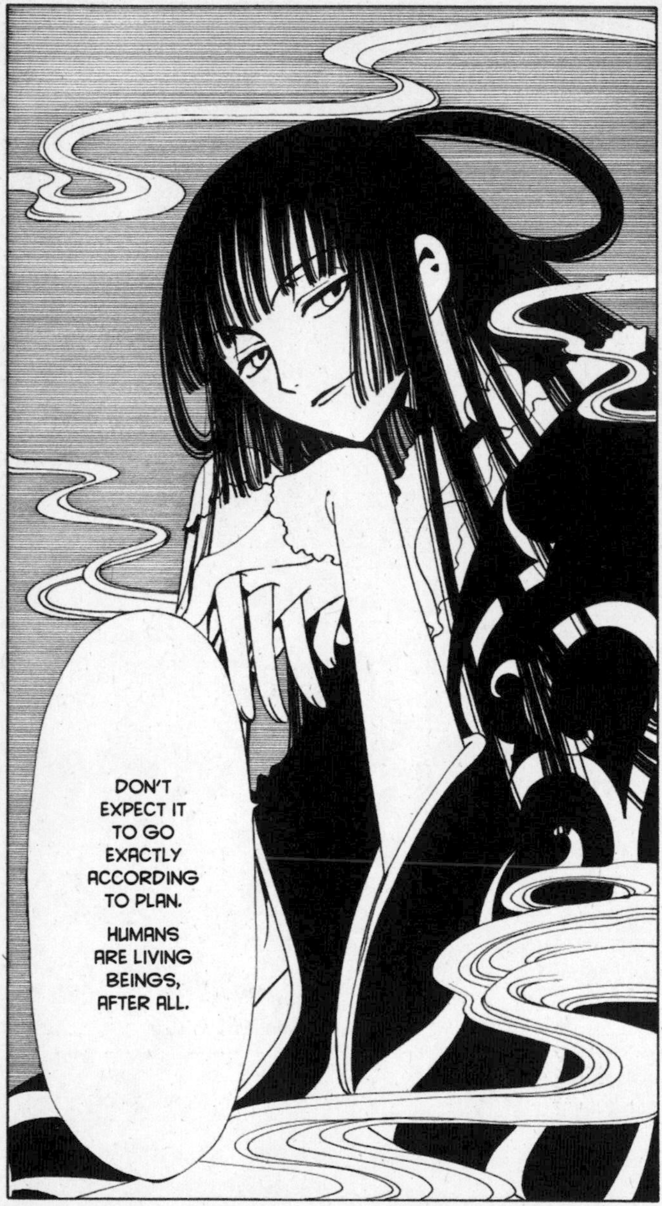
DON'T EXPECT IT TO GO EXACTLY ACCORDING TO PLAN.
HUMANS ARE LIVING BEINGS, AFTER ALL.

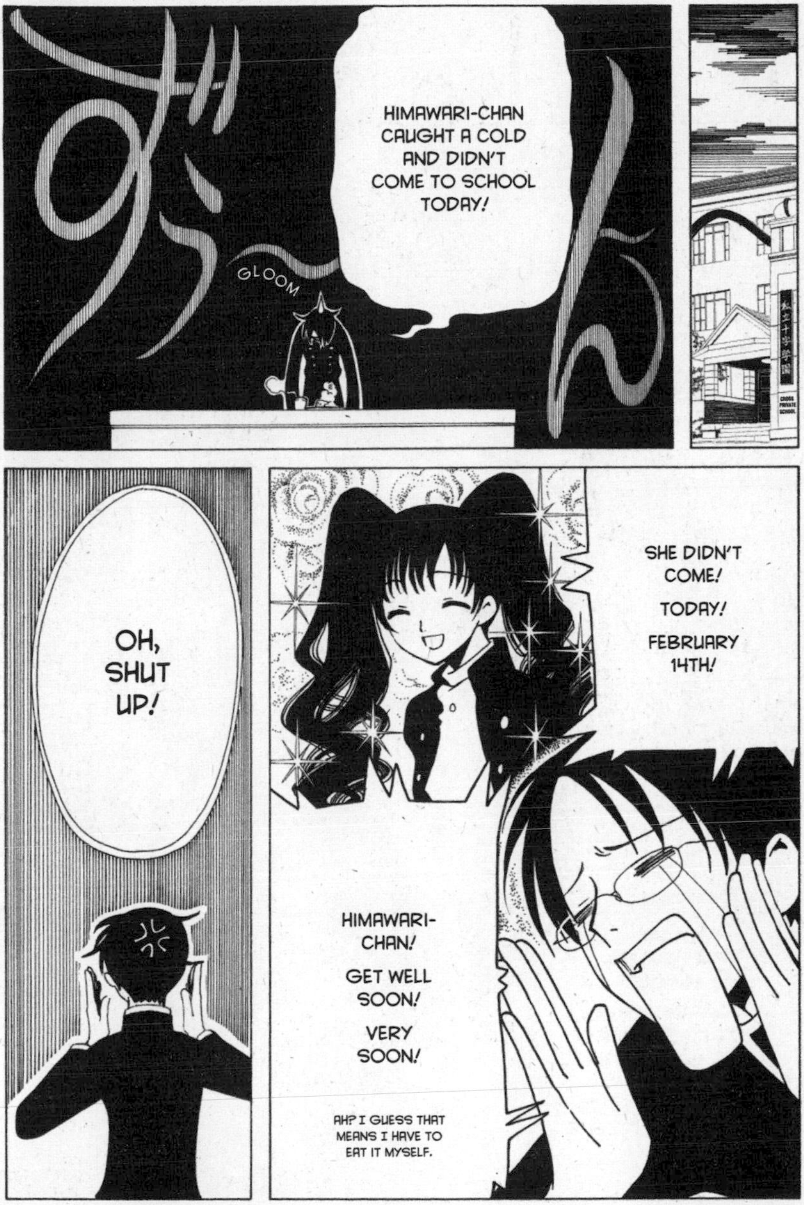
HIMAWARI-CHAN CAUGHT A COLD AND DIDN'T COME TO SCHOOL TODAY!
GLOOM
SHE DIDN'T COME!
TODAY!
FEBRUARY 14TH!
HIMAWARI-CHAN!
GET WELL SOON!
VERY SOON!
AH? I GUESS THAT MEANS I HAVE TO EAT IT MYSELF.
OH, SHUT UP!

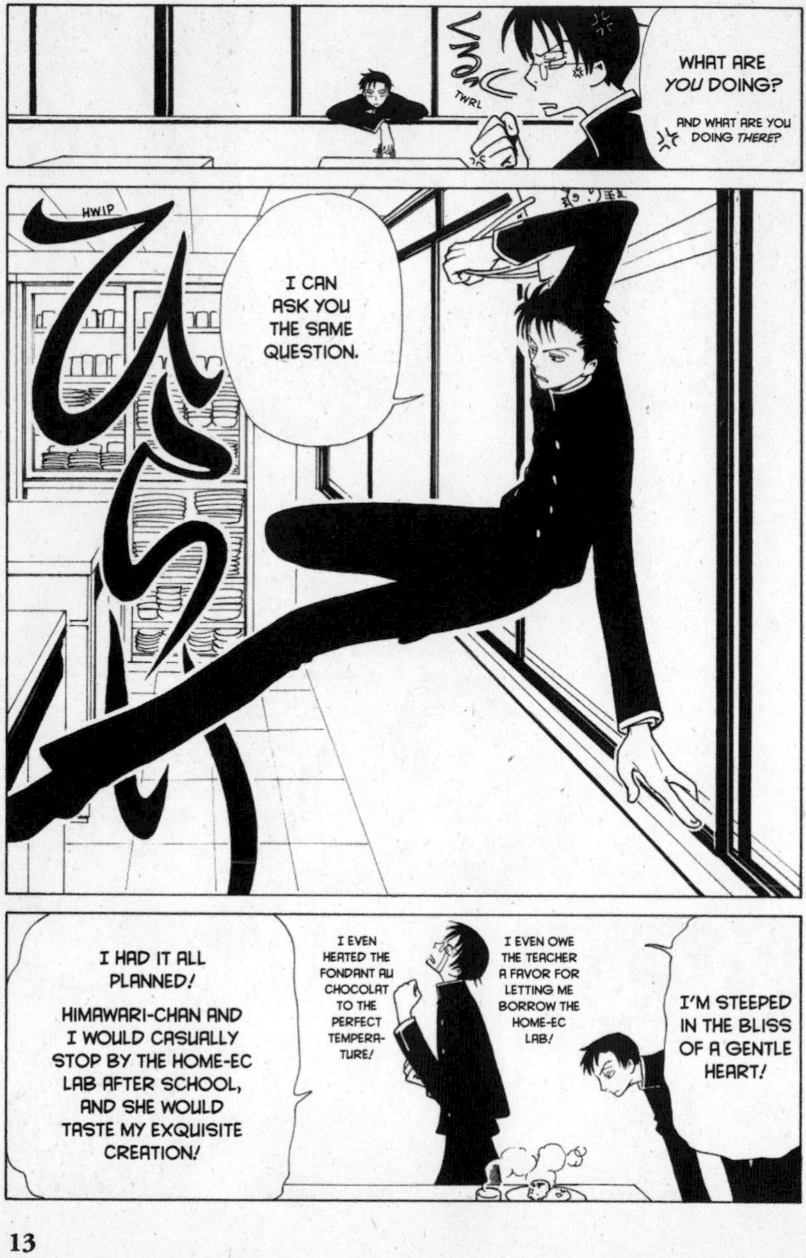
WHAT ARE YOU DOING?
AND WHAT ARE YOU DOING THERE?
TWRL
HWIP
I CAN ASK YOU THE SAME QUESTION.
I'M STEEPED IN THE BLISS OF A GENTLE HEART!
I EVEN OWE THE TEACHER A FAVOR FOR LETTING ME BORROW THE HOME-EC LAB!
I EVEN HEATED THE FONDANT AU CHOCOLAT TO THE PERFECT TEMPERA-TURE!
I HAD IT ALL PLANNED!
HIMAWARI-CHAN AND I WOULD CASUALLY STOP BY THE HOME-EC LAB AFTER SCHOOL, AND SHE WOULD TASTE MY EXQUISITE CREATION!

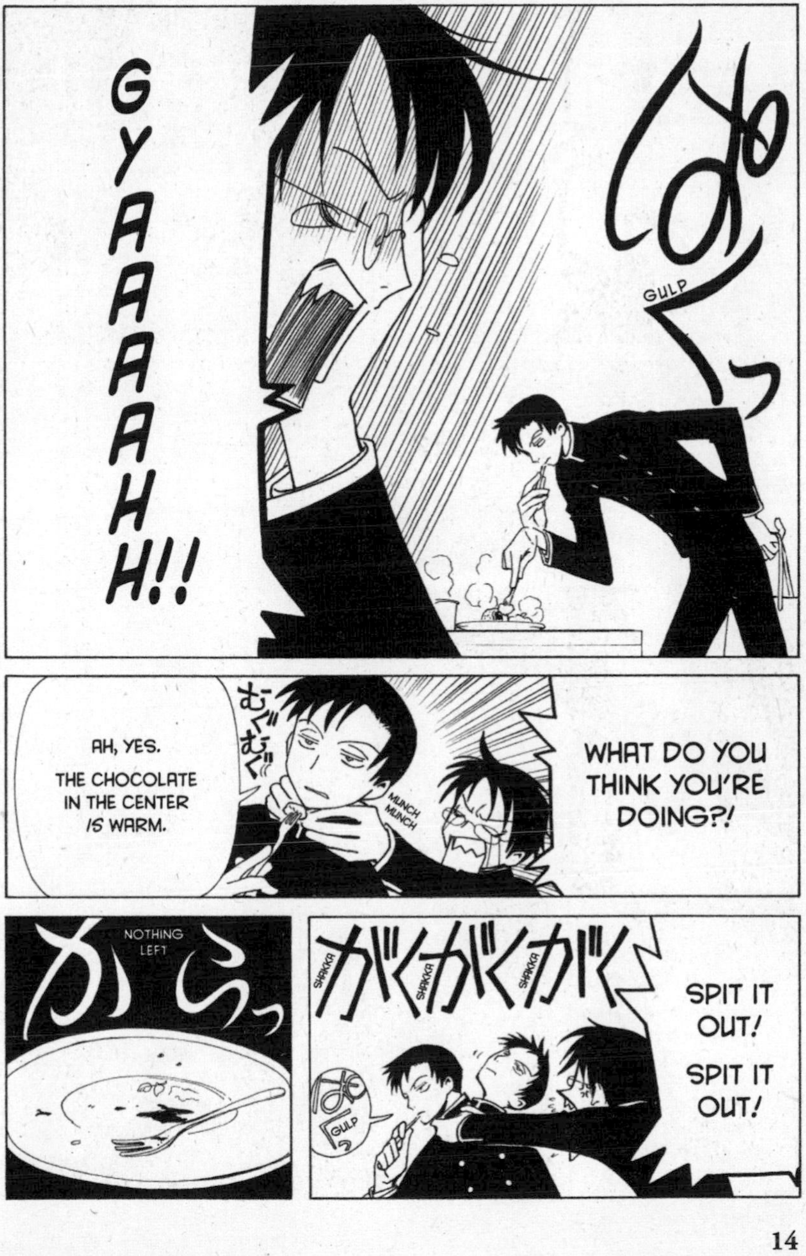
ぱくっ
GULP
GYAAAAHH!!
WHAT DO YOU THINK YOU'RE DOING?!
むぐむぐ
MUNCH MUNCH
AH, YES.
THE CHOCOLATE IN THE CENTER IS WARM.
がくがくがく
SHAKKA SHAKKA SHAKKA
SPIT IT OUT!
SPIT IT OUT!
ぱくっ
GULP
からっ
NOTHING LEFT

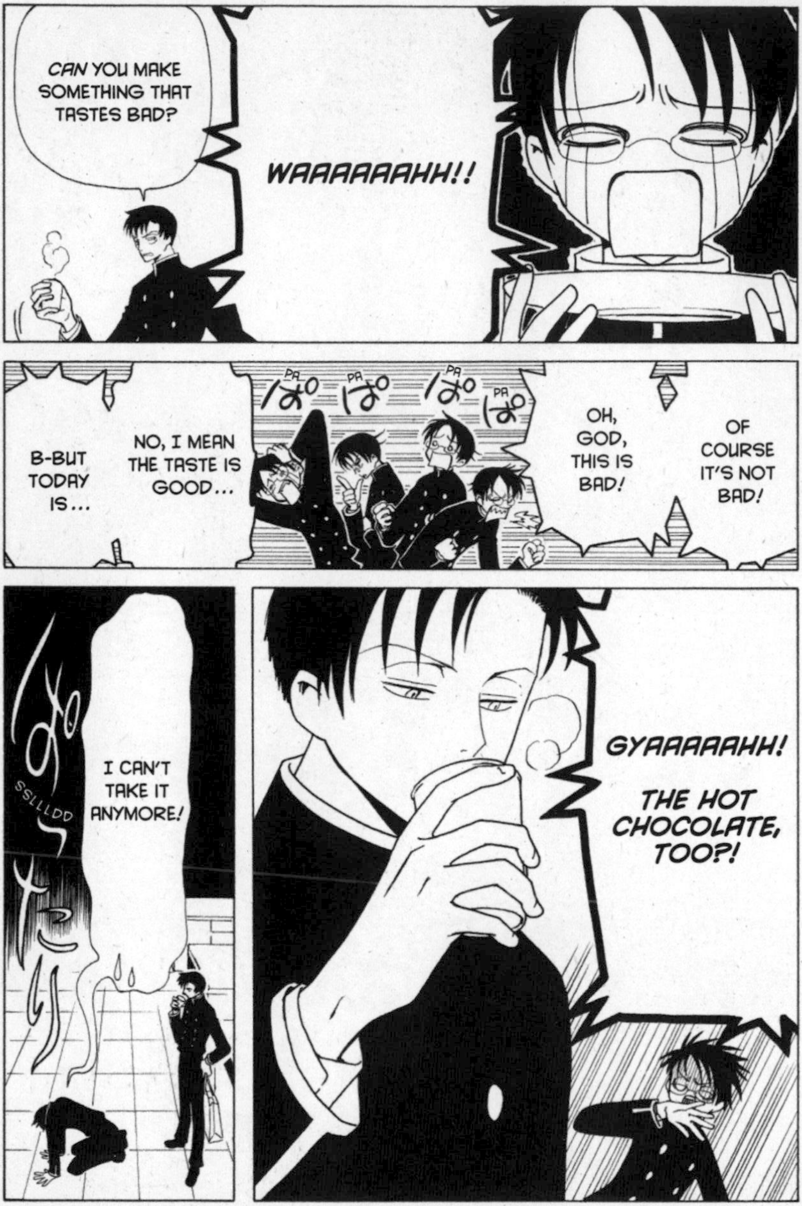
WAAAAAAHH!!
CAN YOU MAKE SOMETHING THAT TASTES BAD?
OF COURSE IT'S NOT BAD!
OH, GOD, THIS IS BAD!
PA PA PA PA
NO, I MEAN THE TASTE IS GOOD...
B-BUT TODAY IS...
GYAAAAAHH!
THE HOT CHOCOLATE, TOO?!
SSLLLDD
I CAN'T TAKE IT ANYMORE!

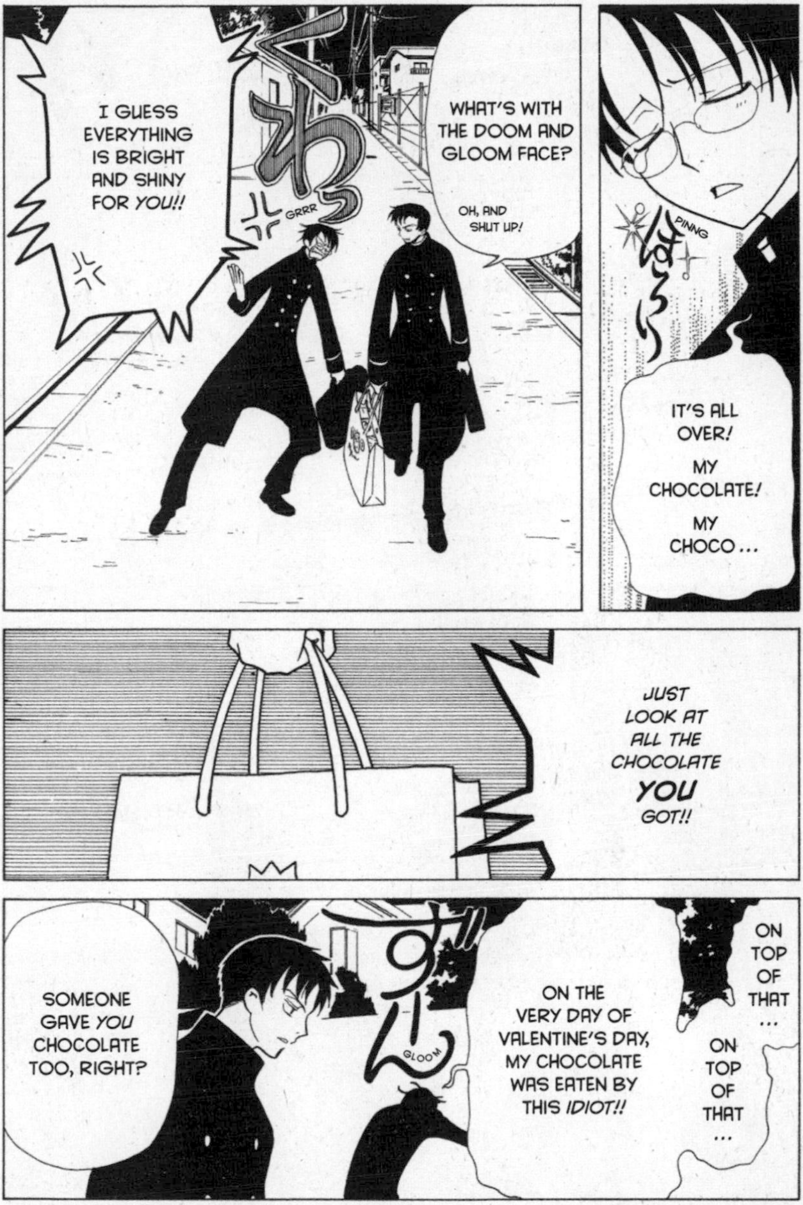
PINNG
IT'S ALL OVER! MY CHOCOLATE! MY CHOCO...
WHAT'S WITH THE DOOM AND GLOOM FACE?
OH, AND SHUT UP!
GRRR
I GUESS EVERYTHING IS BRIGHT AND SHINY FOR YOU!!
JUST LOOK AT ALL THE CHOCOLATE YOU GOT!!
ON TOP OF THAT...
ON TOP OF THAT...
ON THE VERY DAY OF VALENTINE'S DAY, MY CHOCOLATE WAS EATEN BY THIS IDIOT!!
GLOOM
SOMEONE GAVE YOU CHOCOLATE TOO, RIGHT?

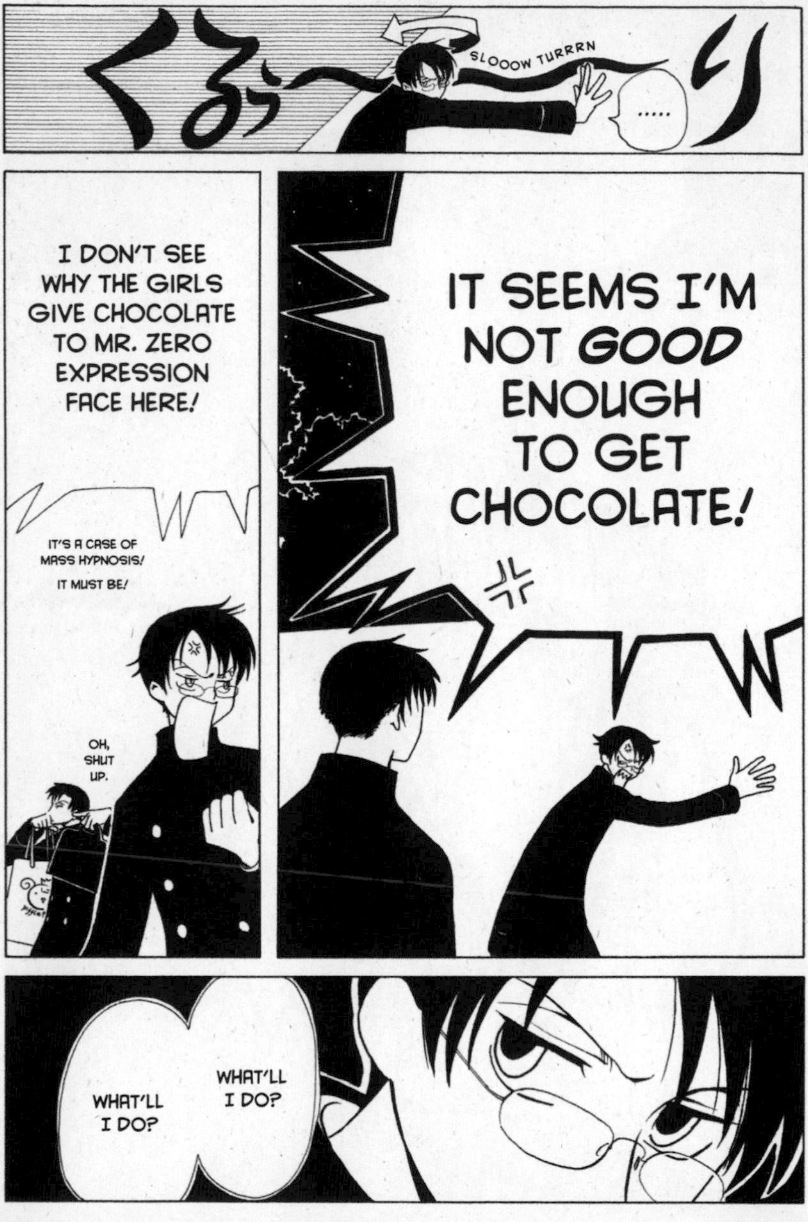
くるぅ〜り
SLOOOW TURRRN
......
IT SEEMS I'M NOT *GOOD* ENOUGH TO GET CHOCOLATE!
I DON'T SEE WHY THE GIRLS GIVE CHOCOLATE TO MR. ZERO EXPRESSION FACE HERE!
IT'S A CASE OF MASS HYPNOSIS!
IT MUST BE!
OH, SHUT UP.
WHAT'LL I DO?
WHAT'LL I DO?

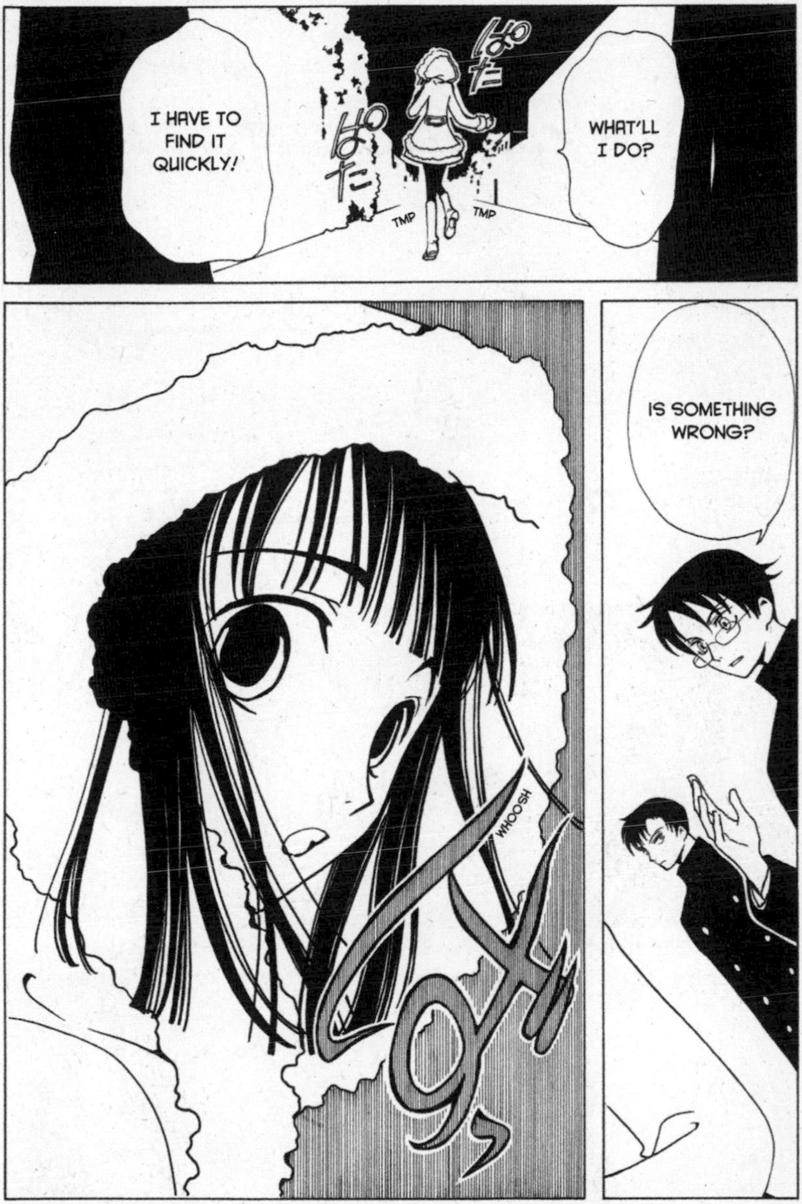
WHAT'LL I DO?
ぱた
ぱた
TMP
TMP
I HAVE TO FIND IT QUICKLY!
IS SOMETHING WRONG?
WHOOSH

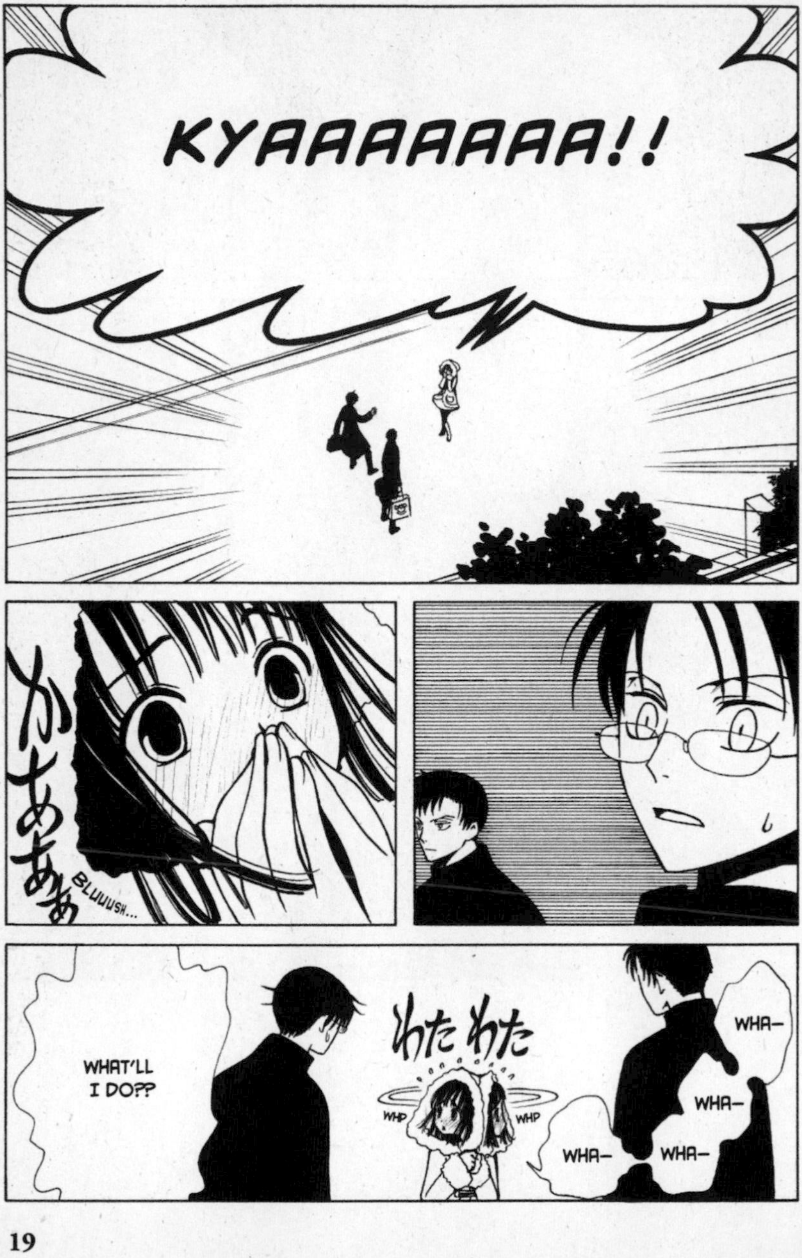
KYAAAAAAAA!!
かあああ
BLUUUSH...
WHA-
WHA-
WHA-
WHA-
わたわた
WHP
WHP
WHAT'LL I DO??

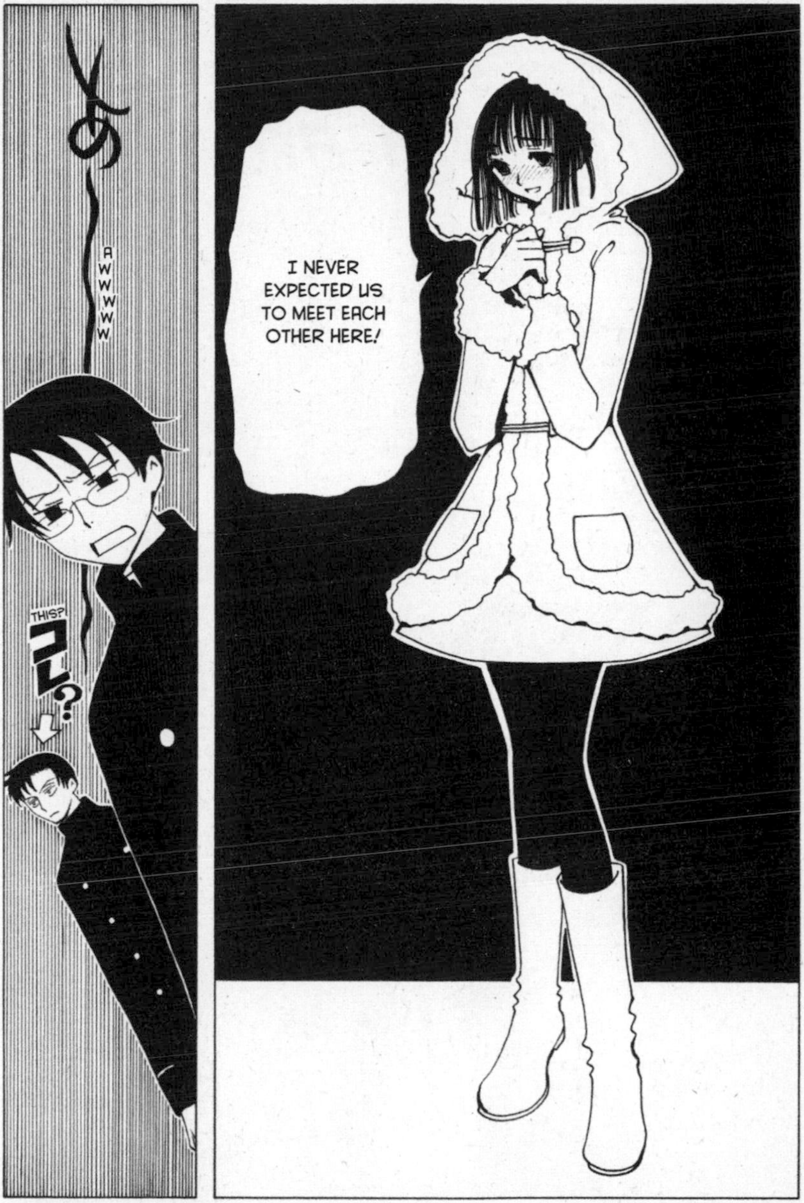
I NEVER EXPECTED US TO MEET EACH OTHER HERE!
あー
AWWWWWW
THIS?
コレ?

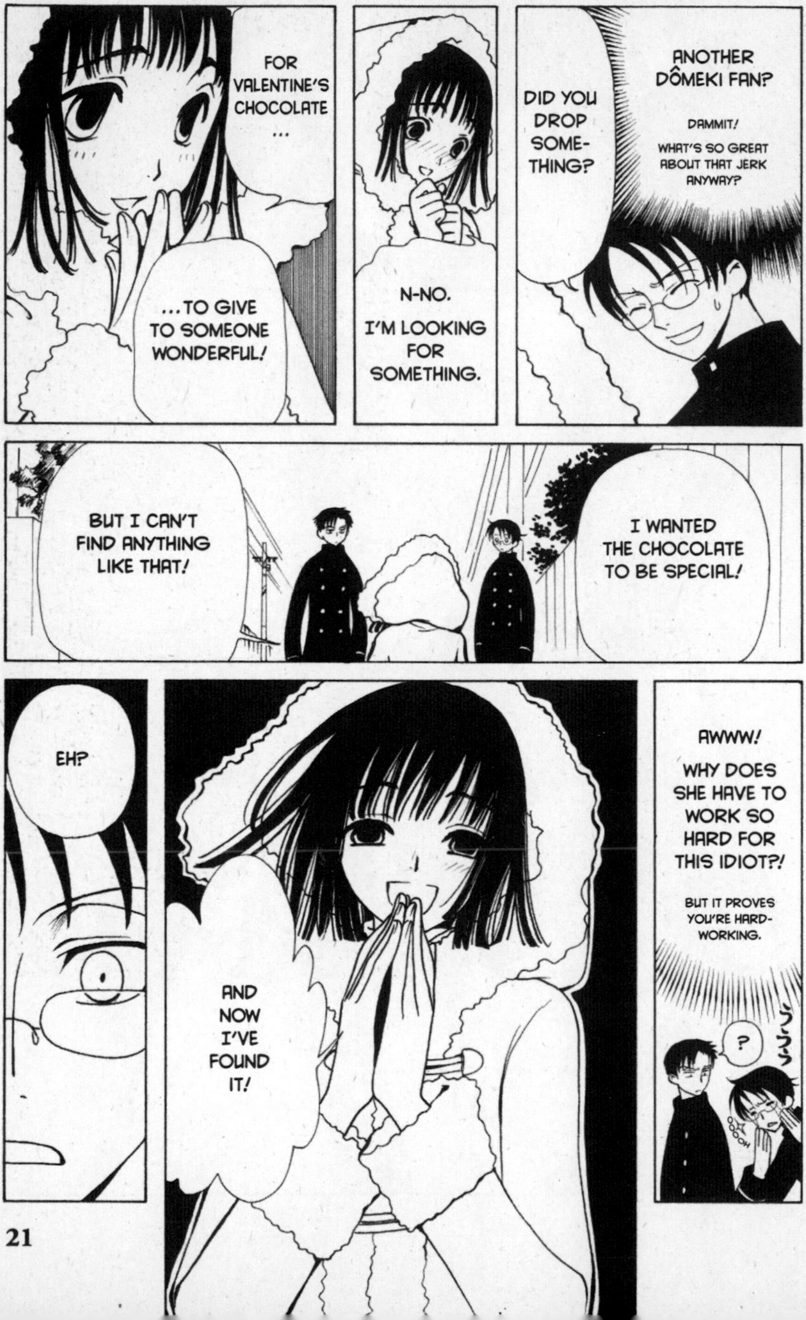
ANOTHER DÔMEKI FAN?
DAMMIT!
WHAT'S SO GREAT ABOUT THAT JERK ANYWAY?
DID YOU DROP SOME-THING?
N-NO.
I'M LOOKING FOR SOMETHING.
FOR VALENTINE'S CHOCOLATE ...
...TO GIVE TO SOMEONE WONDERFUL!
I WANTED THE CHOCOLATE TO BE SPECIAL!
BUT I CAN'T FIND ANYTHING LIKE THAT!
AWWW!
WHY DOES SHE HAVE TO WORK SO HARD FOR THIS IDIOT?!
BUT IT PROVES YOU'RE HARD-WORKING.
?
AND NOW I'VE FOUND IT!
EH?

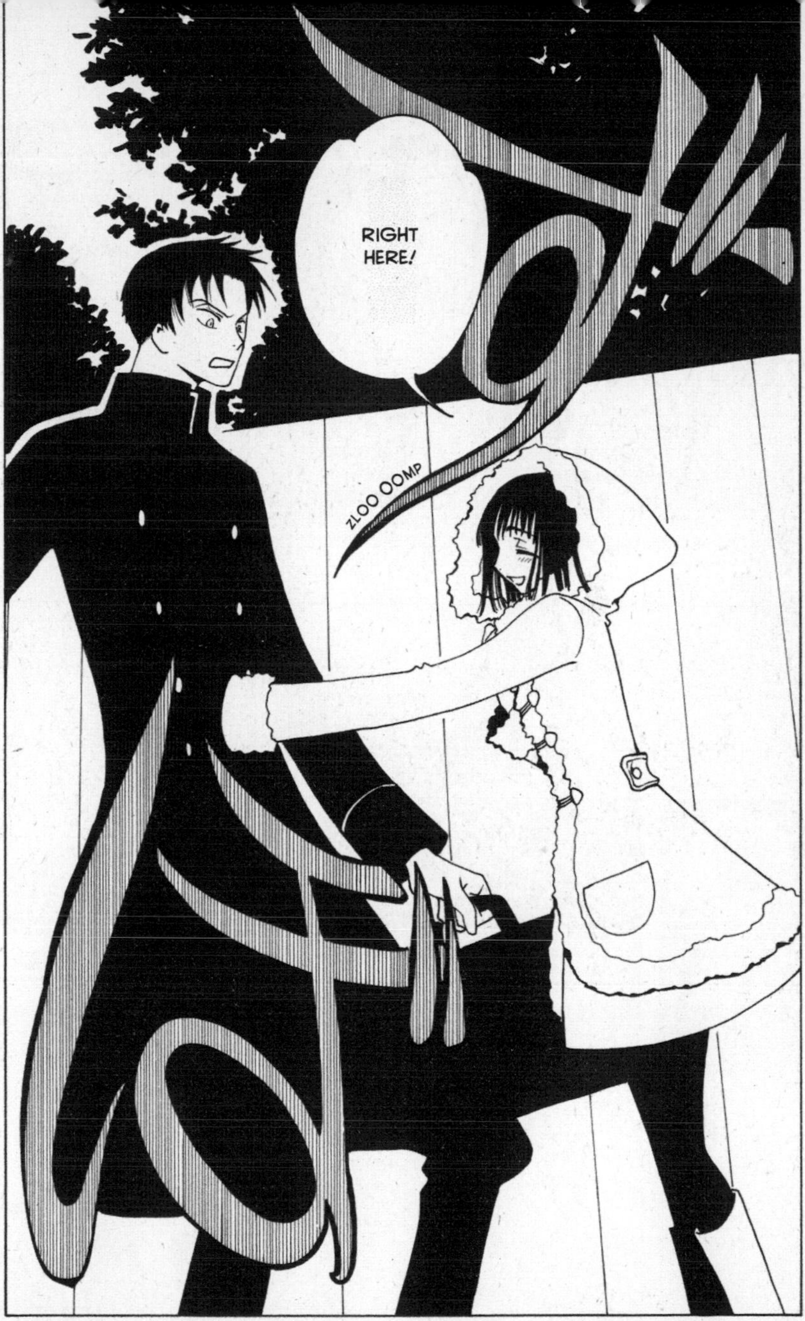
RIGHT HERE!
ZLOO OOMP

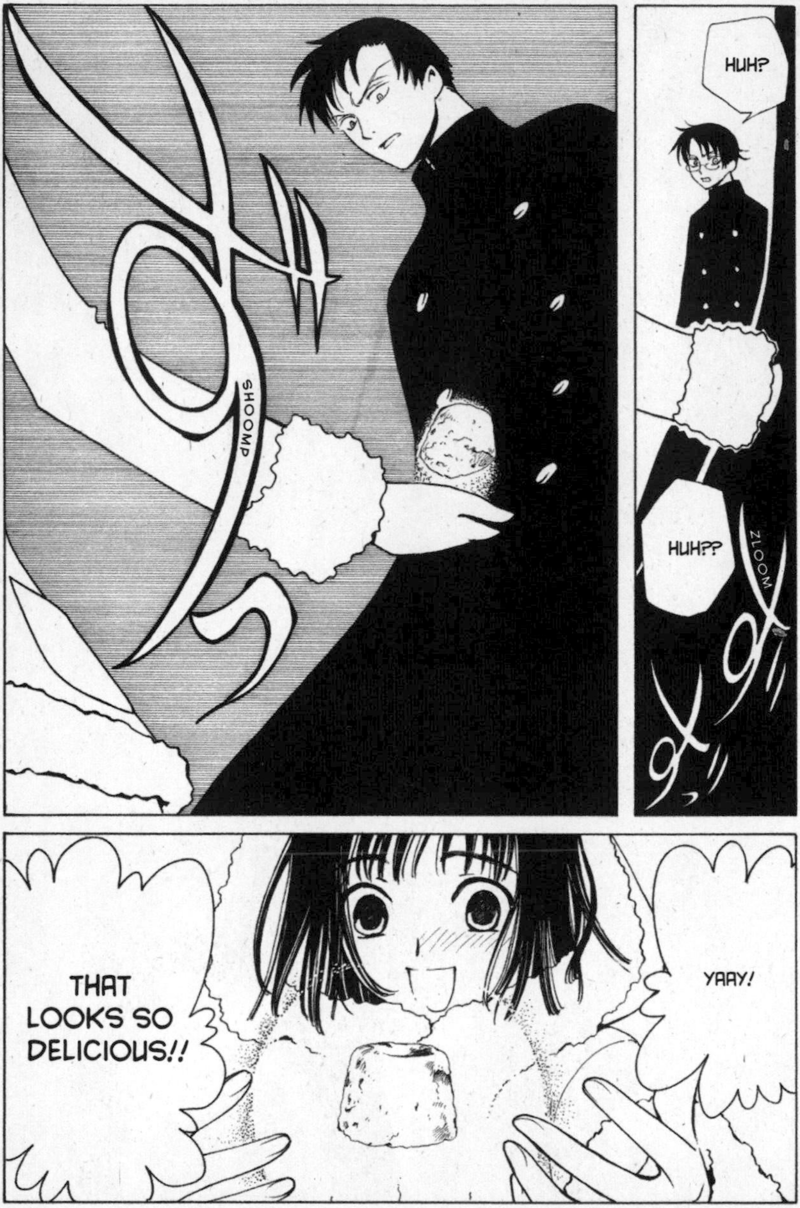
HUH?
HUH??
ZLOOM
SHOOMP
YAAY!
THAT LOOKS SO DELICIOUS!!

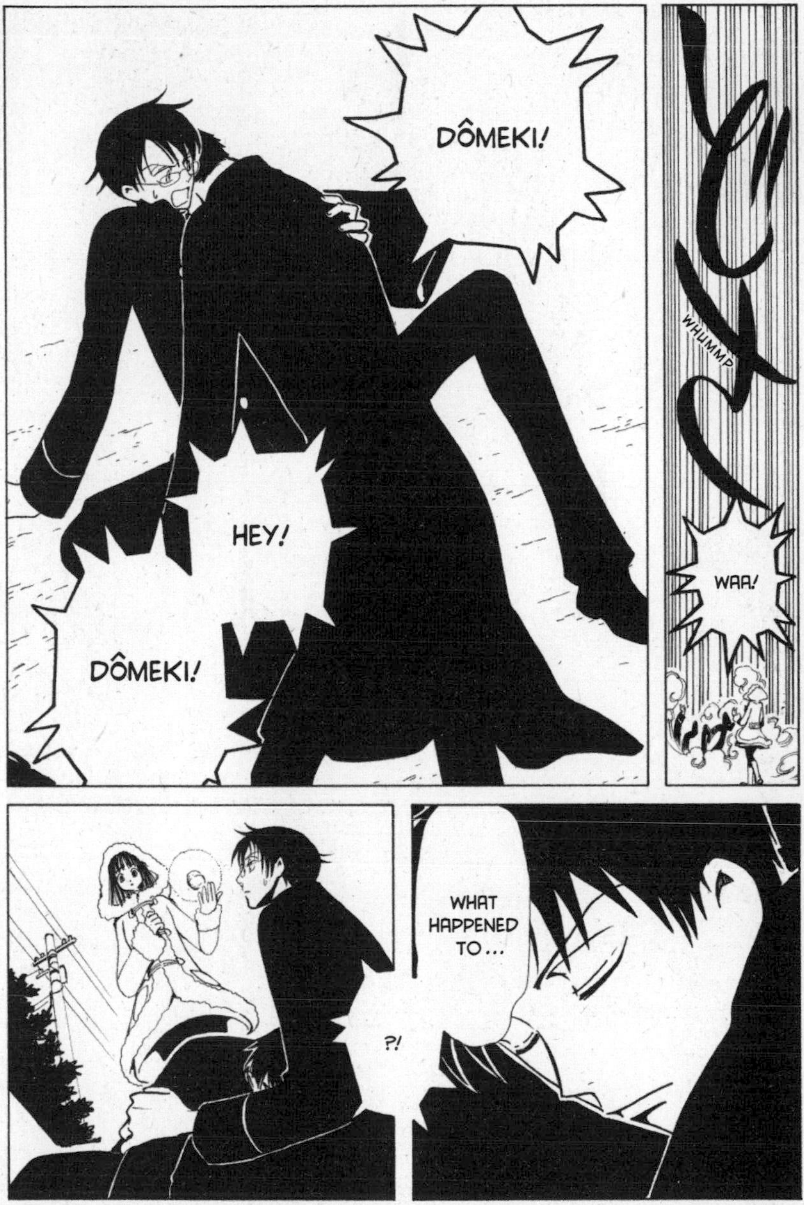
WHUMMP
WAA!
DÔMEKI!
HEY!
DÔMEKI!
WHAT HAPPENED TO...
?!

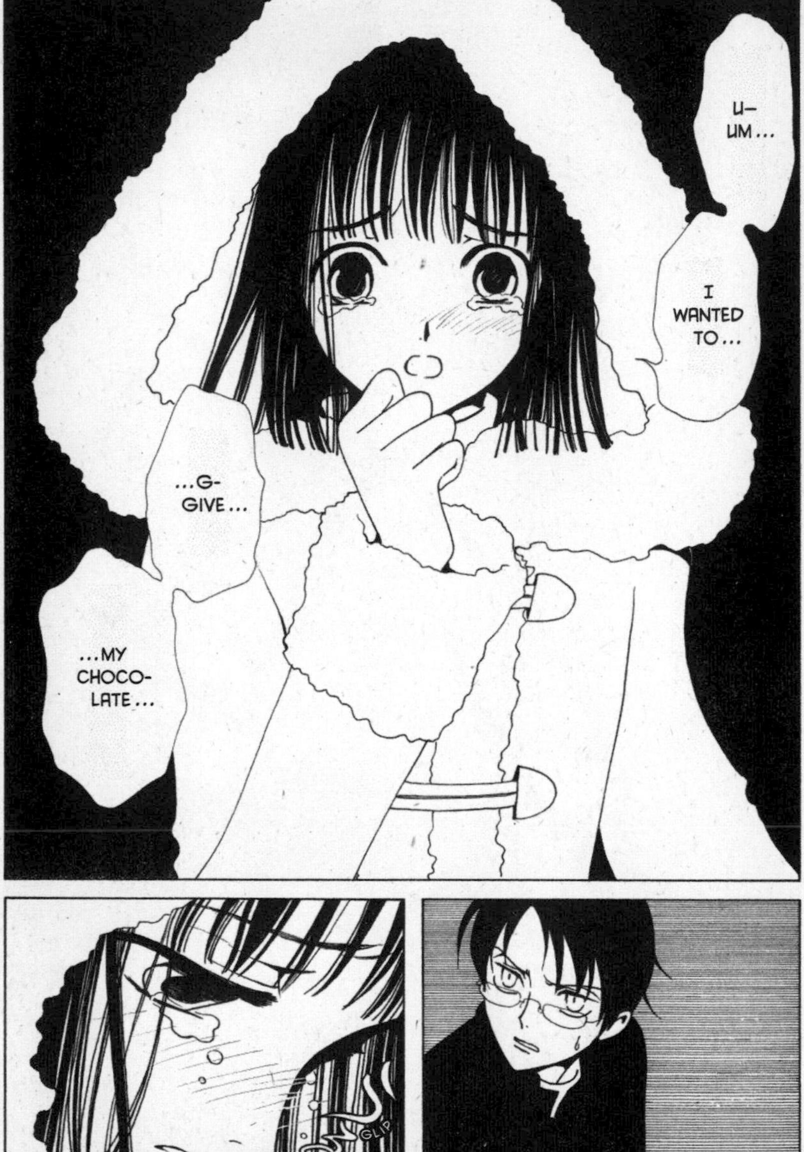
U– UM…
I WANTED TO…
…G- GIVE…
…MY CHOCO- LATE…
GLIP

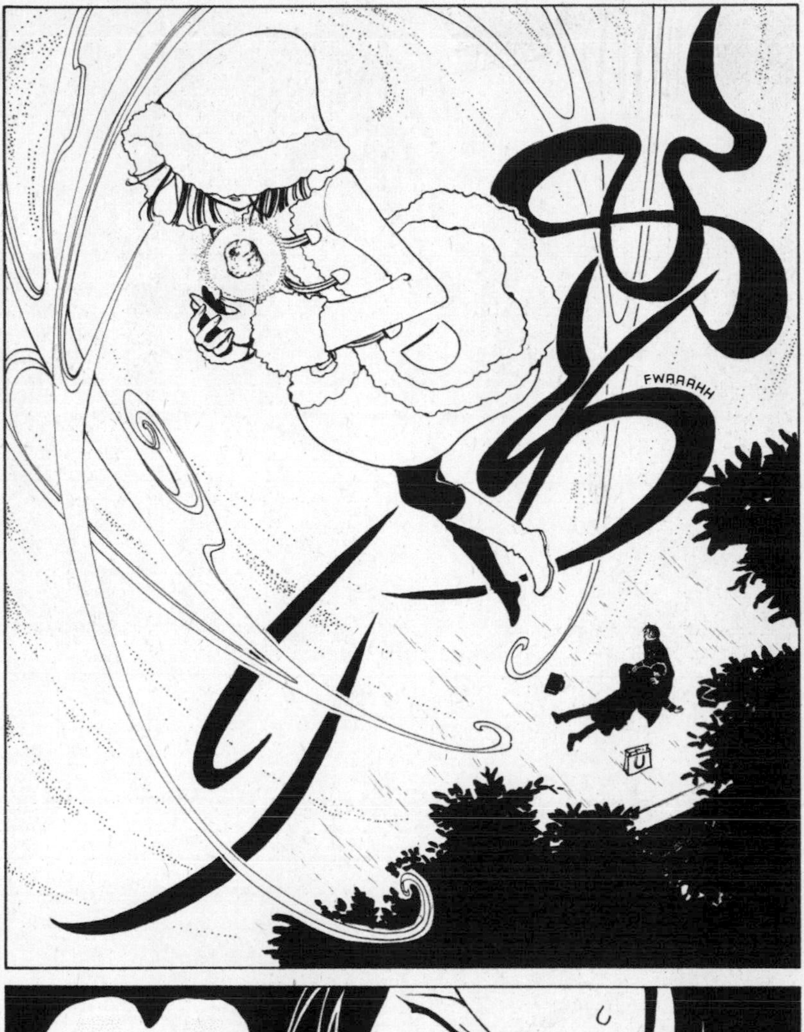
FWAAAAHH
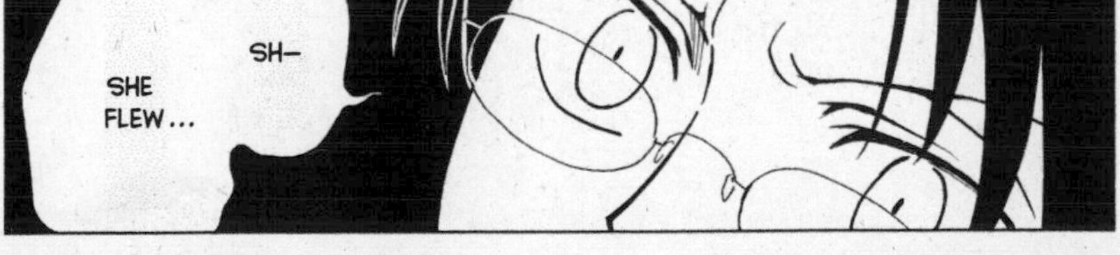
SH-
SHE FLEW...

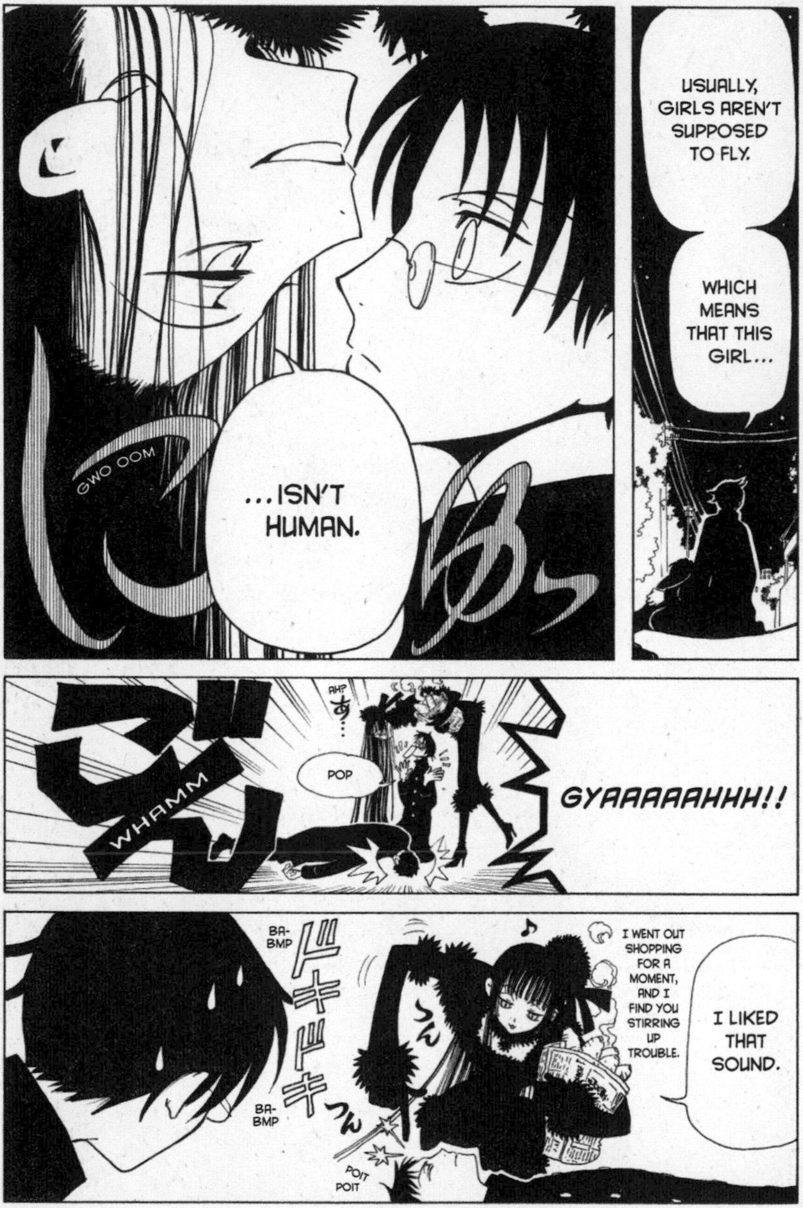
USUALLY, GIRLS AREN'T SUPPOSED TO FLY.
WHICH MEANS THAT THIS GIRL...
GWO OOM
...ISN'T HUMAN.
GYAAAAAHHH!!
AH?
あ…
POP
WHAMM
I LIKED THAT SOUND.
I WENT OUT SHOPPING FOR A MOMENT, AND I FIND YOU STIRRING UP TROUBLE.
BA-BMP
BA-BMP
POIT POIT

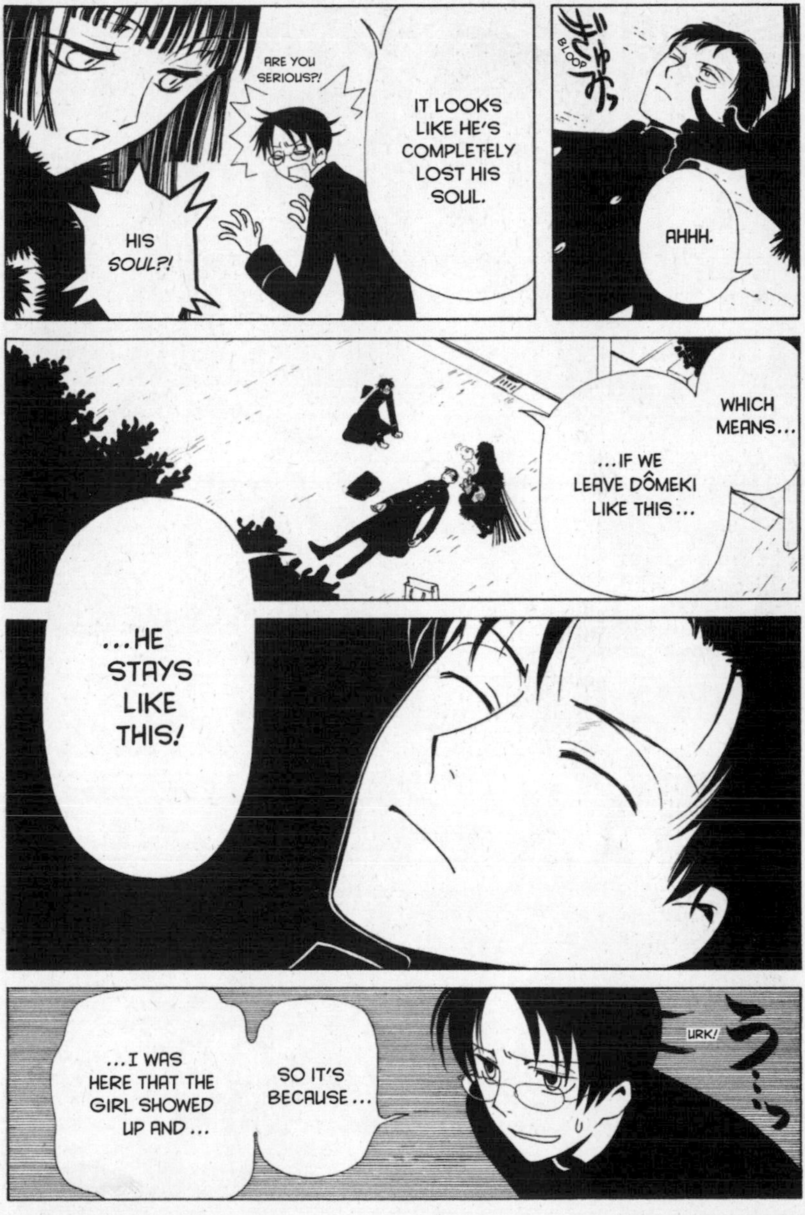
ぎゅおっ
BLOOP
AHHH.
IT LOOKS LIKE HE'S COMPLETELY LOST HIS SOUL.
ARE YOU SERIOUS?!
HIS SOUL?!
WHICH MEANS...
...IF WE LEAVE DÔMEKI LIKE THIS...
...HE STAYS LIKE THIS!
う…っ
URK!
SO IT'S BECAUSE...
...I WAS HERE THAT THE GIRL SHOWED UP AND...

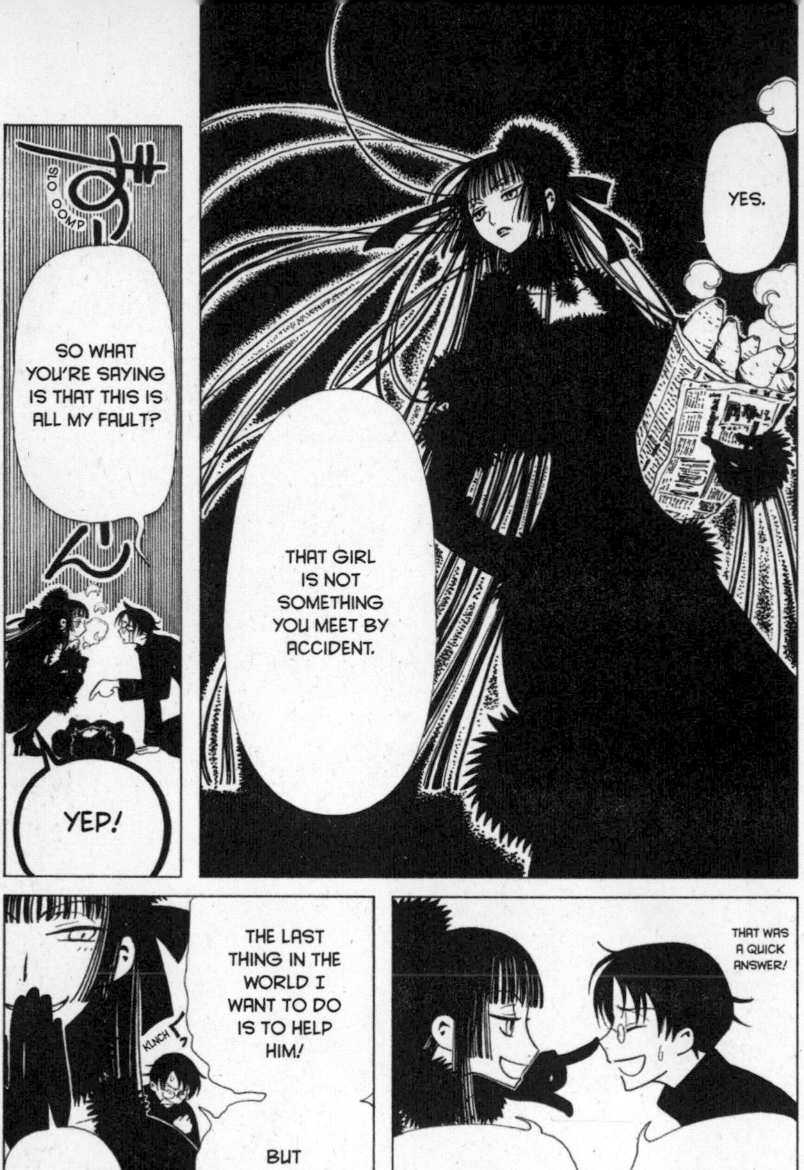
YES.
THAT GIRL IS NOT SOMETHING YOU MEET BY ACCIDENT.
OOMP
SO WHAT YOU'RE SAYING IS THAT THIS IS ALL MY FAULT?
YEP!
WHAT DO WE DO TO BRING HIM BACK TO NORMAL?
THAT WAS A QUICK ANSWER!
I CAN TELL YOU, BUT IT'LL COST YOU PLENTY.
THE LAST THING IN THE WORLD I WANT TO DO IS TO HELP HIM!
KLNCH
BUT I'LL NEVER SLEEP IF HIS CONDITION IS MY FAULT.
THEN WE'RE AGREED.

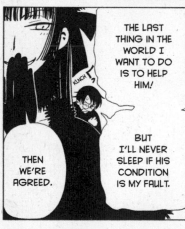

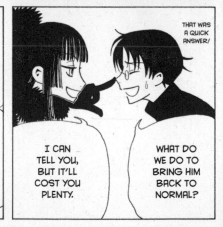

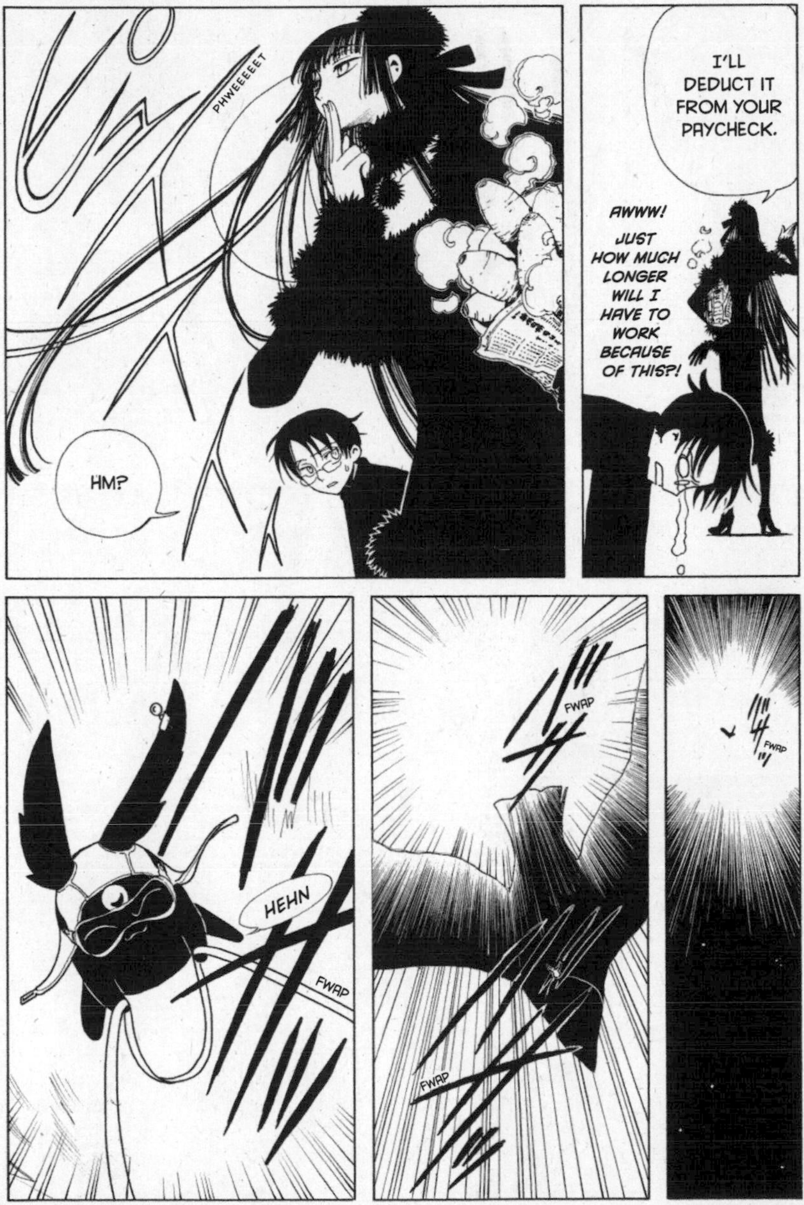
I'LL DEDUCT IT FROM YOUR PAYCHECK.
AWWW! JUST HOW MUCH LONGER WILL I HAVE TO WORK BECAUSE OF THIS?!
PHWEEEEET
HM?
FWAP
FWAP
FWAP
HEHN
FWAP

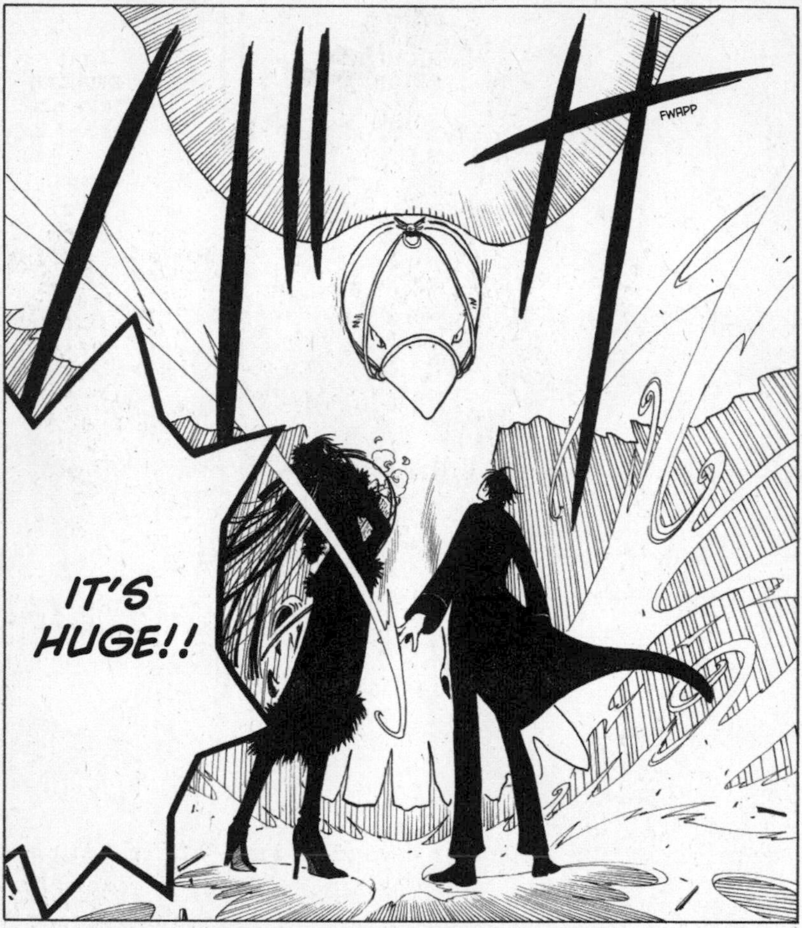
FWAPP
IT'S HUGE!!
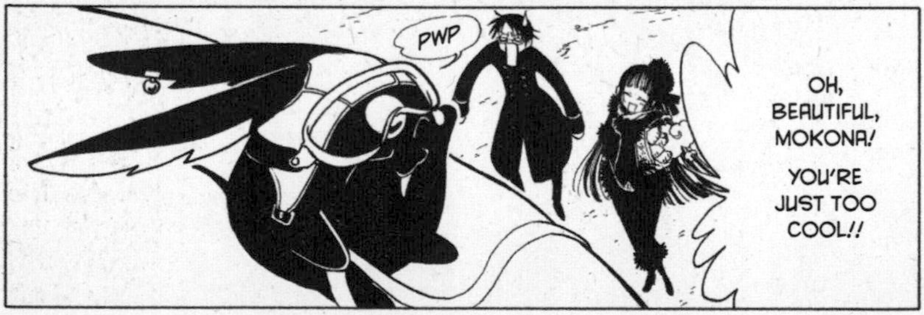
OH, BEAUTIFUL, MOKONA!
YOU'RE JUST TOO COOL!!
PWP

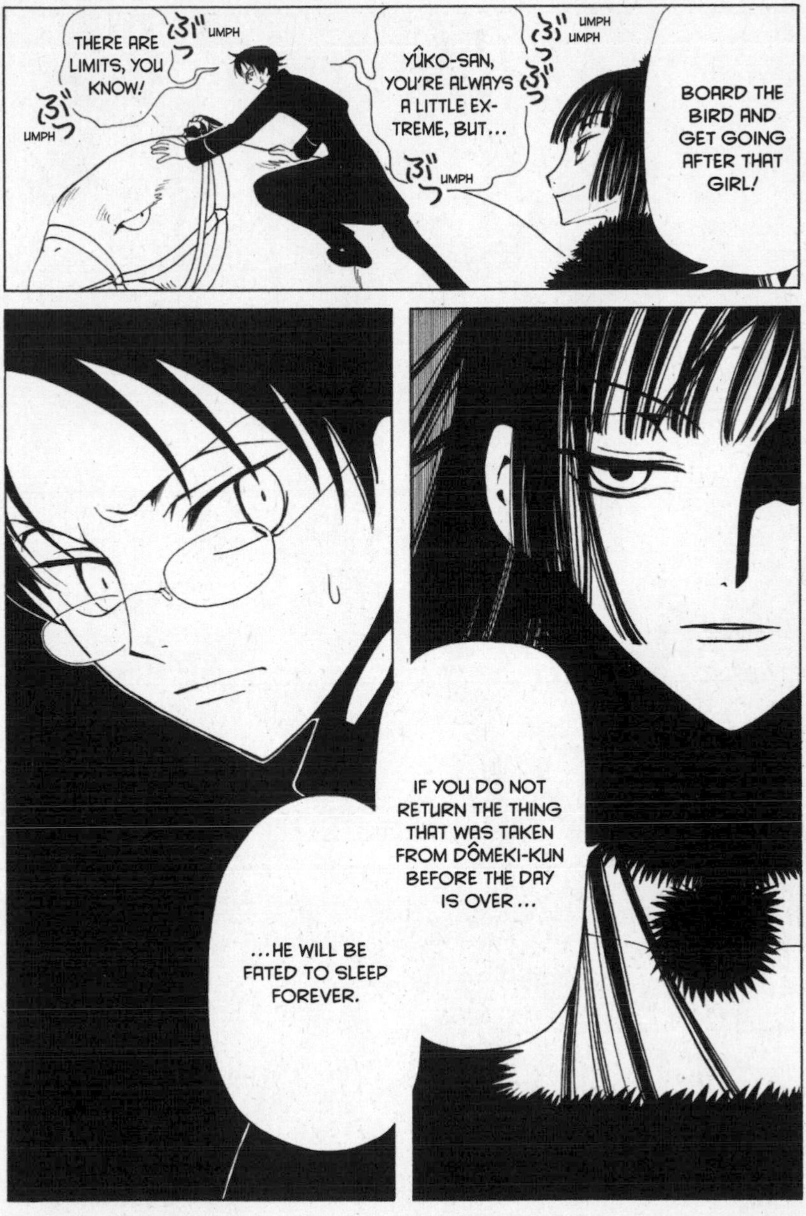
BOARD THE BIRD AND GET GOING AFTER THAT GIRL!
ぶっ UMPH
ぶっ UMPH
YÛKO-SAN, YOU'RE ALWAYS A LITTLE EX-TREME, BUT...
ぶっ UMPH
ぶっ UMPH
THERE ARE LIMITS, YOU KNOW!
ぶっ UMPH
IF YOU DO NOT RETURN THE THING THAT WAS TAKEN FROM DÔMEKI-KUN BEFORE THE DAY IS OVER...
...HE WILL BE FATED TO SLEEP FOREVER.

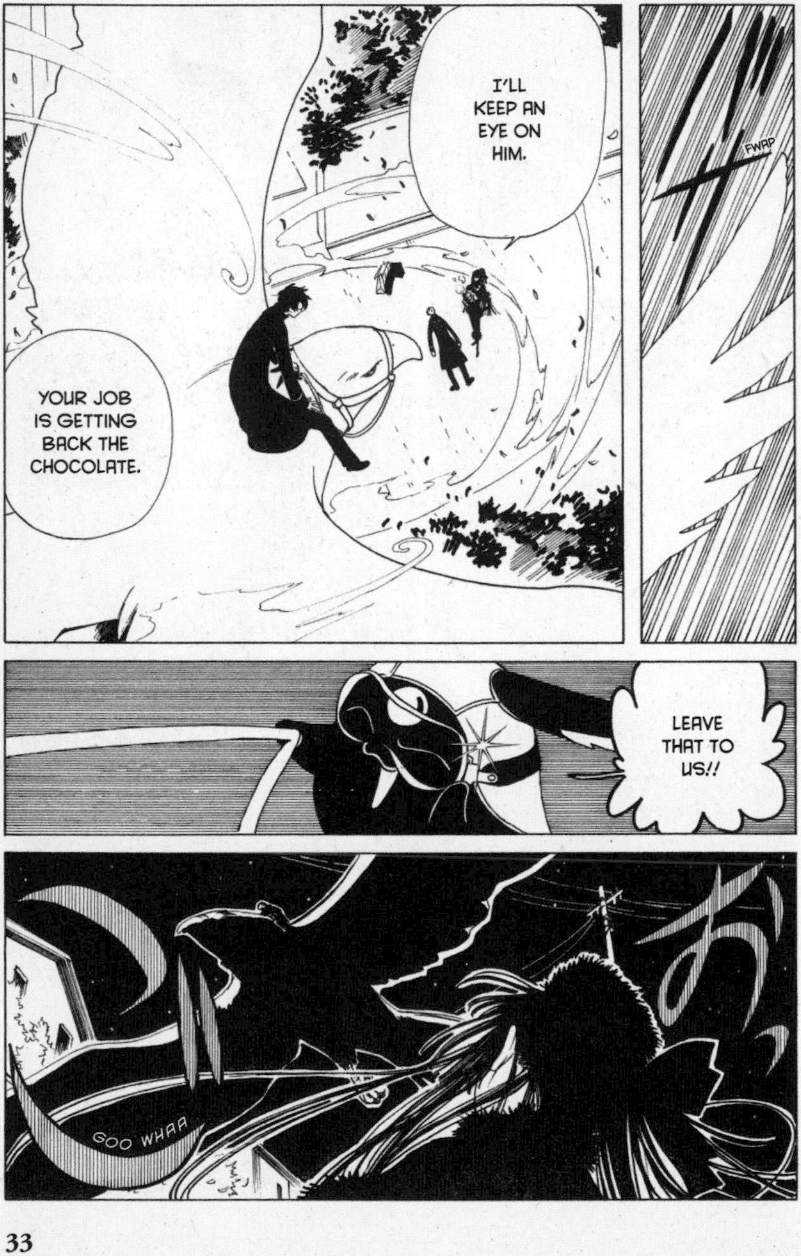
FWAP
I'LL KEEP AN EYE ON HIM.
YOUR JOB IS GETTING BACK THE CHOCOLATE.
LEAVE THAT TO US!!
GOO WHAA

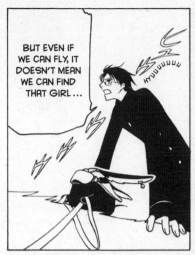

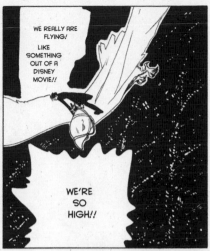

WE REALLY ARE FLYING!
LIKE SOMETHING OUT OF A DISNEY MOVIE!!
WE'RE SO HIGH!!
BUT EVEN IF WE CAN FLY, IT DOESN'T MEAN WE CAN FIND THAT GIRL...
HYUUUUUUU
GASP

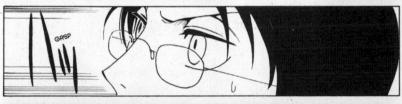

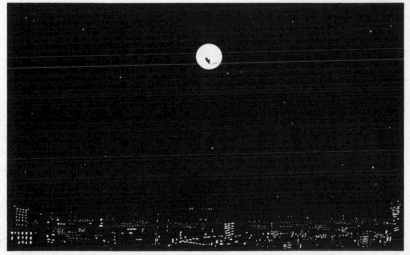

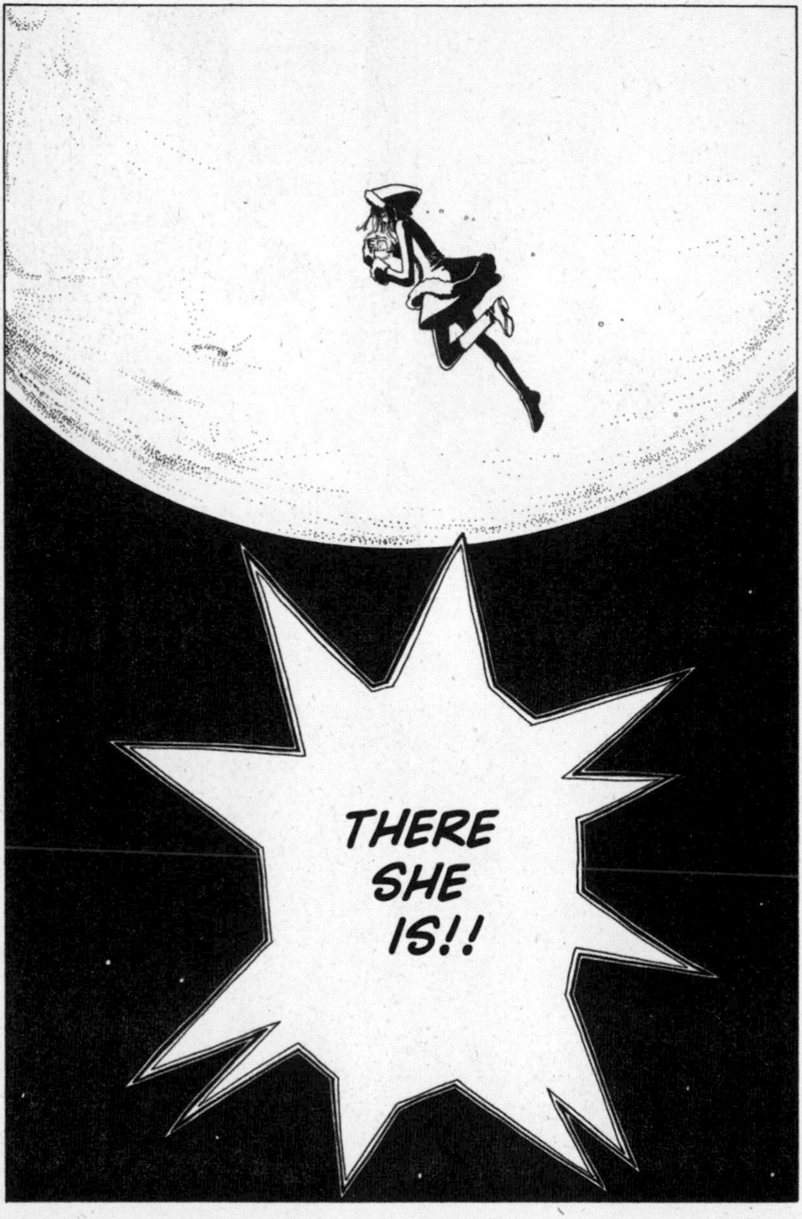
THERE SHE IS!!

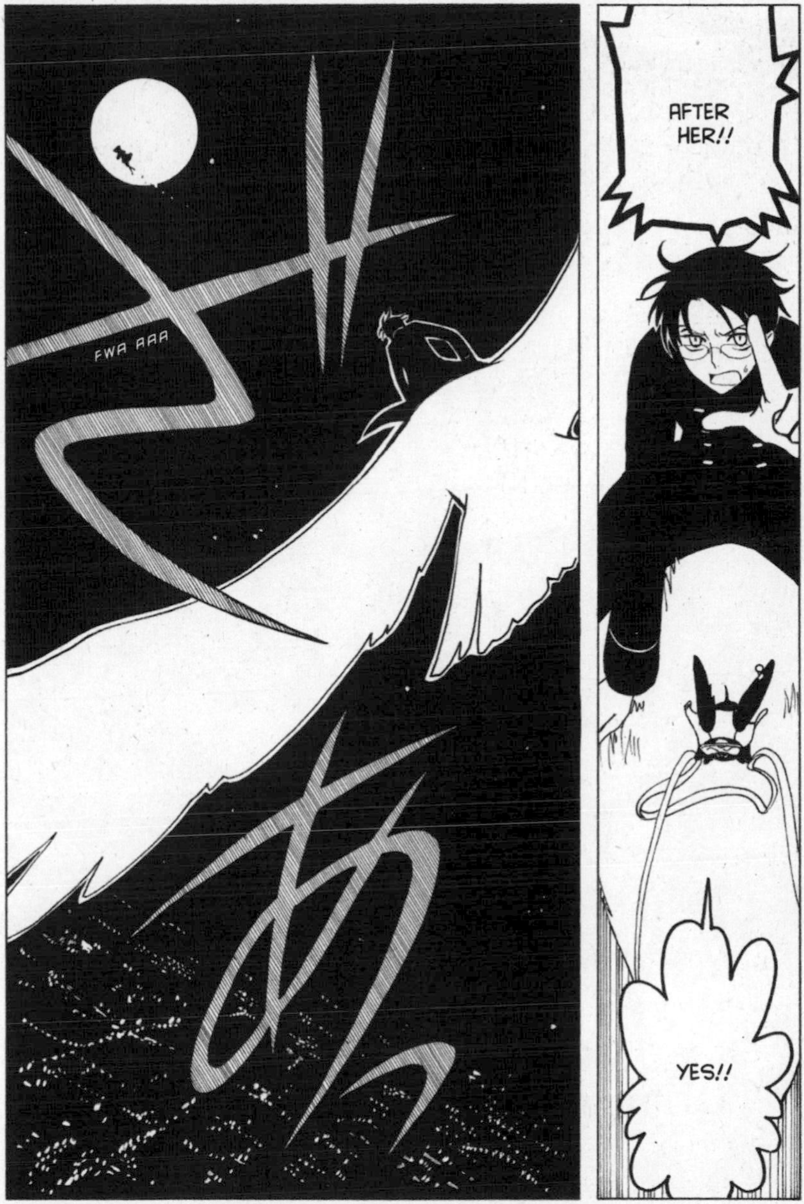
AFTER HER!!
YES!!
FWA AAA

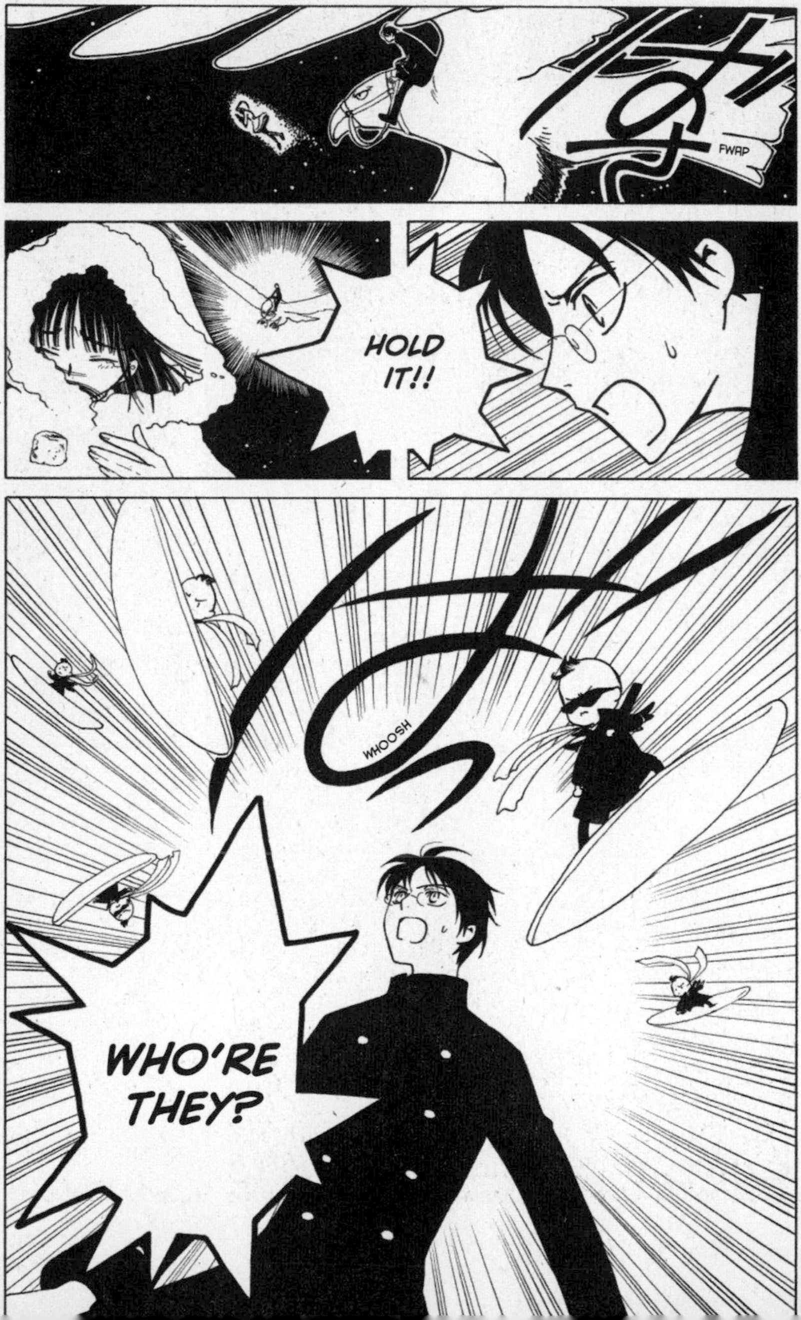
FWAP
HOLD IT!!
WHOOSH
WHO'RE THEY?

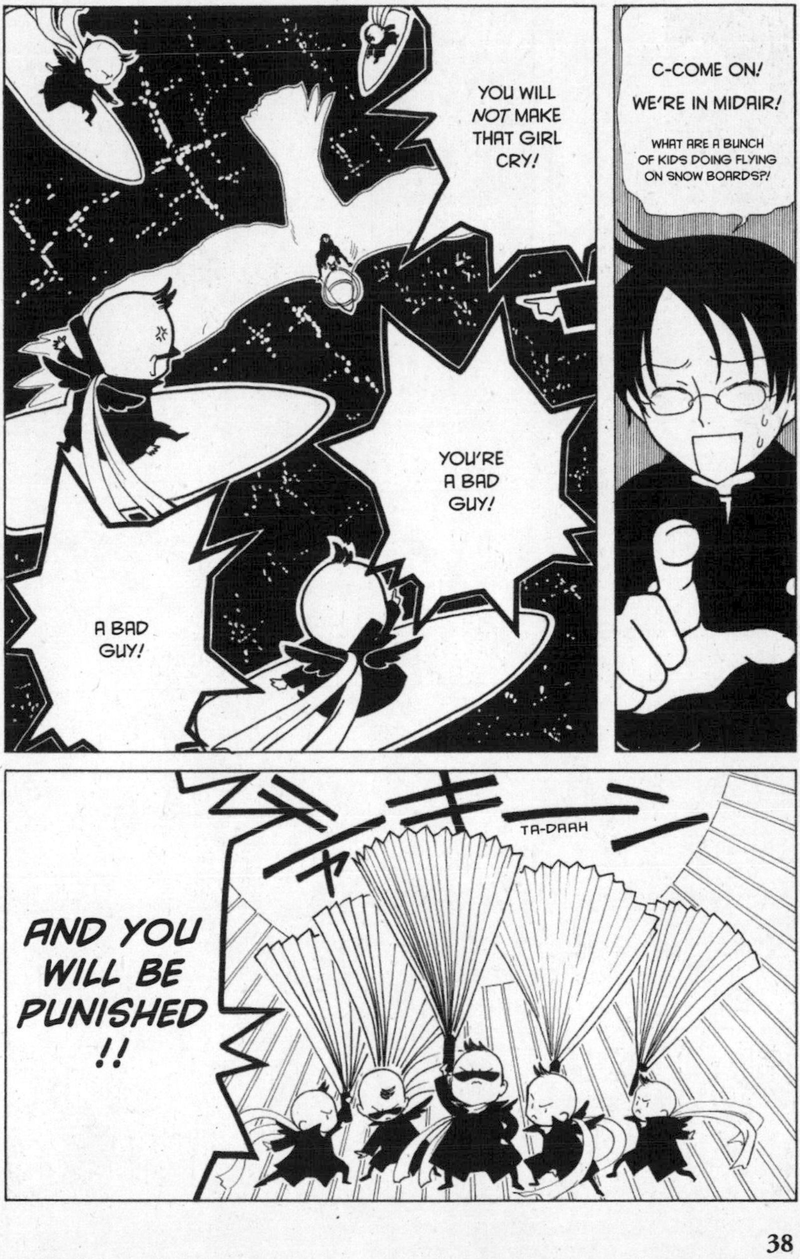
C-COME ON!
WE'RE IN MIDAIR!
WHAT ARE A BUNCH OF KIDS DOING FLYING ON SNOW BOARDS?!
YOU WILL *NOT* MAKE THAT GIRL CRY!
YOU'RE A BAD GUY!
A BAD GUY!
TA-DAAH
AND YOU WILL BE PUNISHED !!

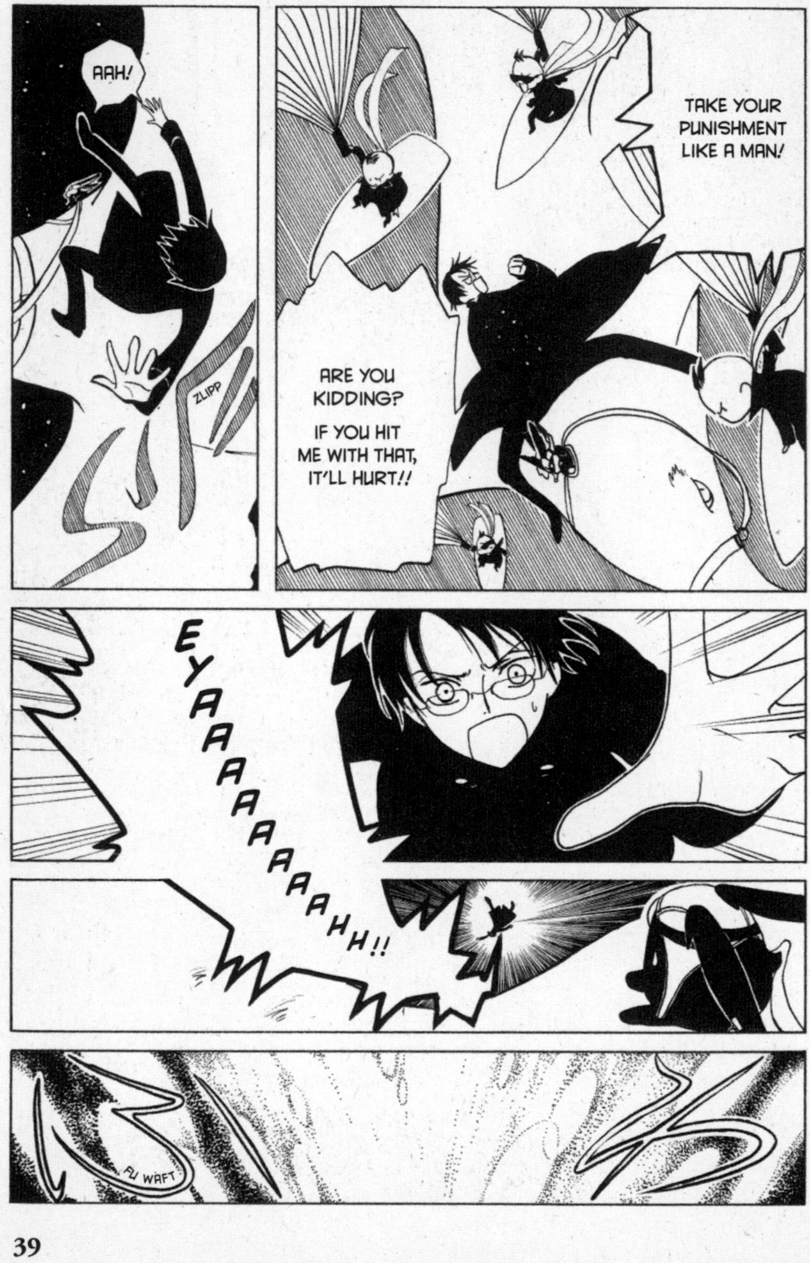
TAKE YOUR PUNISHMENT LIKE A MAN!
ARE YOU KIDDING?
IF YOU HIT ME WITH THAT, IT'LL HURT!!
AAH!
ZLIPP
EYAAAAAAAAHH!!
FU WAFT

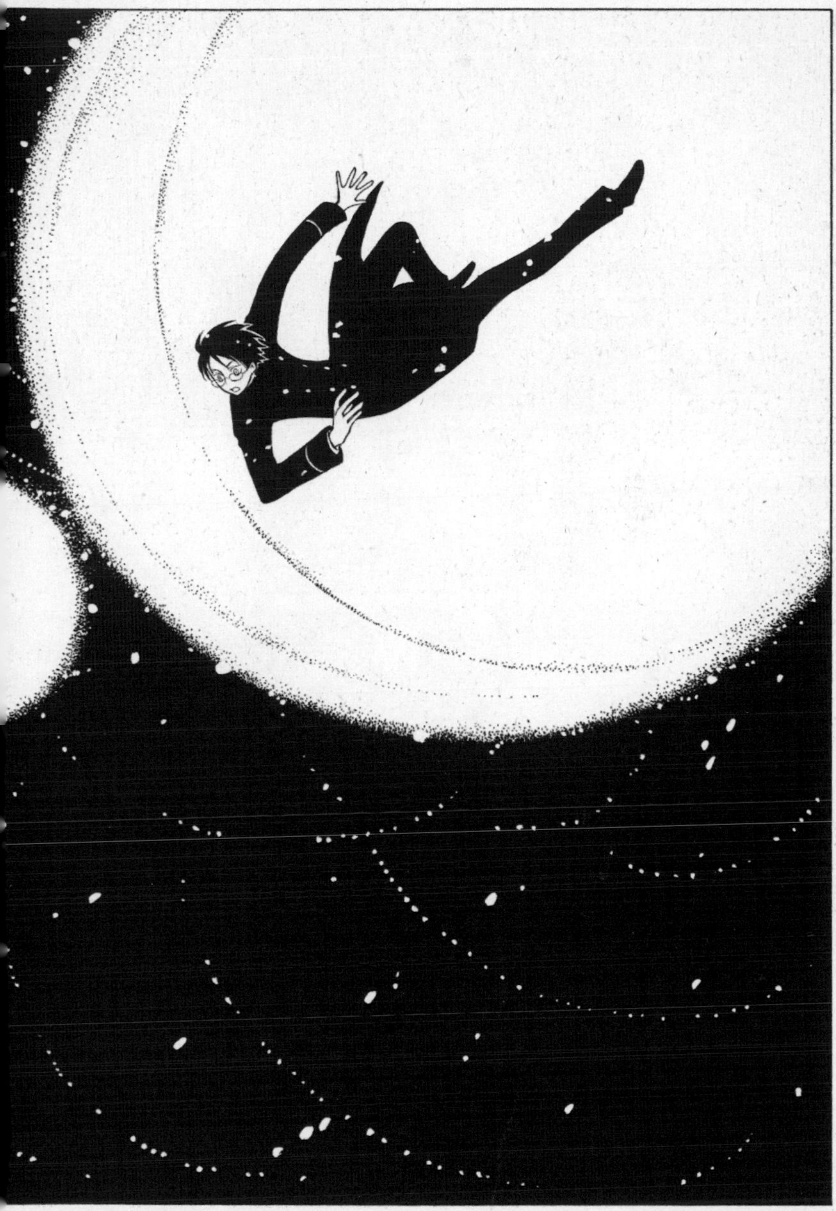

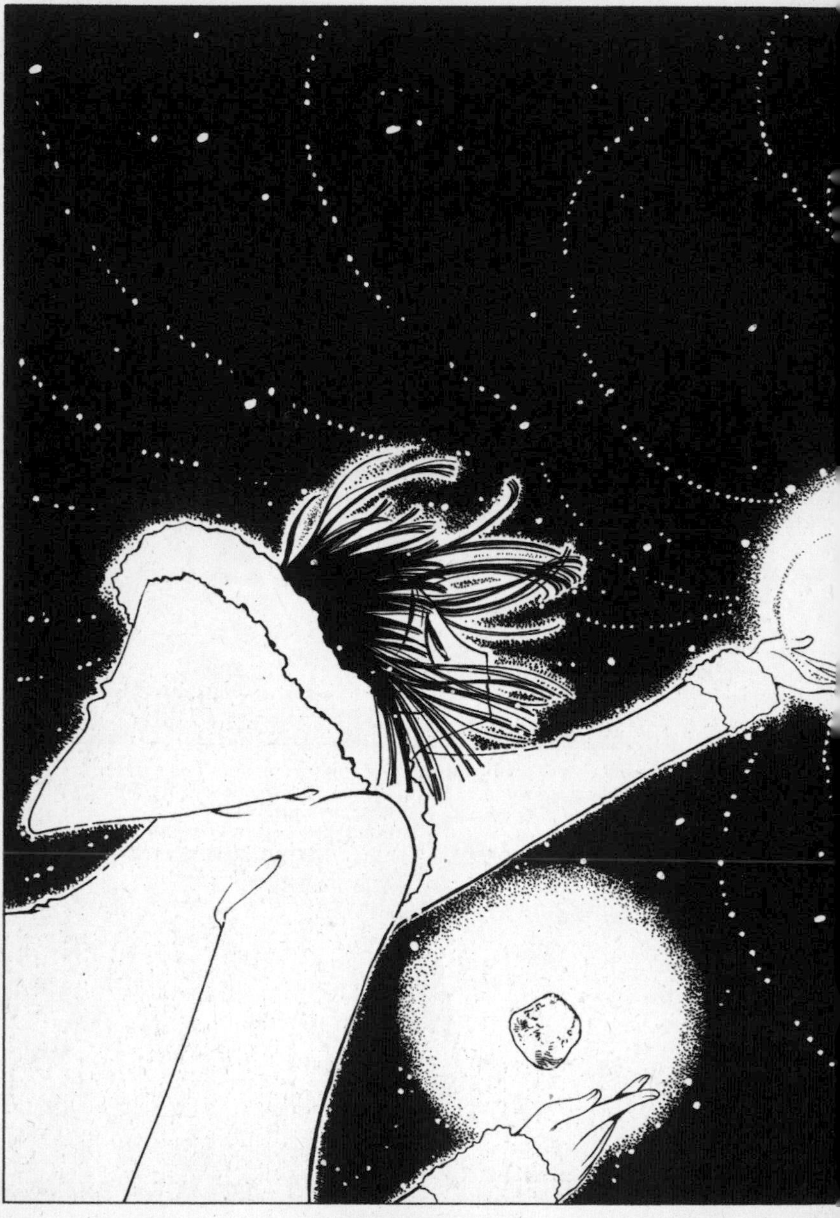

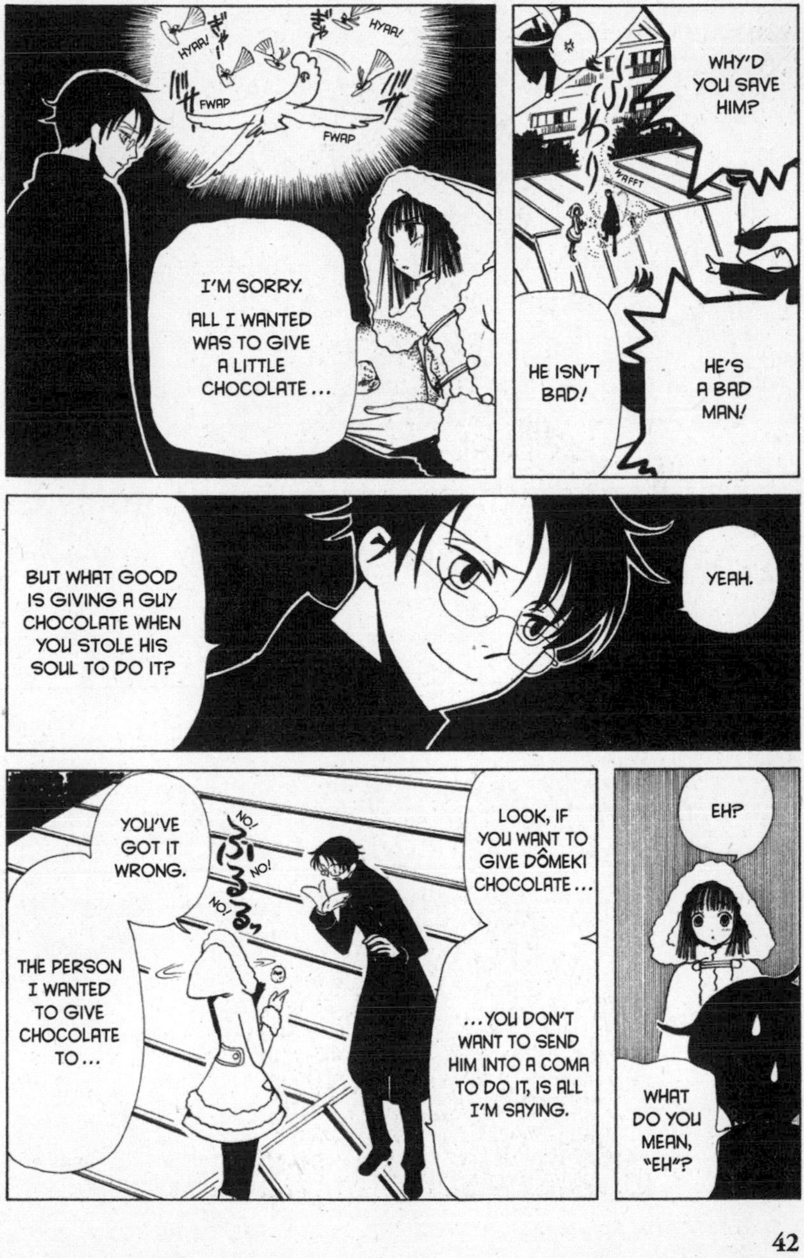
WHY'D YOU SAVE HIM?
HE'S A BAD MAN!
HE ISN'T BAD!
HYAA!
HYAA!
FWAP
FWAP
I'M SORRY.
ALL I WANTED WAS TO GIVE A LITTLE CHOCOLATE...
YEAH.
BUT WHAT GOOD IS GIVING A GUY CHOCOLATE WHEN YOU STOLE HIS SOUL TO DO IT?
EH?
WHAT DO YOU MEAN, "EH"?
LOOK, IF YOU WANT TO GIVE DÔMEKI CHOCOLATE...
...YOU DON'T WANT TO SEND HIM INTO A COMA TO DO IT, IS ALL I'M SAYING.
YOU'VE GOT IT WRONG.
NO! NO! NO!
THE PERSON I WANTED TO GIVE CHOCOLATE TO...

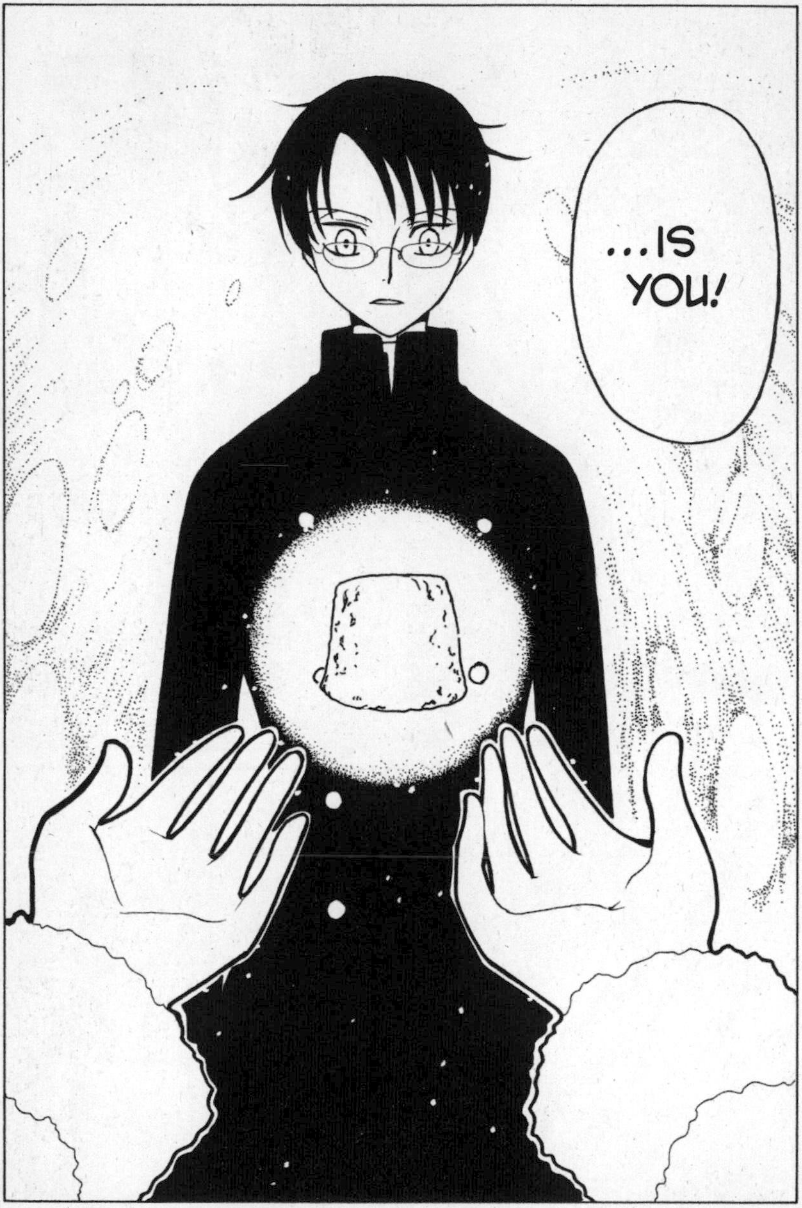
...IS YOU!

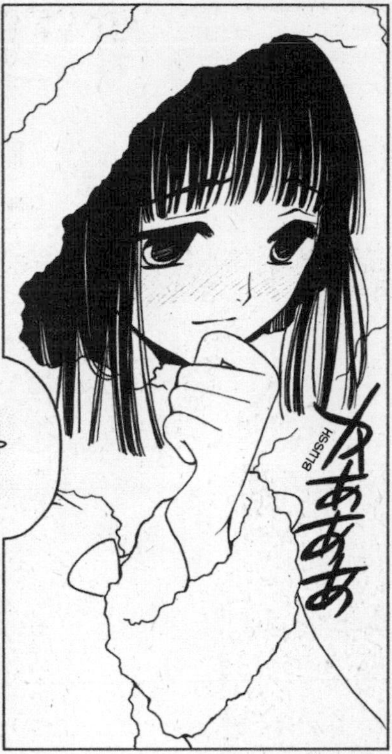
BLUSSH
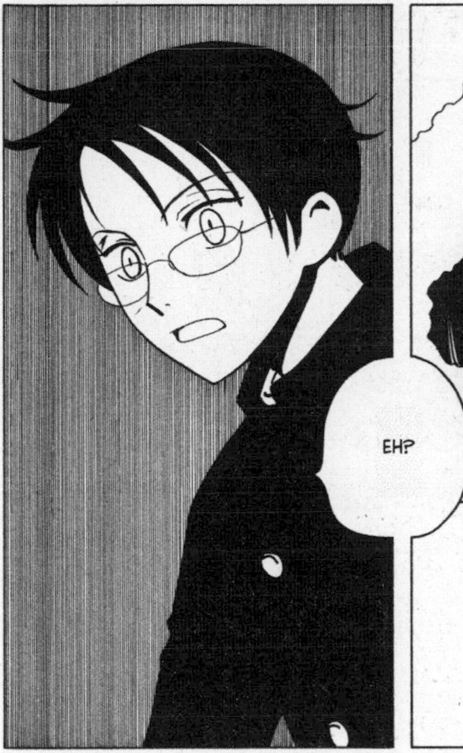
EH?
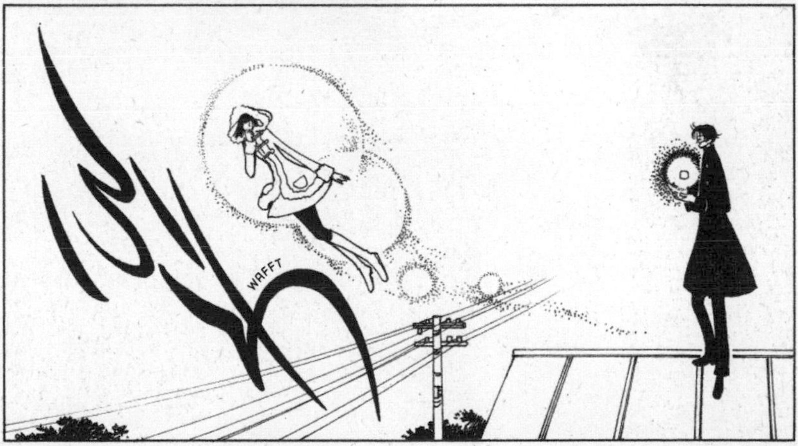
WAFFT

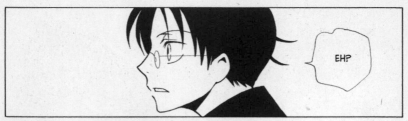

EH?

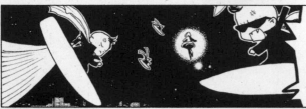

NEXT TIME, IF YOU MAKE HER CRY, YOU ARE *GONNA* GET PUNISHED!

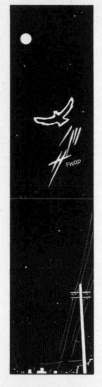

FWAP

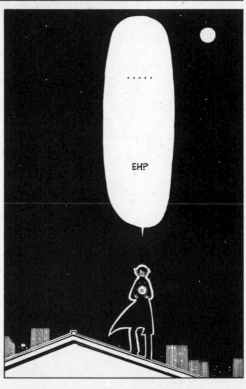

.....

EH?

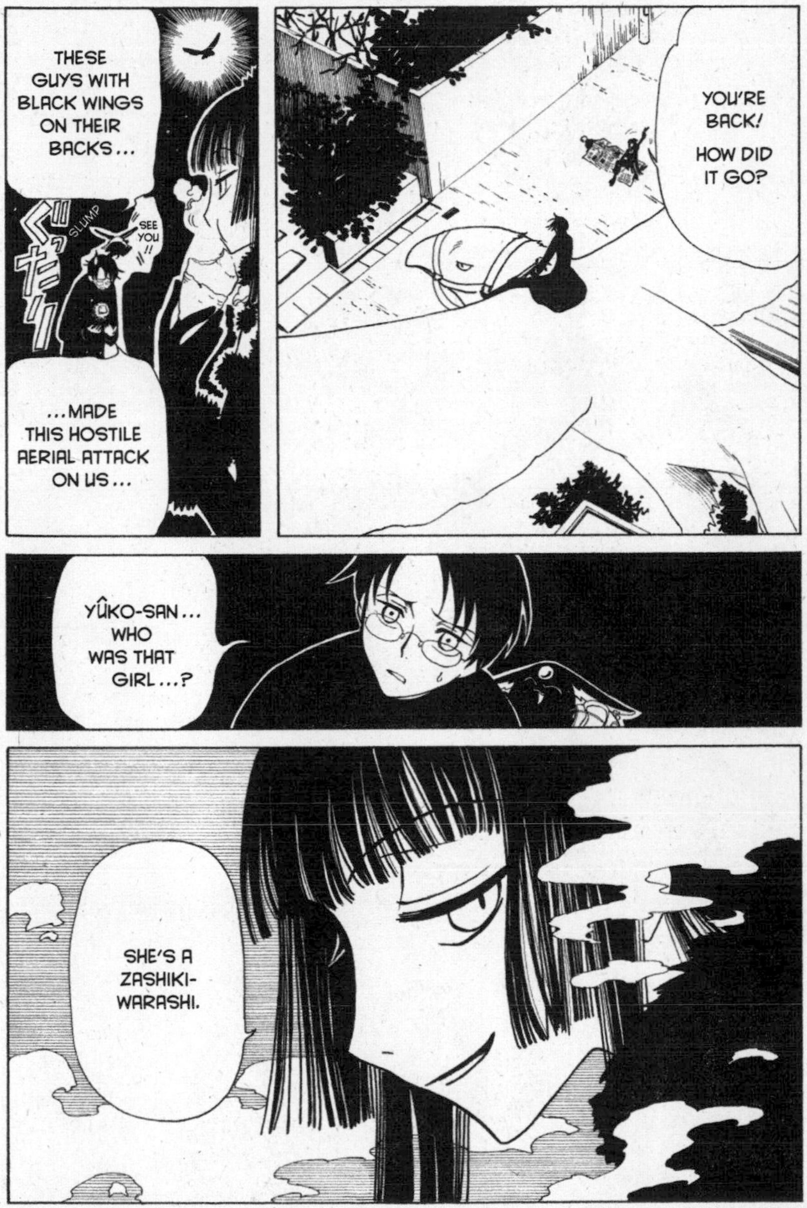
YOU'RE BACK!
HOW DID IT GO?
THESE GUYS WITH BLACK WINGS ON THEIR BACKS...
SEE YOU!!
SLUMP
...MADE THIS HOSTILE AERIAL ATTACK ON US...
YÛKO-SAN... WHO WAS THAT GIRL...?
SHE'S A ZASHIKI-WARASHI.

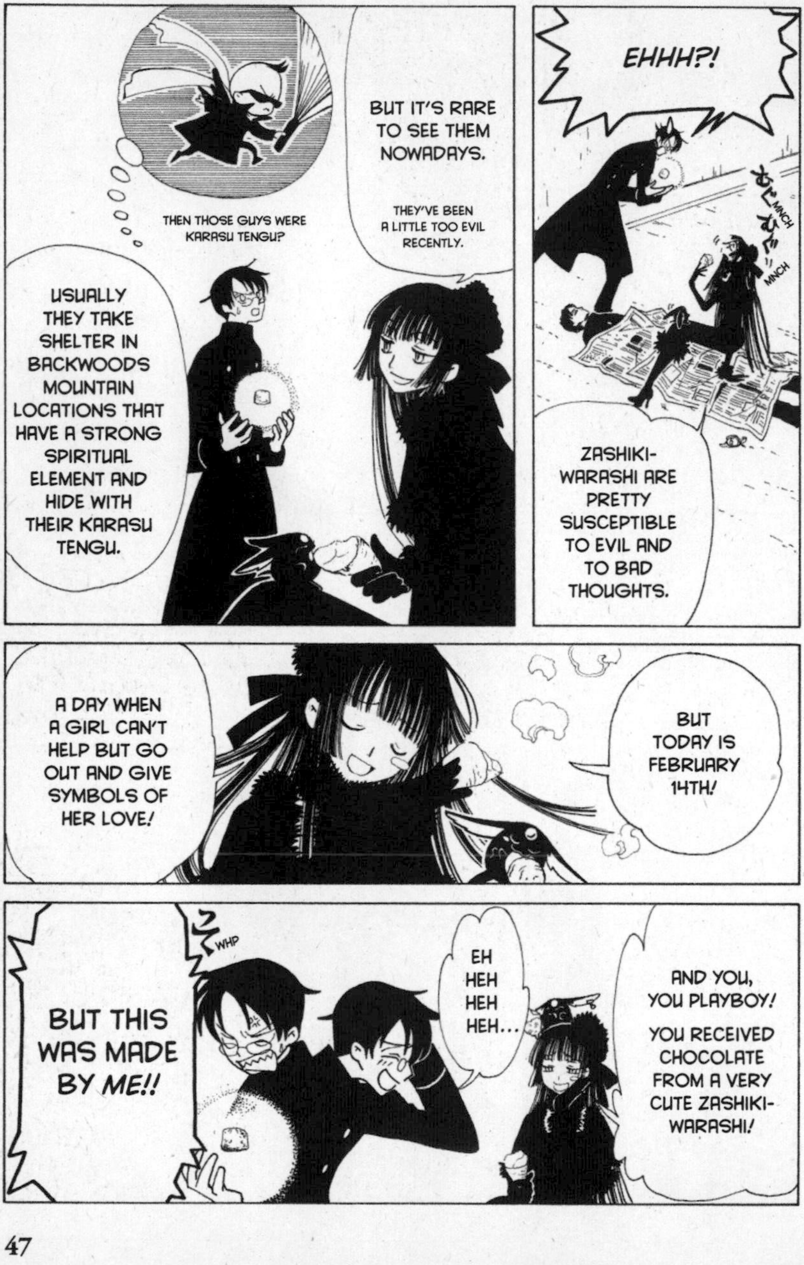
EHHH?!
MNCH
MNCH
ZASHIKI-WARASHI ARE PRETTY SUSCEPTIBLE TO EVIL AND TO BAD THOUGHTS.
BUT IT'S RARE TO SEE THEM NOWADAYS.
THEY'VE BEEN A LITTLE TOO EVIL RECENTLY.
THEN THOSE GUYS WERE KARASU TENGU?
USUALLY THEY TAKE SHELTER IN BACKWOODS MOUNTAIN LOCATIONS THAT HAVE A STRONG SPIRITUAL ELEMENT AND HIDE WITH THEIR KARASU TENGU.
BUT TODAY IS FEBRUARY 14TH!
A DAY WHEN A GIRL CAN'T HELP BUT GO OUT AND GIVE SYMBOLS OF HER LOVE!
AND YOU, YOU PLAYBOY!
YOU RECEIVED CHOCOLATE FROM A VERY CUTE ZASHIKI-WARASHI!
EH HEH HEH HEH...
WHP
BUT THIS WAS MADE BY ME!!

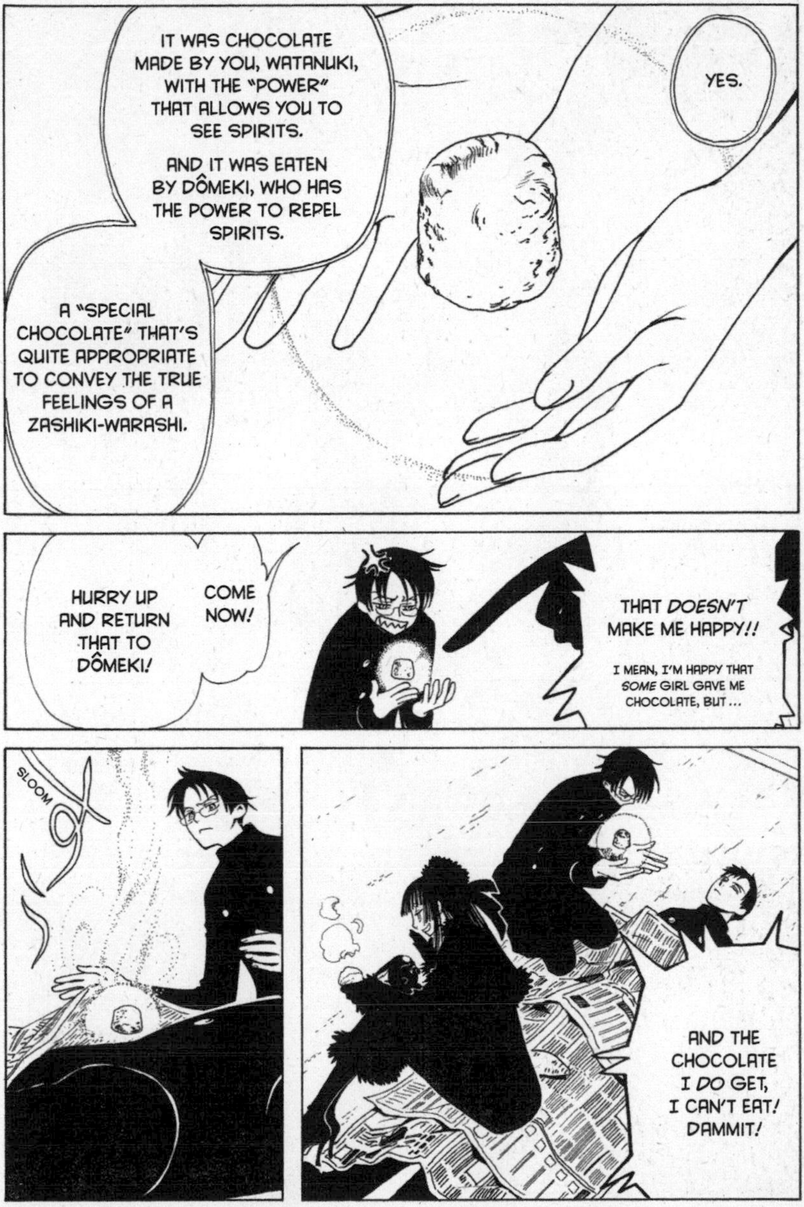
YES.
IT WAS CHOCOLATE MADE BY YOU, WATANUKI, WITH THE "POWER" THAT ALLOWS YOU TO SEE SPIRITS.
AND IT WAS EATEN BY DÔMEKI, WHO HAS THE POWER TO REPEL SPIRITS.
A "SPECIAL CHOCOLATE" THAT'S QUITE APPROPRIATE TO CONVEY THE TRUE FEELINGS OF A ZASHIKI-WARASHI.
THAT *DOESN'T* MAKE ME HAPPY!!
I MEAN, I'M HAPPY THAT *SOME* GIRL GAVE ME CHOCOLATE, BUT...
COME NOW!
HURRY UP AND RETURN THAT TO DÔMEKI!
AND THE CHOCOLATE I *DO* GET, I CAN'T EAT! DAMMIT!
SLOOM

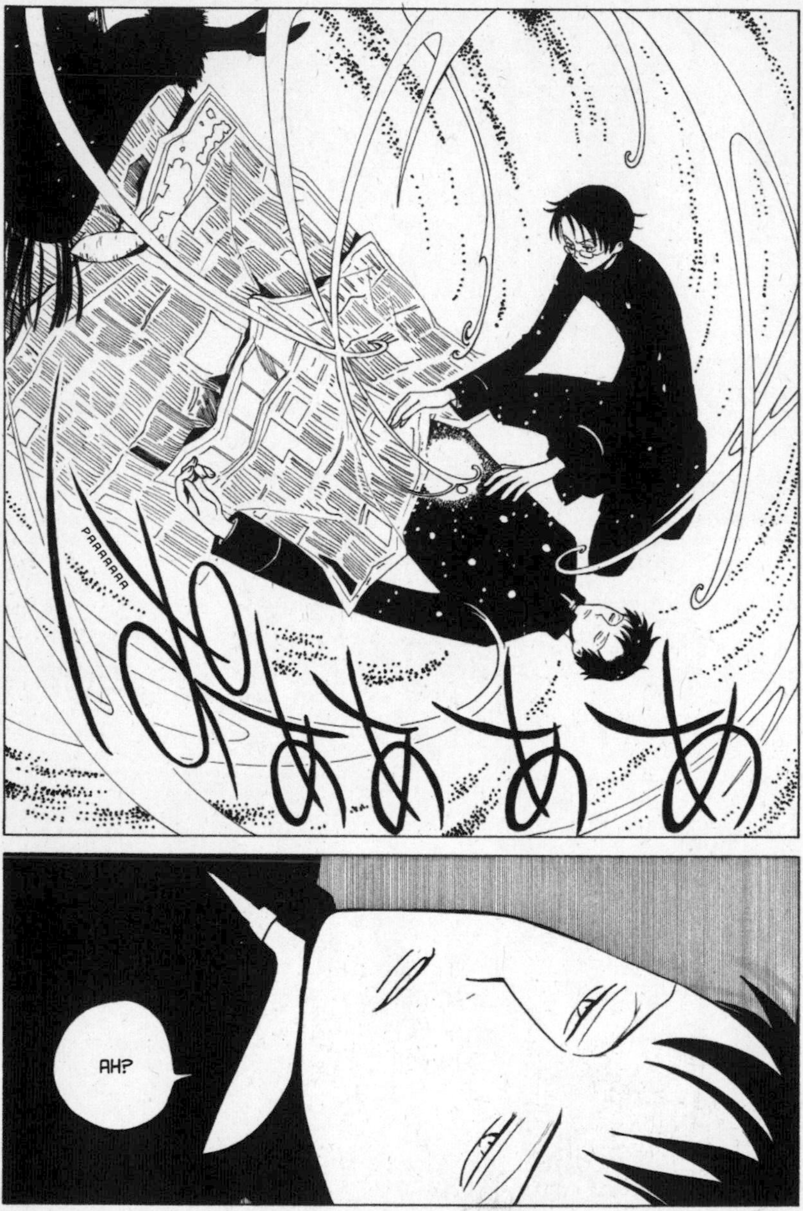
あああああ
PAAAAAAA
AH?

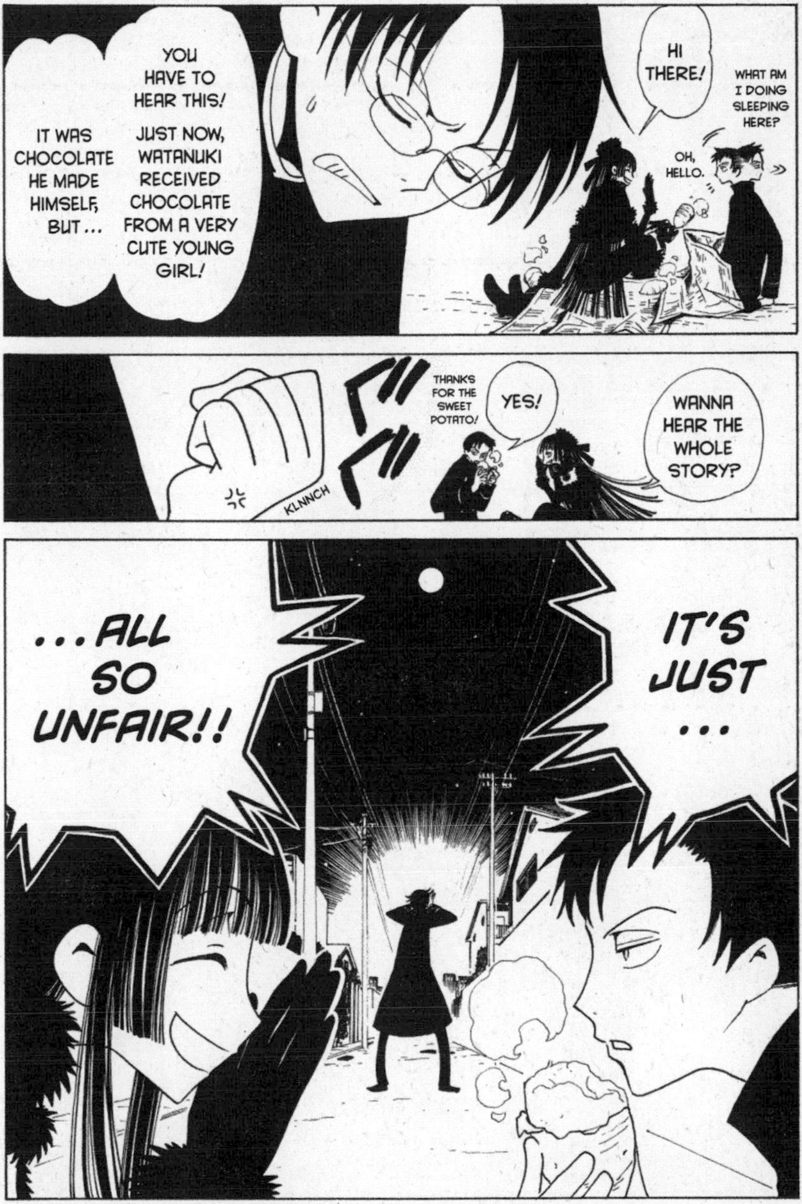
WHAT AM I DOING SLEEPING HERE?
HI THERE!
OH, HELLO.
YOU HAVE TO HEAR THIS!
JUST NOW, WATANUKI RECEIVED CHOCOLATE FROM A VERY CUTE YOUNG GIRL!
IT WAS CHOCOLATE HE MADE HIMSELF, BUT...
WANNA HEAR THE WHOLE STORY?
YES!
THANKS FOR THE SWEET POTATO!
KLNNCH
IT'S JUST...
...ALL SO UNFAIR!!

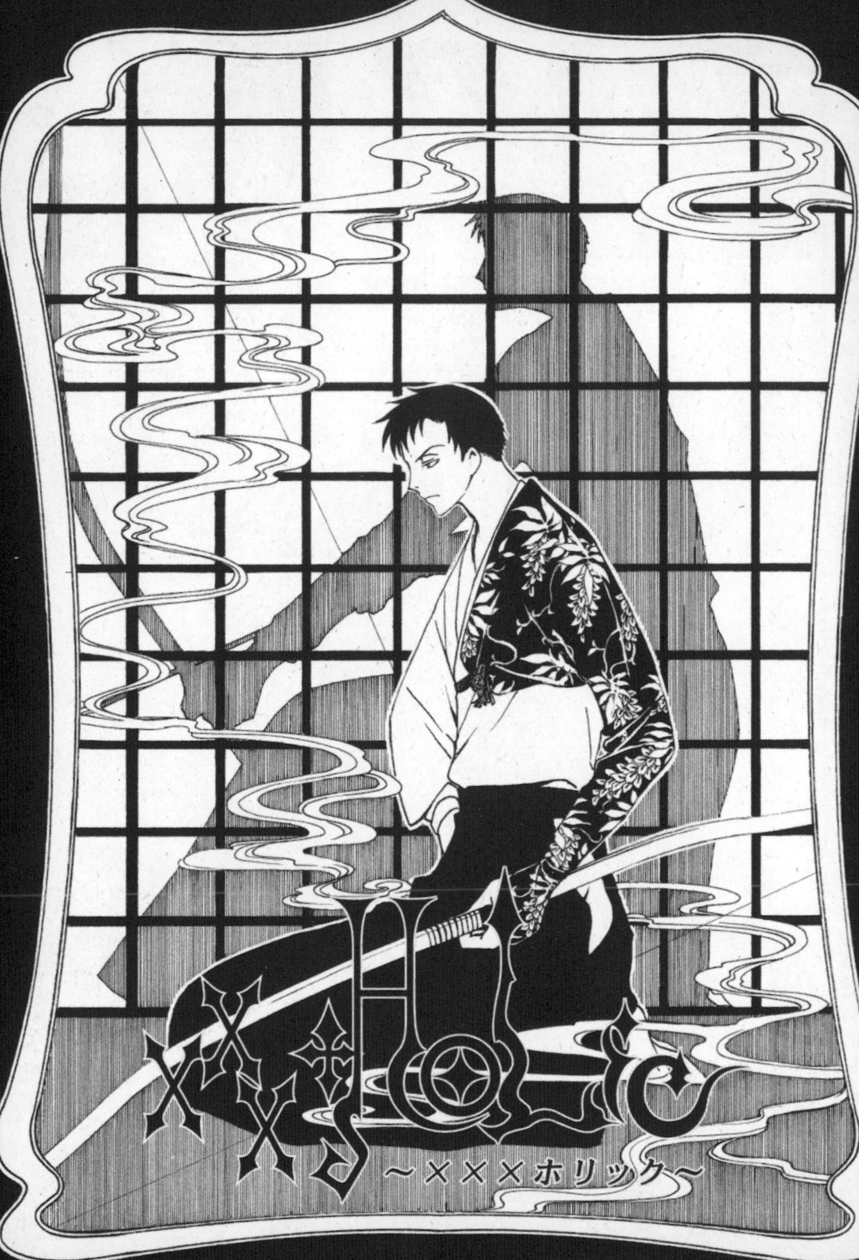
xxxHOLiC
~×××ホリック~

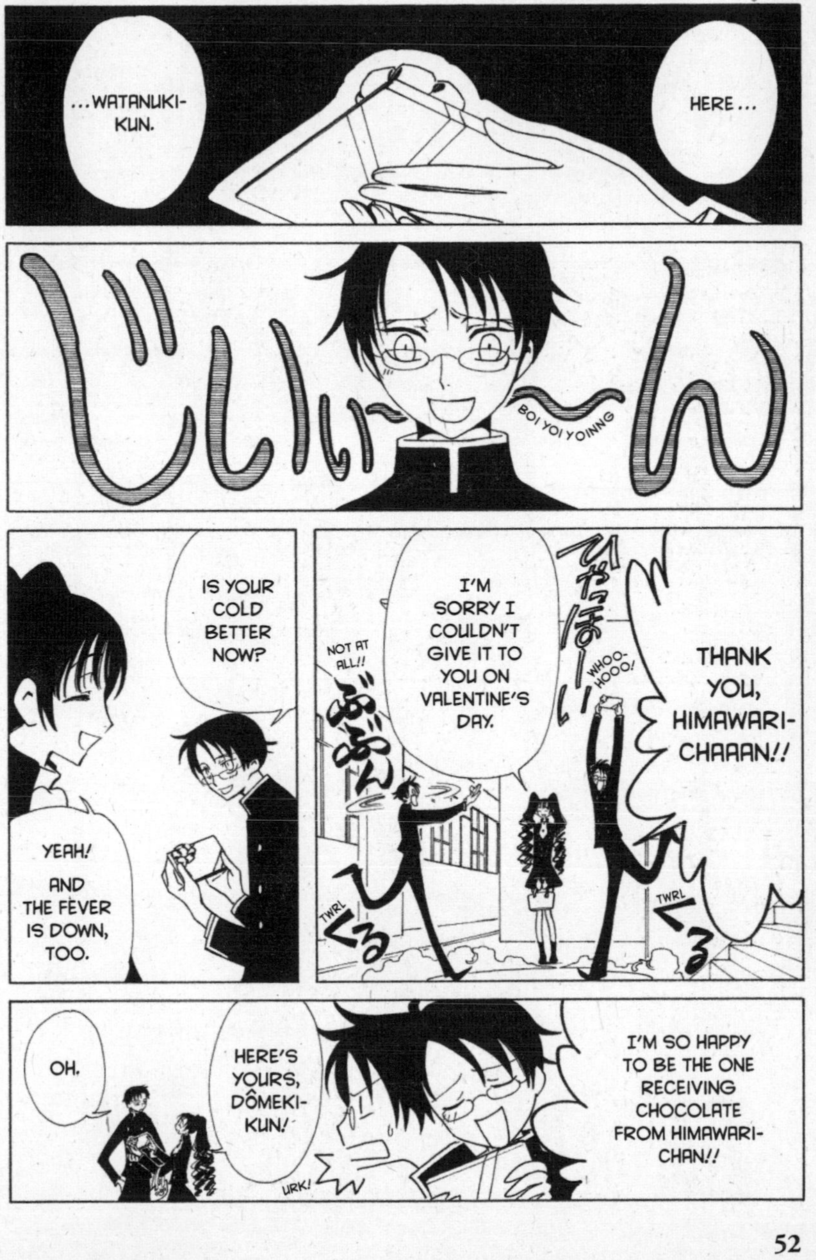
HERE...
...WATANUKI-KUN.
じぃぃ〜ん
BOI YOI YOINNG
ひゃっほーい
WHOO-HOOO!
THANK YOU, HIMAWARI-CHAAAN!!
I'M SORRY I COULDN'T GIVE IT TO YOU ON VALENTINE'S DAY.
NOT AT ALL!!
ぶぶん
TWRL
くる
TWRL
くる
IS YOUR COLD BETTER NOW?
YEAH!
AND THE FEVER IS DOWN, TOO.
I'M SO HAPPY TO BE THE ONE RECEIVING CHOCOLATE FROM HIMAWARI-CHAN!!
URK!
HERE'S YOURS, DÔMEKI-KUN!
OH.

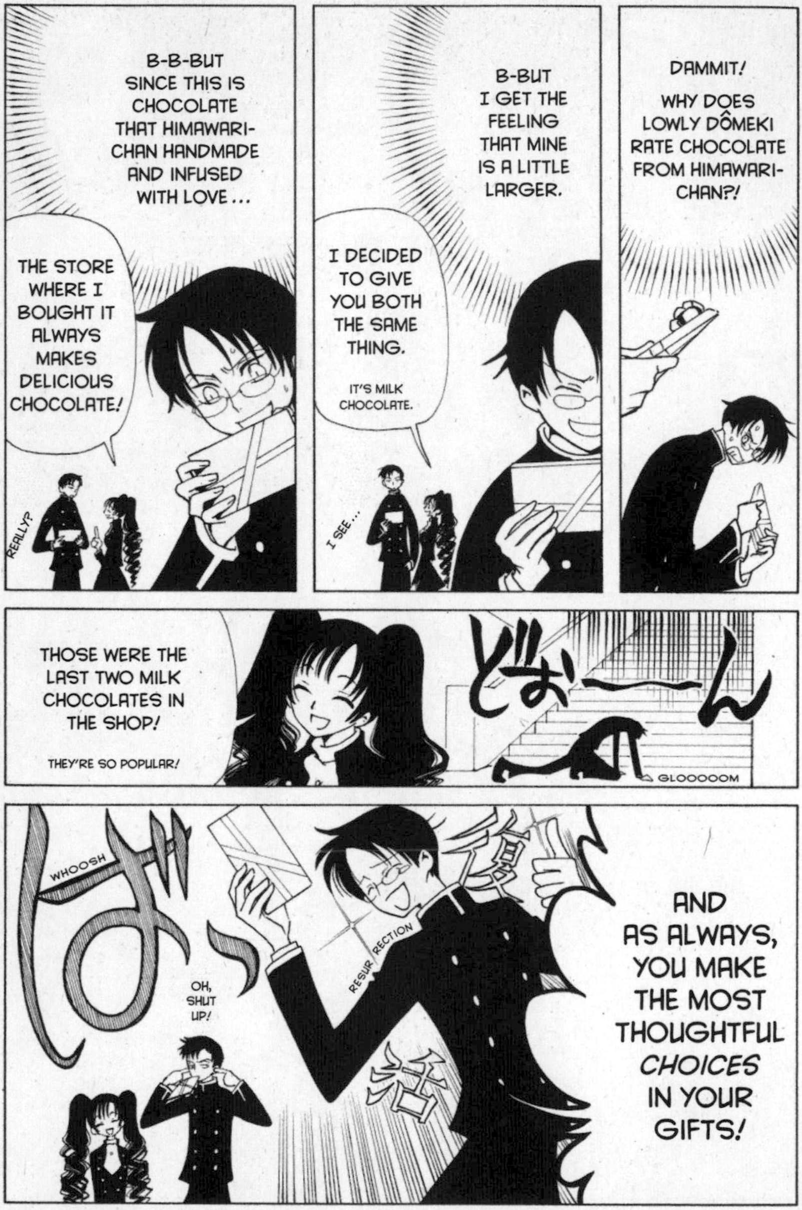
DAMMIT!
WHY DOES LOWLY DÔMEKI RATE CHOCOLATE FROM HIMAWARI-CHAN?!
B-BUT I GET THE FEELING THAT MINE IS A LITTLE LARGER.
I DECIDED TO GIVE YOU BOTH THE SAME THING.
IT'S MILK CHOCOLATE.
I SEE...
B-B-BUT SINCE THIS IS CHOCOLATE THAT HIMAWARI-CHAN HANDMADE AND INFUSED WITH LOVE...
THE STORE WHERE I BOUGHT IT ALWAYS MAKES DELICIOUS CHOCOLATE!
REALLY?
どぉーーん
GLOOOOOM
THOSE WERE THE LAST TWO MILK CHOCOLATES IN THE SHOP!
THEY'RE SO POPULAR!
AND AS ALWAYS, YOU MAKE THE MOST THOUGHTFUL *CHOICES* IN YOUR GIFTS!
RESUR RECTION
OH, SHUT UP!
WHOOSH

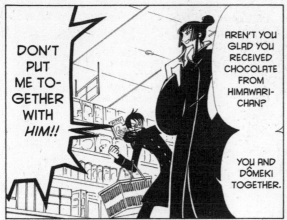

Supermarket
AREN'T YOU GLAD YOU RECEIVED CHOCOLATE FROM HIMAWARI-CHAN?
YOU AND DÔMEKI TOGETHER.
DON'T PUT ME TO-GETHER WITH *HIM!!*
THAT MAKES THE THIRD CHOCOLATE YOU RECEIVED THIS YEAR.
HUH?
HOW DO YOU GET THREE?
ATARIME
THE ZASHIKI-WARASHI GAVE YOU ONE.
HIMAWARI-CHAN GAVE YOU ONE.
AND?
THAT MAKES TWO.
AND THE CHOCOLATE I GAVE YOU.

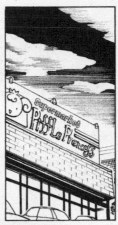

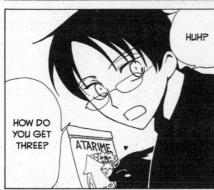

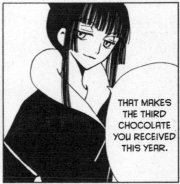

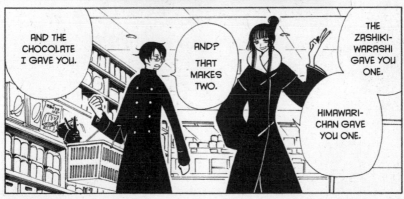

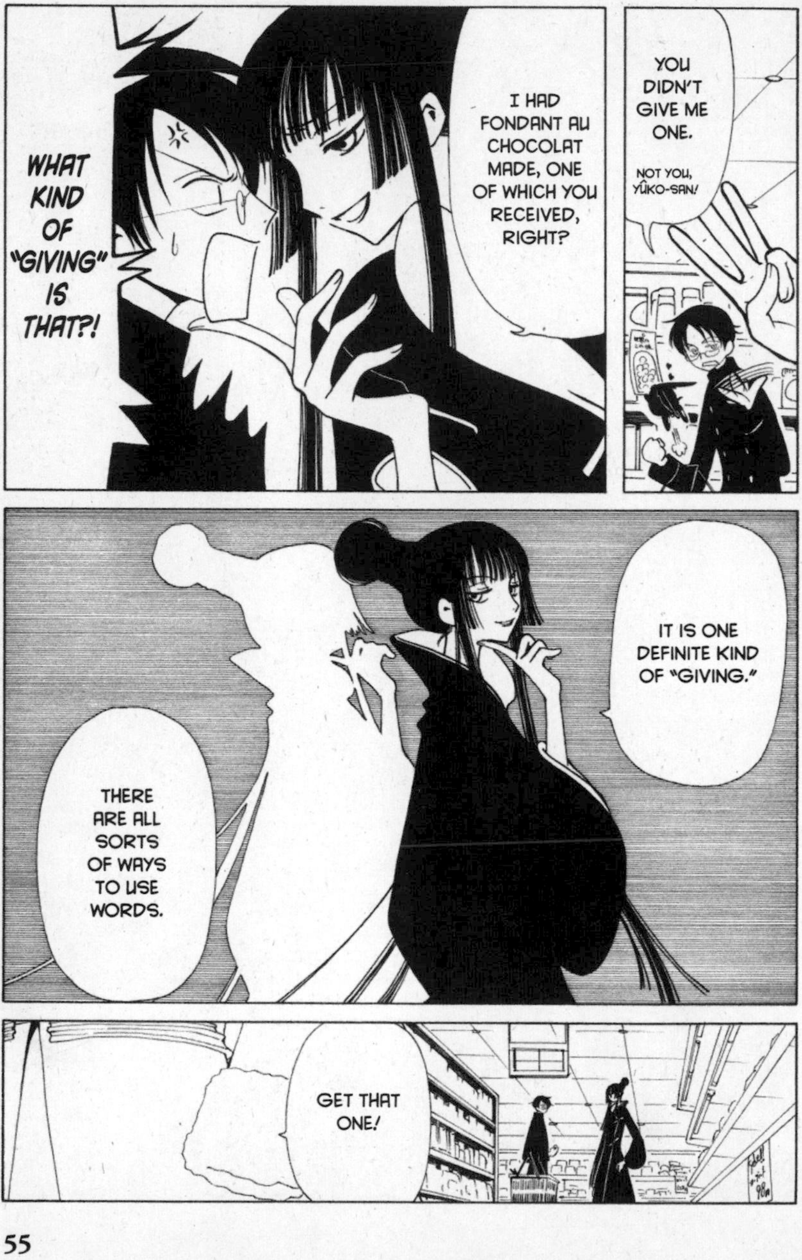
YOU DIDN'T GIVE ME ONE.
NOT YOU, YÛKO-SAN!
I HAD FONDANT AU CHOCOLAT MADE, ONE OF WHICH YOU RECEIVED, RIGHT?
WHAT KIND OF "GIVING" IS THAT?!
IT IS ONE DEFINITE KIND OF "GIVING."
THERE ARE ALL SORTS OF WAYS TO USE WORDS.
GET THAT ONE!

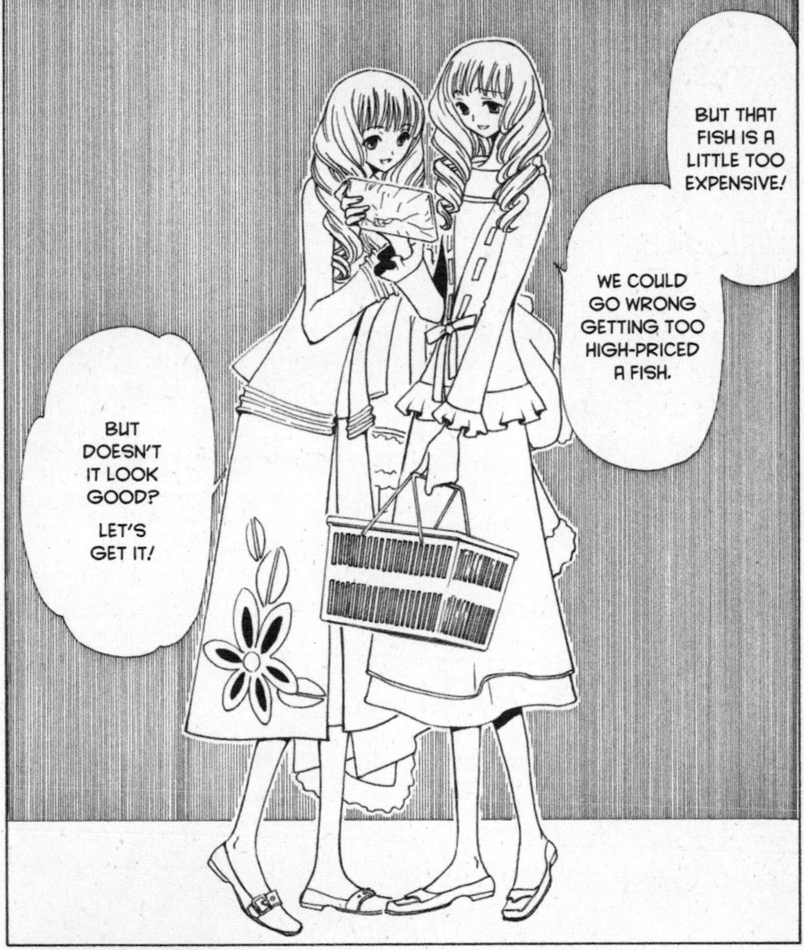
BUT THAT FISH IS A LITTLE TOO EXPENSIVE!
WE COULD GO WRONG GETTING TOO HIGH-PRICED A FISH.
BUT DOESN'T IT LOOK GOOD?
LET'S GET IT!

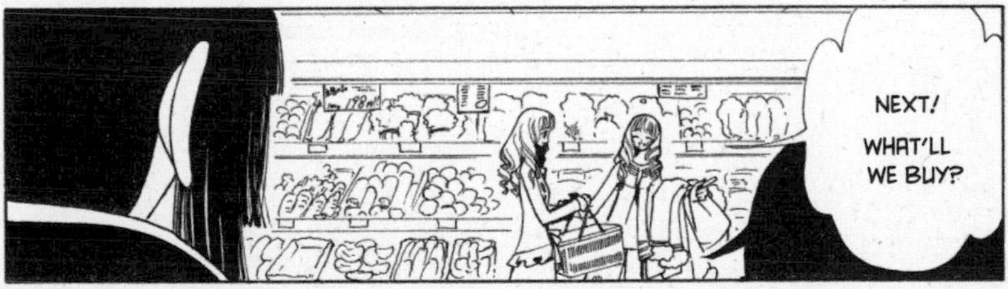
NEXT!
WHAT'LL WE BUY?

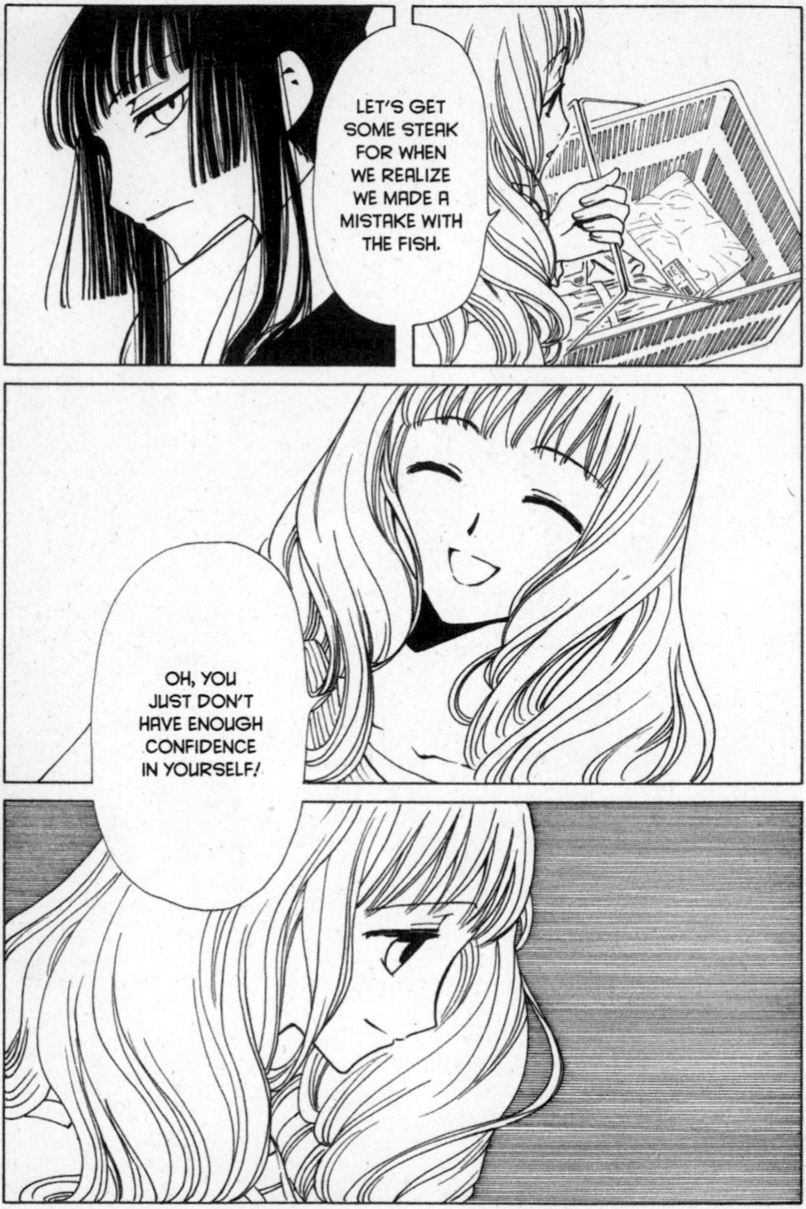
LET'S GET SOME STEAK FOR WHEN WE REALIZE WE MADE A MISTAKE WITH THE FISH.
OH, YOU JUST DON'T HAVE ENOUGH CONFIDENCE IN YOURSELF!

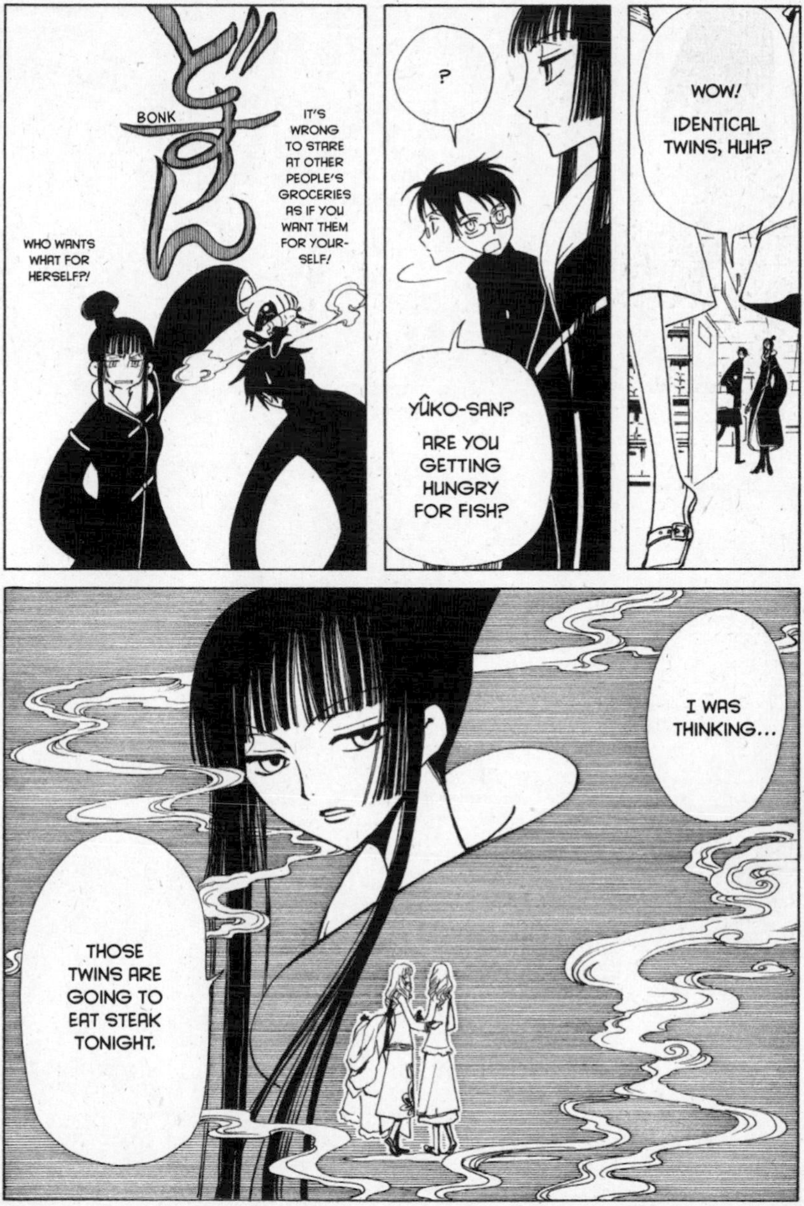
WOW!
IDENTICAL TWINS, HUH?
?
YÛKO-SAN?
ARE YOU GETTING HUNGRY FOR FISH?
IT'S WRONG TO STARE AT OTHER PEOPLE'S GROCERIES AS IF YOU WANT THEM FOR YOURSELF!
BONK
WHO WANTS WHAT FOR HERSELF?!
I WAS THINKING...
THOSE TWINS ARE GOING TO EAT STEAK TONIGHT.

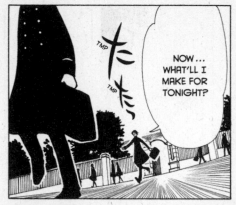

私立十字学園
CROSS PRIVATE SCHOOL
TMP
TMP
NOW... WHAT'LL I MAKE FOR TONIGHT?
LAST NIGHT I MADE MABO-DÔFU, DIDN'T I...
AND I THREW SHUMAI AND OTHER CHINESE DISHES IN ON THE SIDE.
MAYBE I'LL GO WITH YAKITORI TONIGHT?
YÛKO-SAN BEING YÛKO-SAN, SHE'LL WANT SOMETHING THAT'S GOOD WITH ALCOHOL.
THE TWINS FROM YESTERDAY!
AT LEAST, ONE OF THEM.
GLANCE

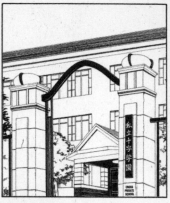

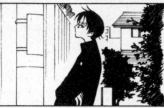

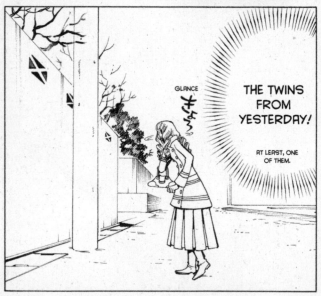

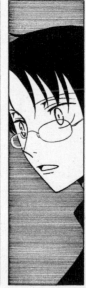

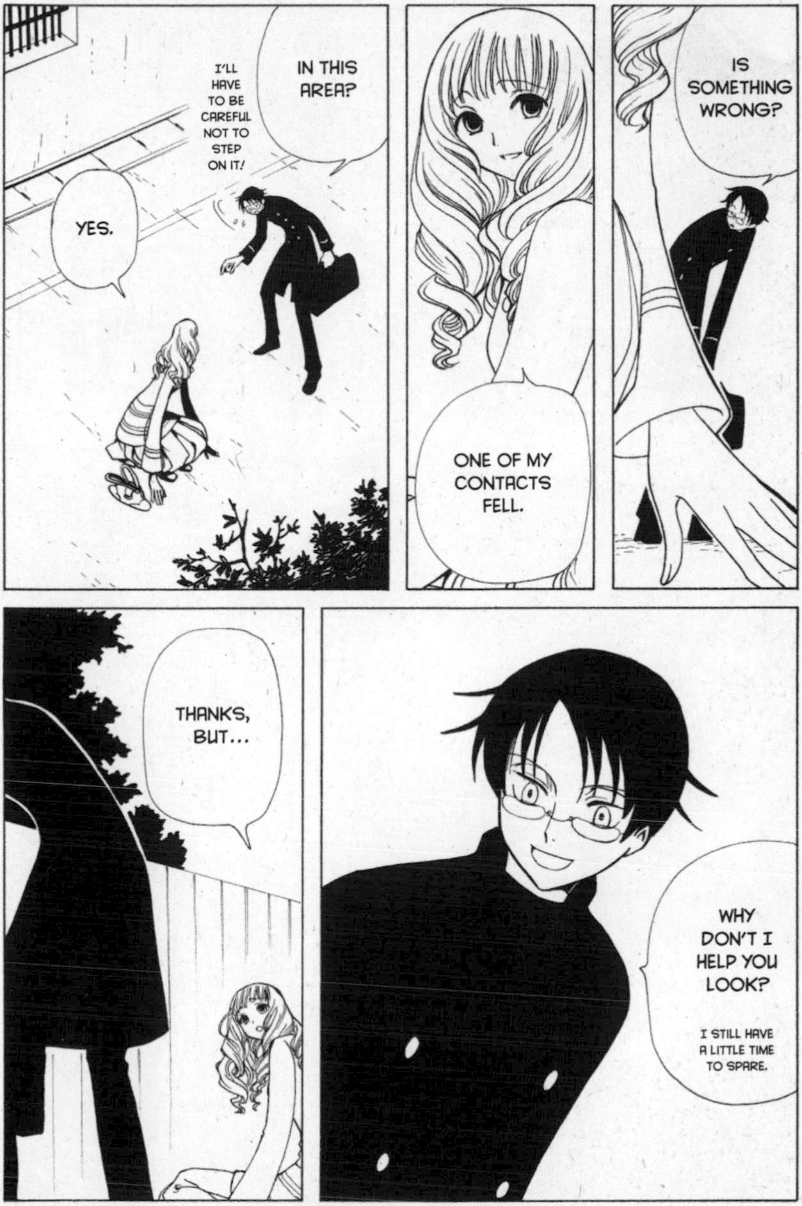
IS SOMETHING WRONG?
ONE OF MY CONTACTS FELL.
IN THIS AREA?
I'LL HAVE TO BE CAREFUL NOT TO STEP ON IT!
YES.
WHY DON'T I HELP YOU LOOK?
I STILL HAVE A LITTLE TIME TO SPARE.
THANKS, BUT...

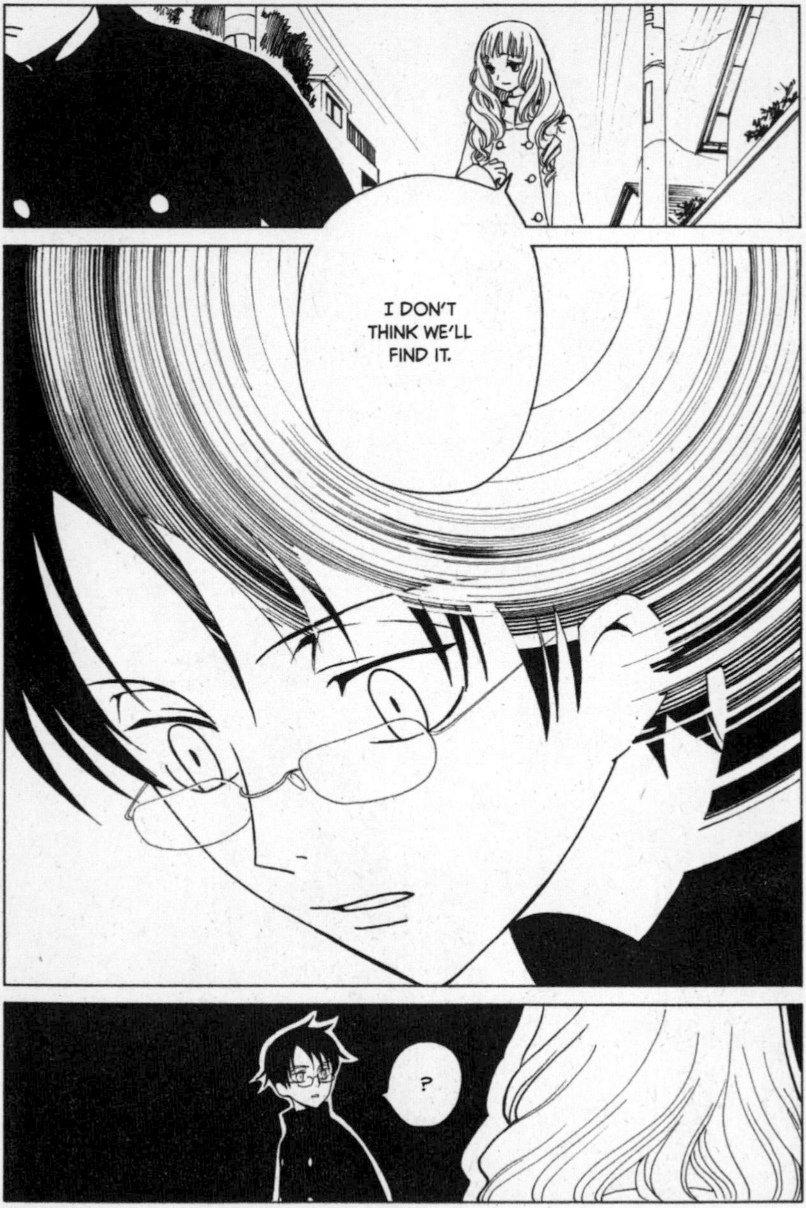
I DON'T THINK WE'LL FIND IT.
?

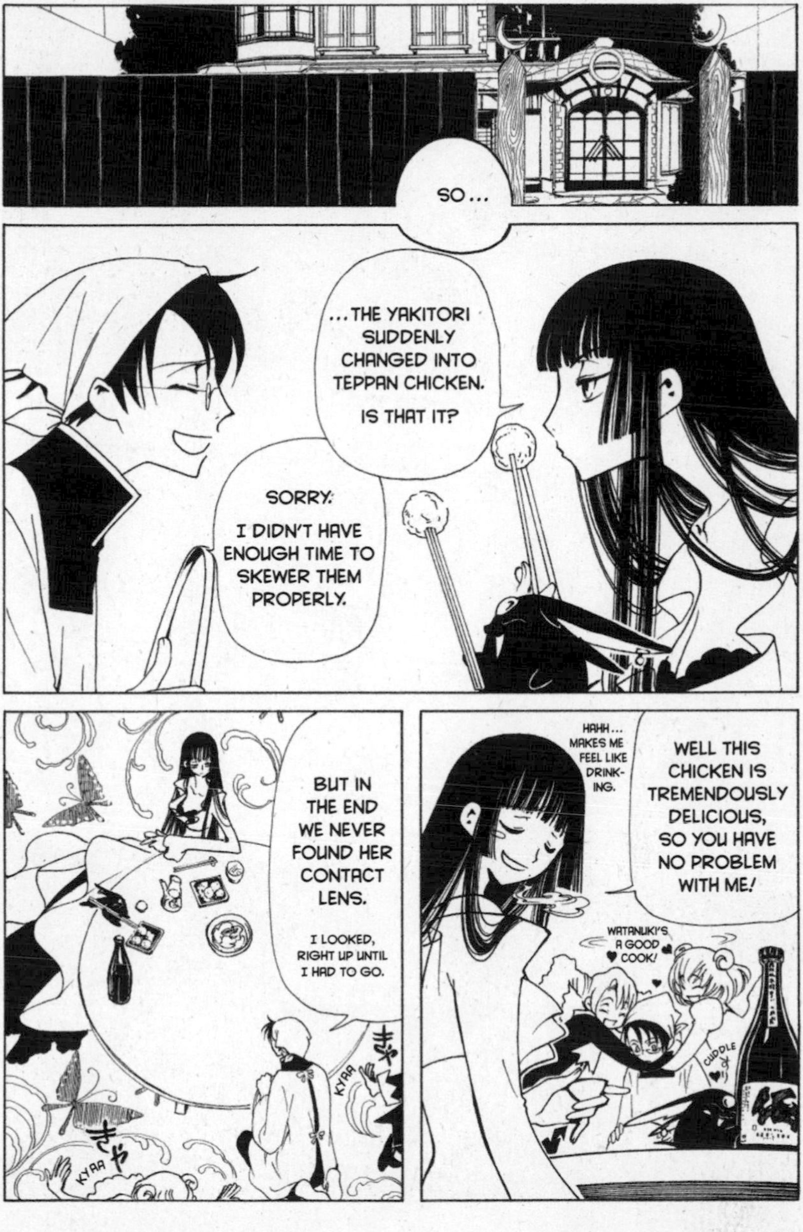
SO…
…THE YAKITORI SUDDENLY CHANGED INTO TEPPAN CHICKEN.
IS THAT IT?
SORRY.
I DIDN'T HAVE ENOUGH TIME TO SKEWER THEM PROPERLY.
WELL THIS CHICKEN IS TREMENDOUSLY DELICIOUS, SO YOU HAVE NO PROBLEM WITH ME!
HAHH… MAKES ME FEEL LIKE DRINK-ING.
WATANUKI'S A GOOD COOK!
CUDDLE
BUT IN THE END WE NEVER FOUND HER CONTACT LENS.
I LOOKED, RIGHT UP UNTIL I HAD TO GO.
きゃ
KYAA
きゃ
KYAA

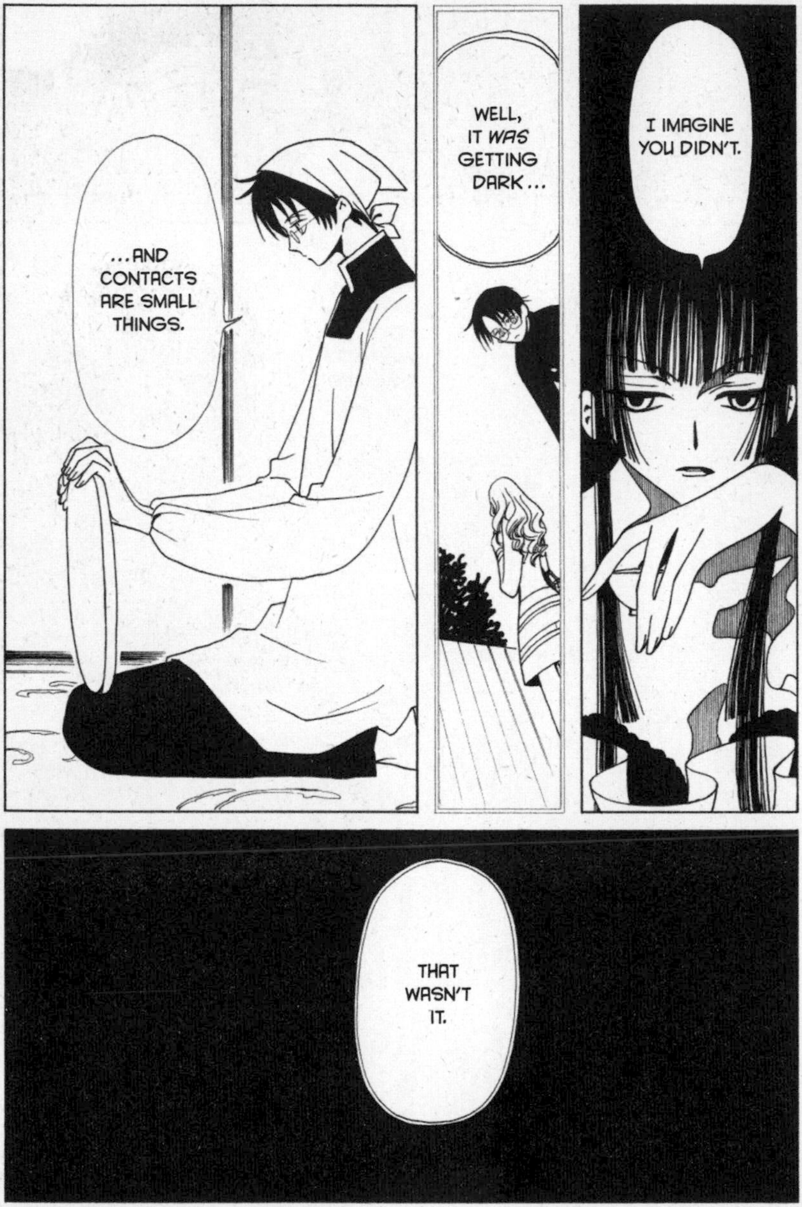
I IMAGINE YOU DIDN'T.
WELL, IT *WAS* GETTING DARK...
...AND CONTACTS ARE SMALL THINGS.
THAT WASN'T IT.

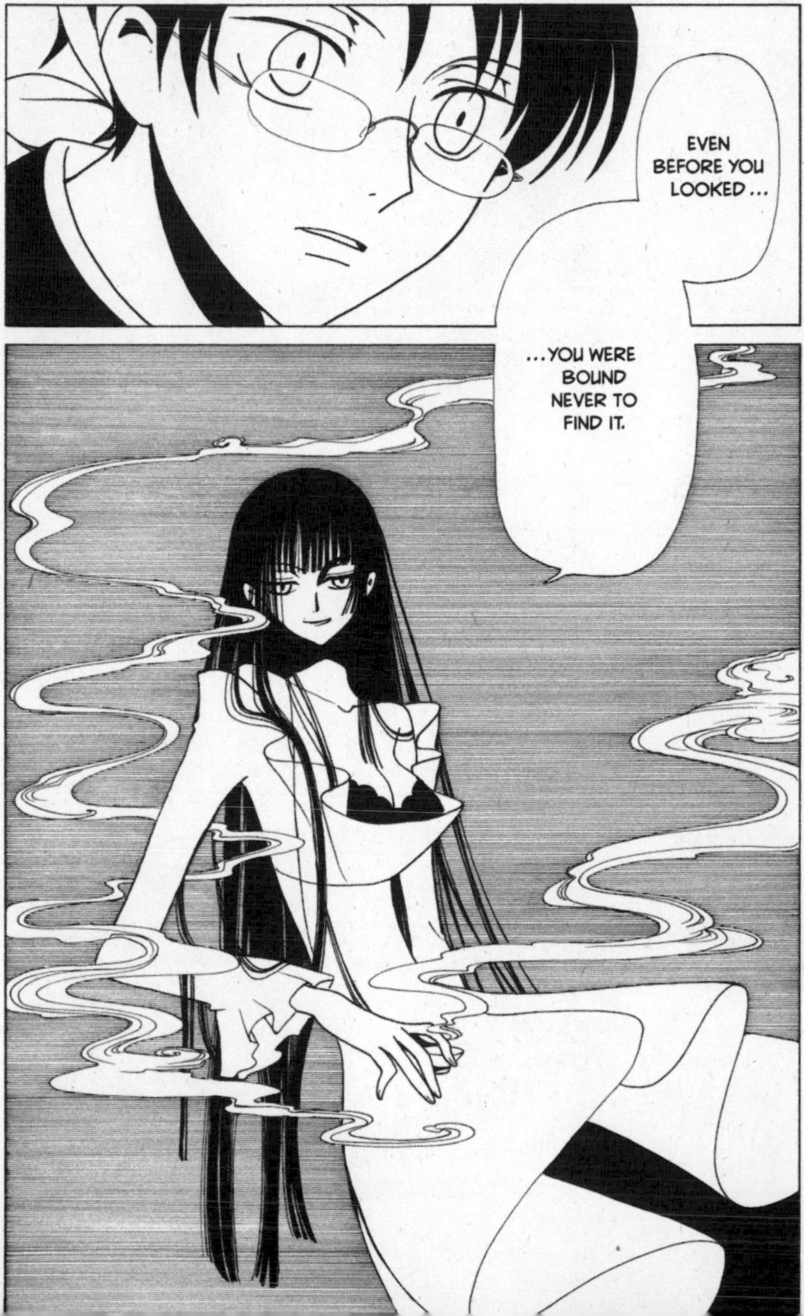
EVEN BEFORE YOU LOOKED...
...YOU WERE BOUND NEVER TO FIND IT.

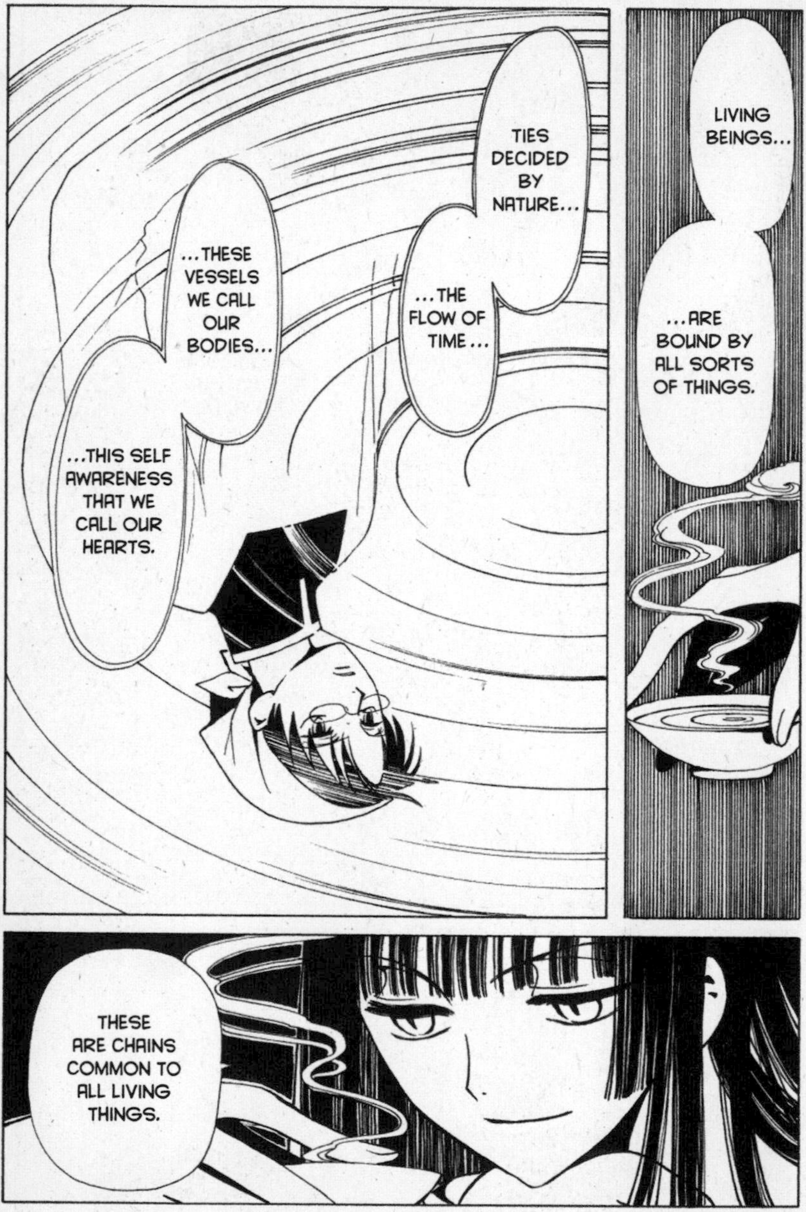
LIVING BEINGS...
...ARE BOUND BY ALL SORTS OF THINGS.
TIES DECIDED BY NATURE...
...THE FLOW OF TIME...
...THESE VESSELS WE CALL OUR BODIES...
...THIS SELF AWARENESS THAT WE CALL OUR HEARTS.
THESE ARE CHAINS COMMON TO ALL LIVING THINGS.

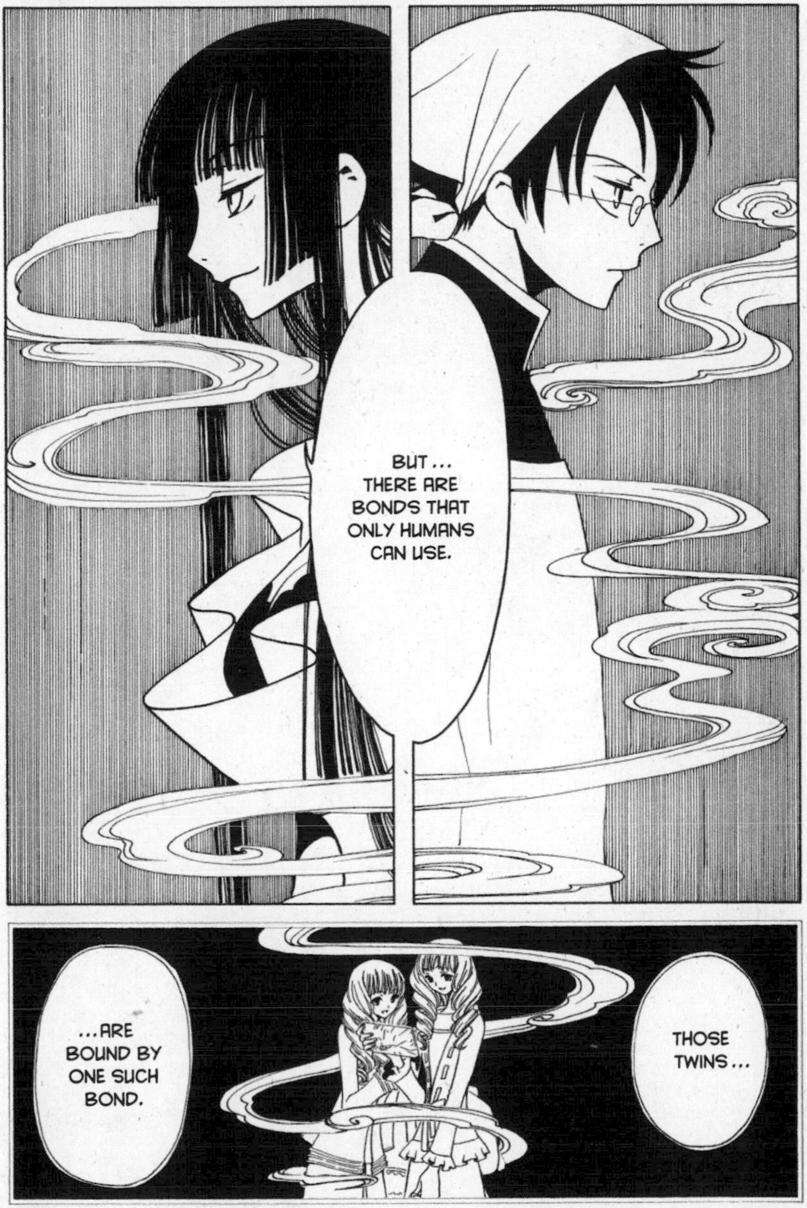
BUT... THERE ARE BONDS THAT ONLY HUMANS CAN USE.
THOSE TWINS...
...ARE BOUND BY ONE SUCH BOND.

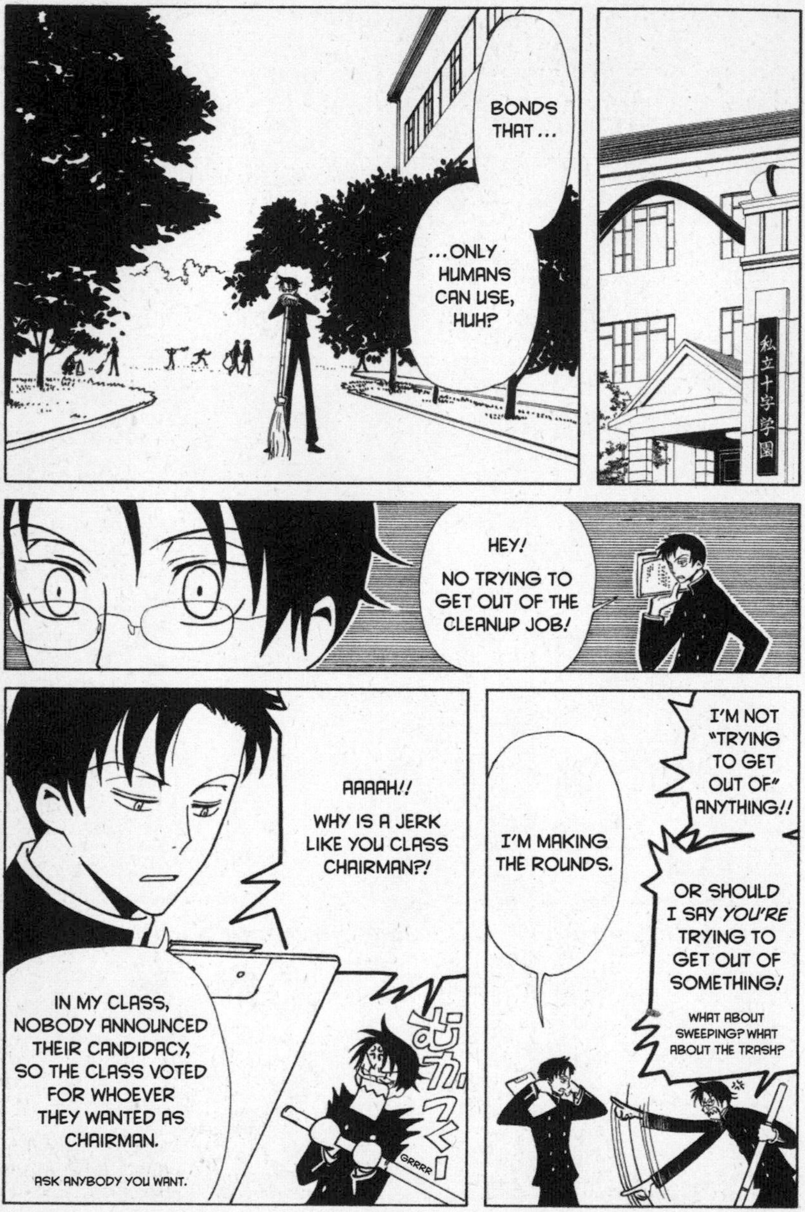
私立十字学園
BONDS THAT...
...ONLY HUMANS CAN USE, HUH?
HEY!
NO TRYING TO GET OUT OF THE CLEANUP JOB!
I'M NOT "TRYING TO GET OUT OF" ANYTHING!!
I'M MAKING THE ROUNDS.
OR SHOULD I SAY *YOU'RE* TRYING TO GET OUT OF SOMETHING!
WHAT ABOUT SWEEPING? WHAT ABOUT THE TRASH?
AAAAH!!
WHY IS A JERK LIKE YOU CLASS CHAIRMAN?!
IN MY CLASS, NOBODY ANNOUNCED THEIR CANDIDACY, SO THE CLASS VOTED FOR WHOEVER THEY WANTED AS CHAIRMAN.
ASK ANYBODY YOU WANT.
GRRRR

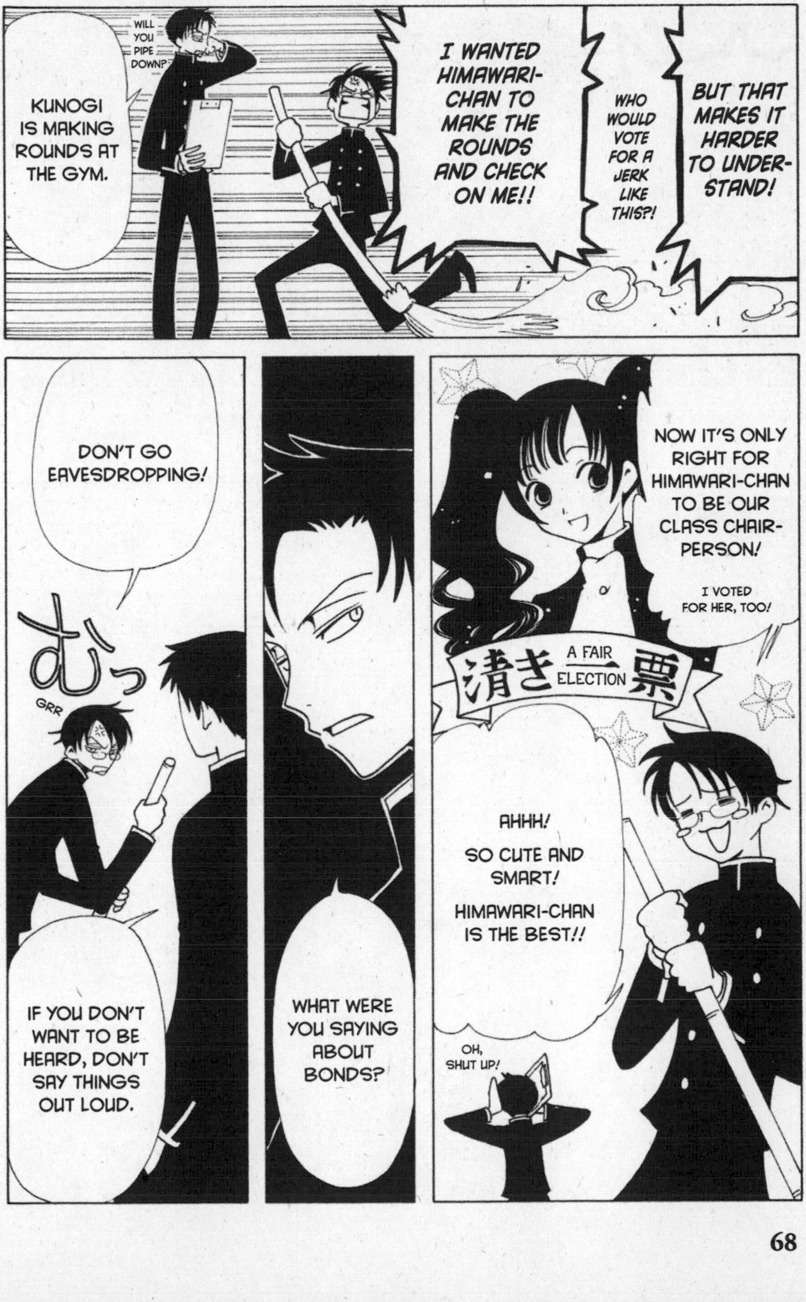

BUT THAT MAKES IT HARDER TO UNDER-STAND!
WHO WOULD VOTE FOR A JERK LIKE THIS?!
I WANTED HIMAWARI-CHAN TO MAKE THE ROUNDS AND CHECK ON ME!!
WILL YOU PIPE DOWN?
KUNOGI IS MAKING ROUNDS AT THE GYM.
NOW IT'S ONLY RIGHT FOR HIMAWARI-CHAN TO BE OUR CLASS CHAIR-PERSON!
I VOTED FOR HER, TOO!
清き一票
A FAIR ELECTION
AHHH!
SO CUTE AND SMART!
HIMAWARI-CHAN IS THE BEST!!
OH, SHUT UP!
WHAT WERE YOU SAYING ABOUT BONDS?
DON'T GO EAVESDROPPING!
むっ
GRR
IF YOU DON'T WANT TO BE HEARD, DON'T SAY THINGS OUT LOUD.

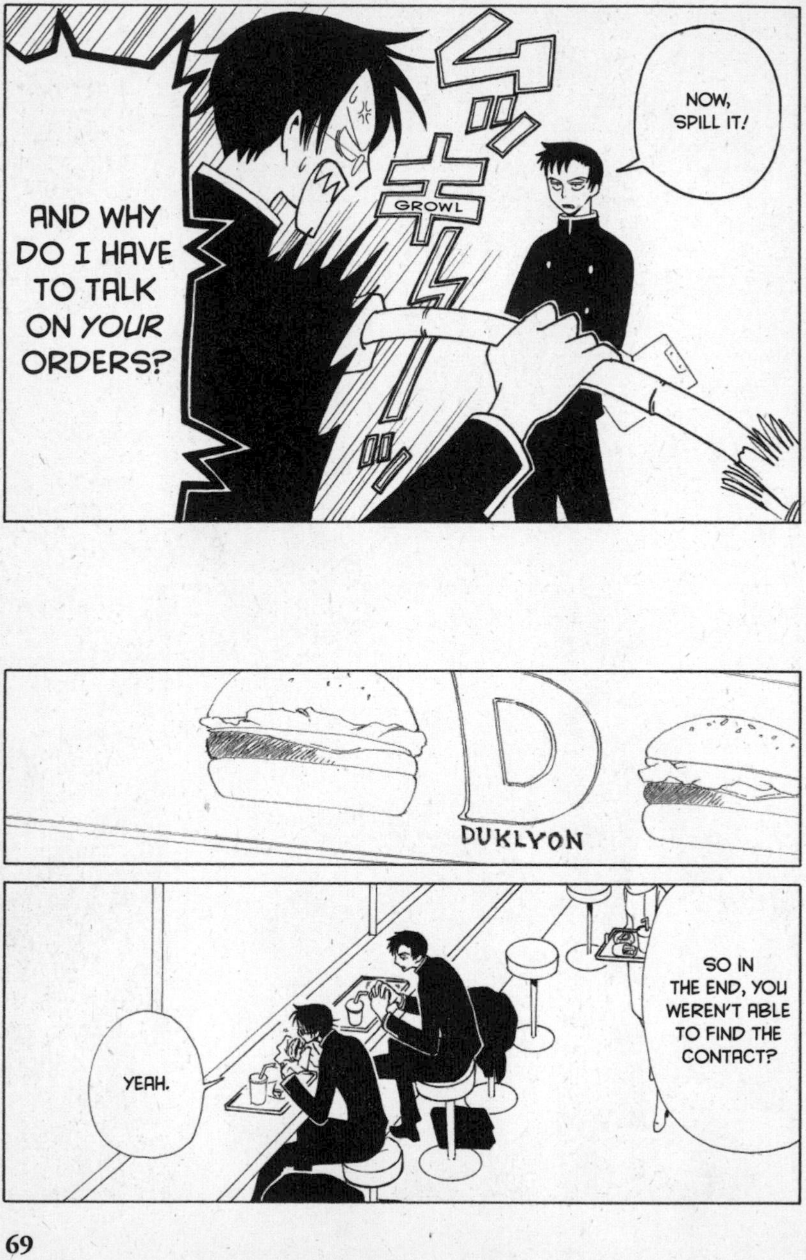
NOW, SPILL IT!
GROWL
AND WHY DO I HAVE TO TALK ON *YOUR* ORDERS?
DUKLYON
SO IN THE END, YOU WEREN'T ABLE TO FIND THE CONTACT?
YEAH.

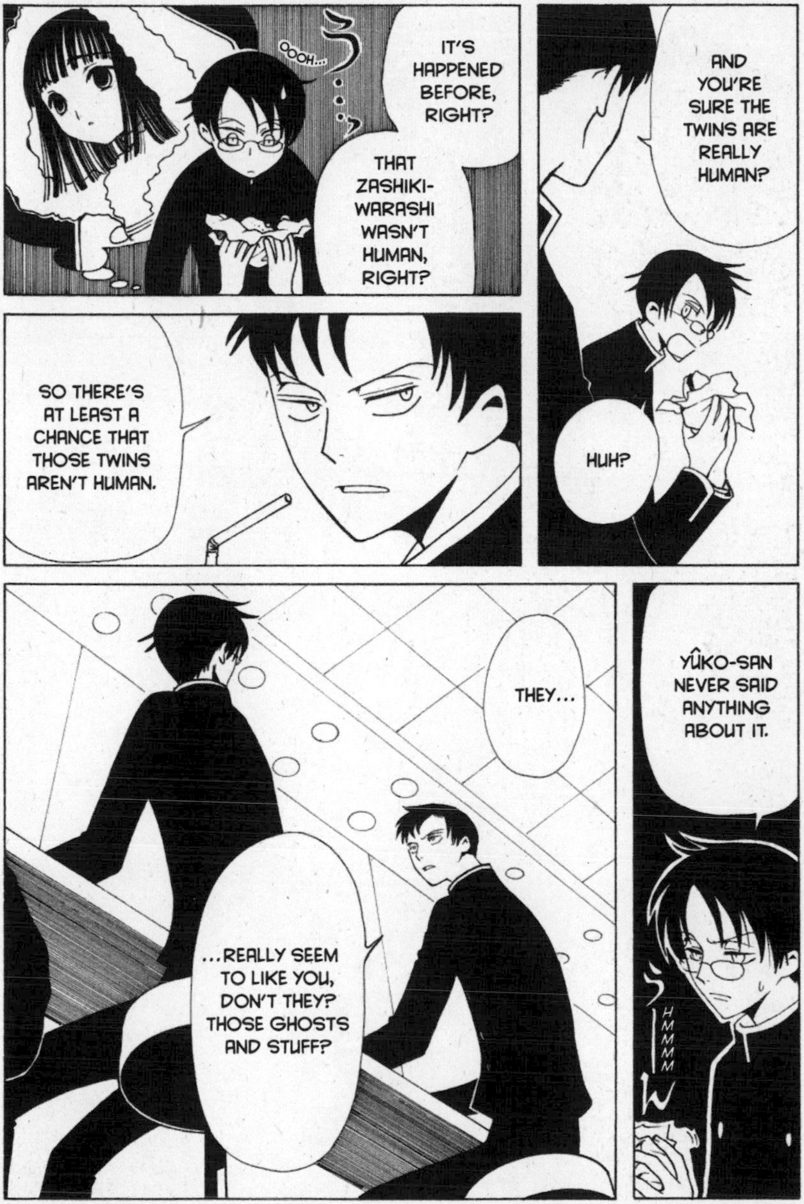
AND YOU'RE SURE THE TWINS ARE REALLY HUMAN?
HUH?
OOOH...
IT'S HAPPENED BEFORE, RIGHT?
THAT ZASHIKI-WARASHI WASN'T HUMAN, RIGHT?
SO THERE'S AT LEAST A CHANCE THAT THOSE TWINS AREN'T HUMAN.
YÛKO-SAN NEVER SAID ANYTHING ABOUT IT.
HMMMM
THEY...
...REALLY SEEM TO LIKE YOU, DON'T THEY? THOSE GHOSTS AND STUFF?

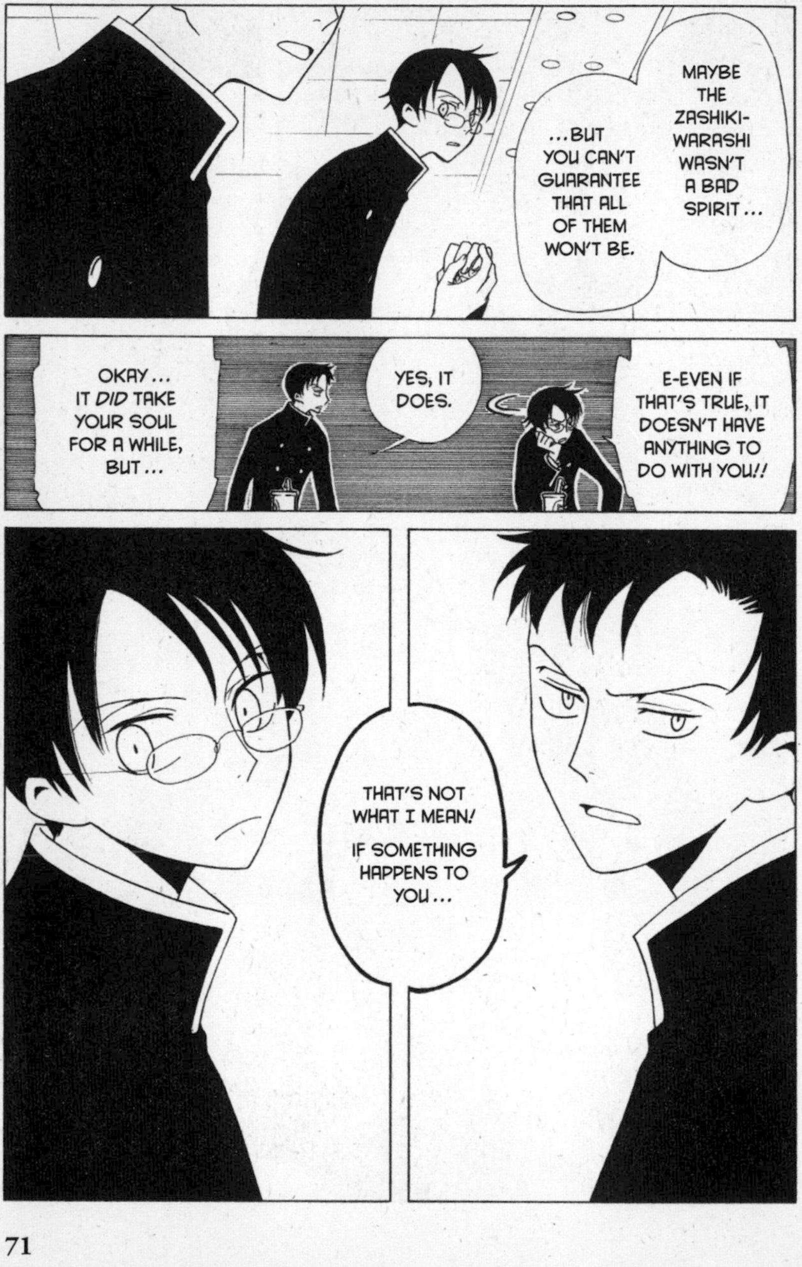
MAYBE THE ZASHIKI-WARASHI WASN'T A BAD SPIRIT...
...BUT YOU CAN'T GUARANTEE THAT ALL OF THEM WON'T BE.
E-EVEN IF THAT'S TRUE, IT DOESN'T HAVE ANYTHING TO DO WITH YOU!!
YES, IT DOES.
OKAY... IT *DID* TAKE YOUR SOUL FOR A WHILE, BUT...
THAT'S NOT WHAT I MEAN!
IF SOMETHING HAPPENS TO YOU...

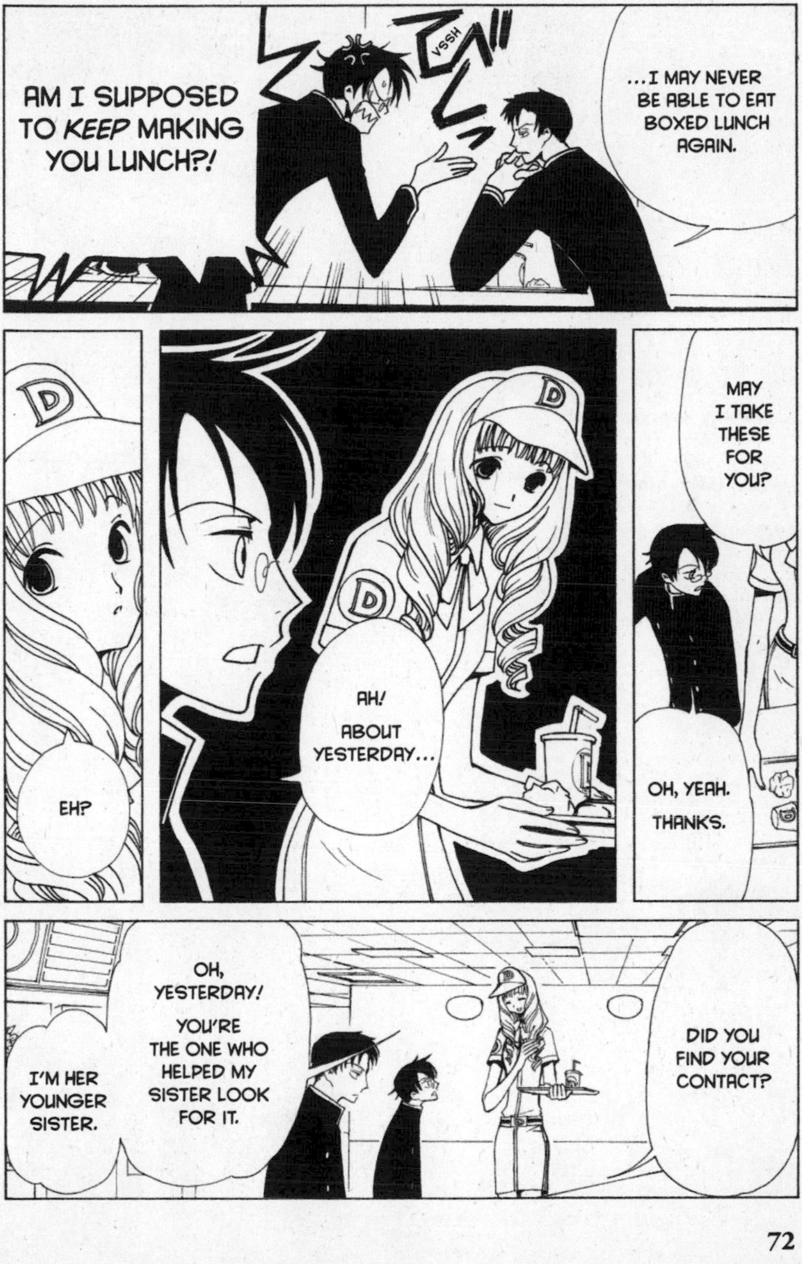
...I MAY NEVER BE ABLE TO EAT BOXED LUNCH AGAIN.
VSSH
AM I SUPPOSED TO *KEEP* MAKING YOU LUNCH?!
MAY I TAKE THESE FOR YOU?
OH, YEAH. THANKS.
AH!
ABOUT YESTERDAY...
EH?
DID YOU FIND YOUR CONTACT?
OH, YESTERDAY!
YOU'RE THE ONE WHO HELPED MY SISTER LOOK FOR IT.
I'M HER YOUNGER SISTER.

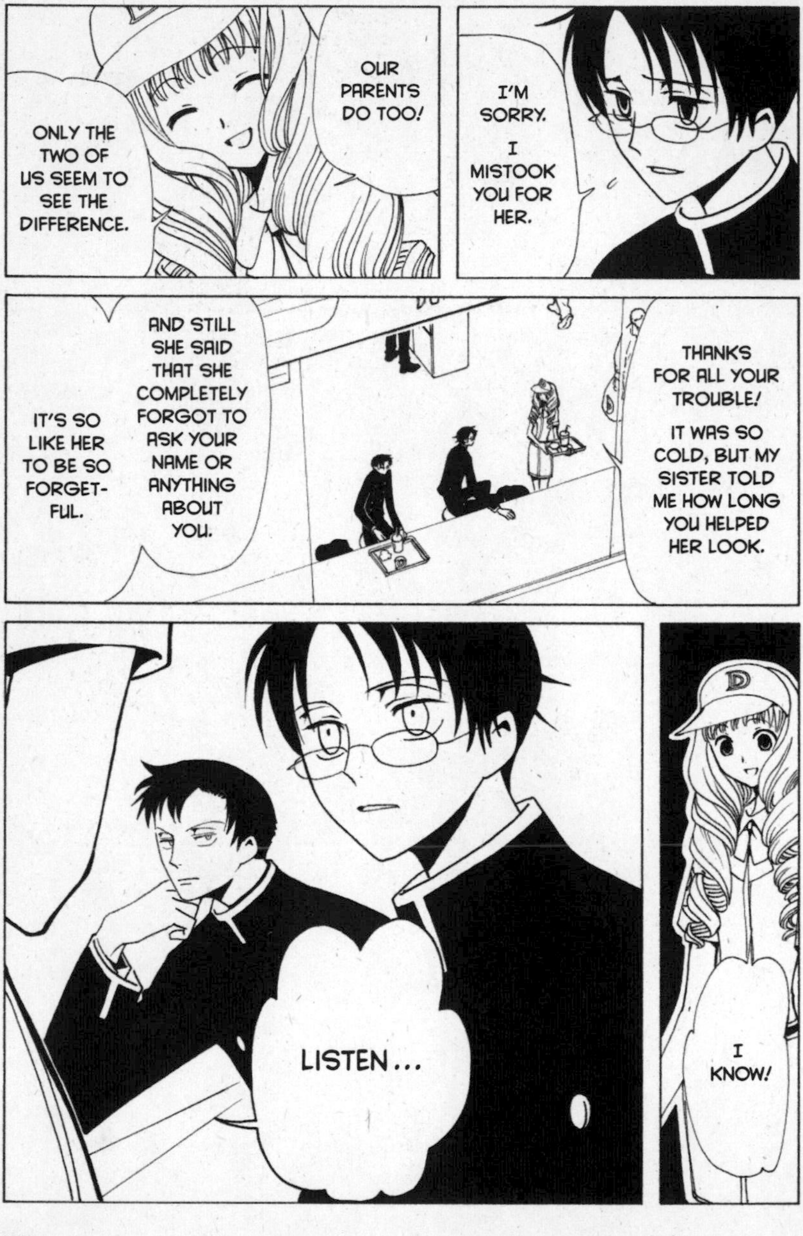
I'M SORRY.
I MISTOOK YOU FOR HER.
OUR PARENTS DO TOO!
ONLY THE TWO OF US SEEM TO SEE THE DIFFERENCE.
THANKS FOR ALL YOUR TROUBLE!
IT WAS SO COLD, BUT MY SISTER TOLD ME HOW LONG YOU HELPED HER LOOK.
AND STILL SHE SAID THAT SHE COMPLETELY FORGOT TO ASK YOUR NAME OR ANYTHING ABOUT YOU.
IT'S SO LIKE HER TO BE SO FORGET-FUL.
I KNOW!
LISTEN...

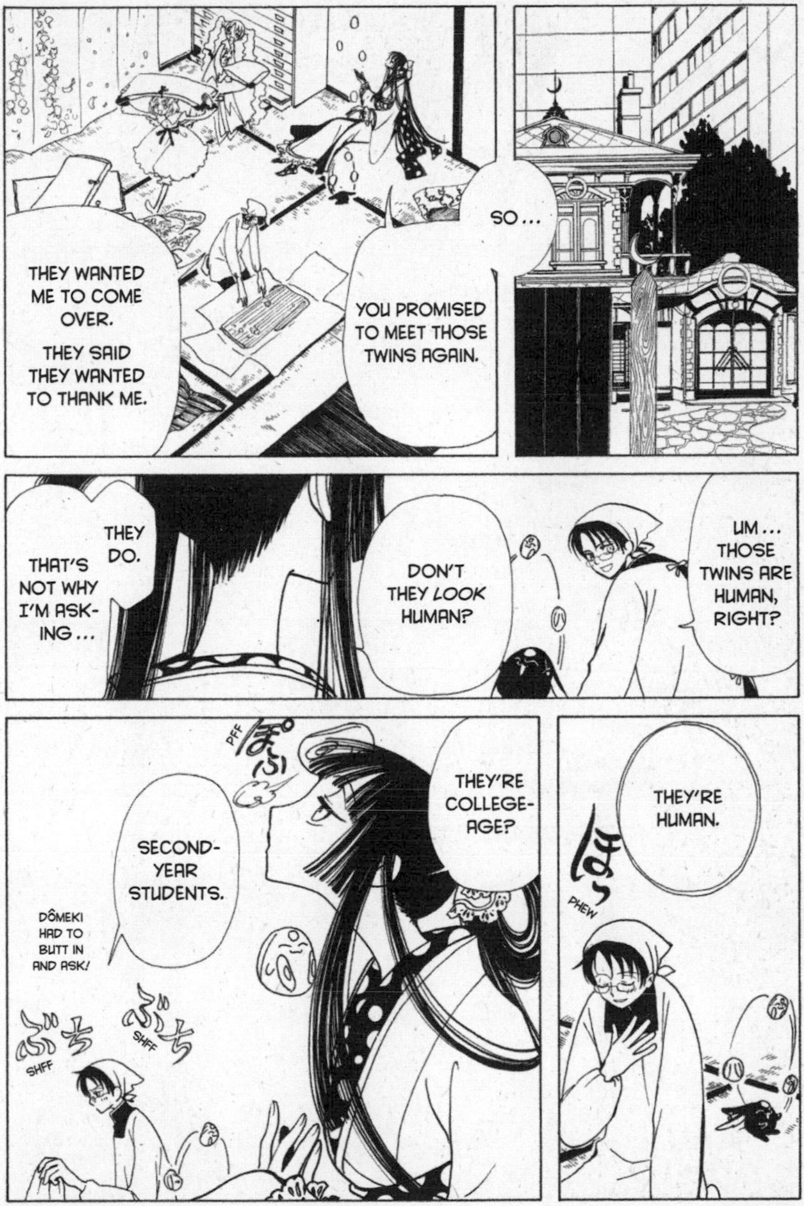
SO...
YOU PROMISED TO MEET THOSE TWINS AGAIN.
THEY WANTED ME TO COME OVER.
THEY SAID THEY WANTED TO THANK ME.
UM... THOSE TWINS ARE HUMAN, RIGHT?
DON'T THEY *LOOK* HUMAN?
THEY DO.
THAT'S NOT WHY I'M ASKING...
THEY'RE HUMAN.
ほっ
PHEW
THEY'RE COLLEGE-AGE?
ぷふ
PFF
SECOND-YEAR STUDENTS.
DÔMEKI HAD TO BUTT IN AND ASK!
ぶち
SHFF
ぶち
SHFF

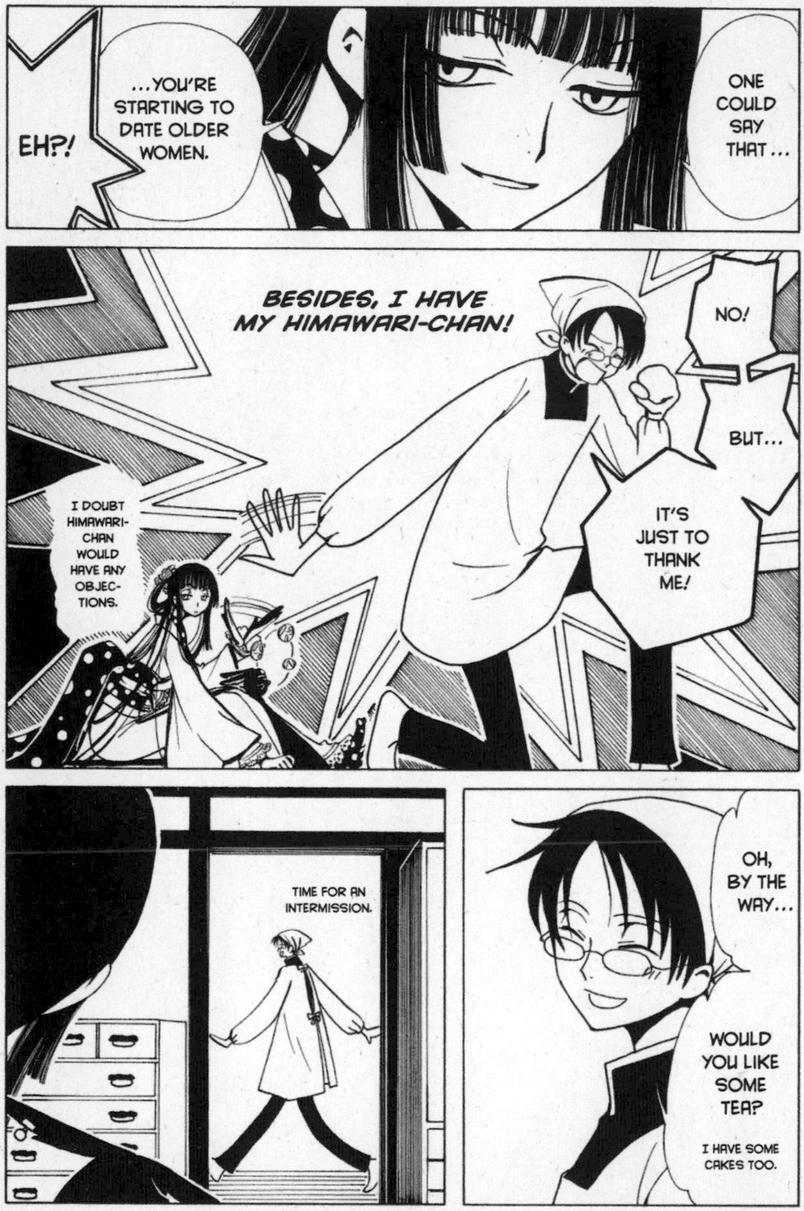
ONE COULD SAY THAT…
…YOU'RE STARTING TO DATE OLDER WOMEN.
EH?!
NO!
BUT…
IT'S JUST TO THANK ME!
BESIDES, I HAVE MY HIMAWARI-CHAN!
I DOUBT HIMAWARI-CHAN WOULD HAVE ANY OBJECTIONS.
OH, BY THE WAY…
WOULD YOU LIKE SOME TEA?
I HAVE SOME CAKES TOO.
TIME FOR AN INTERMISSION.

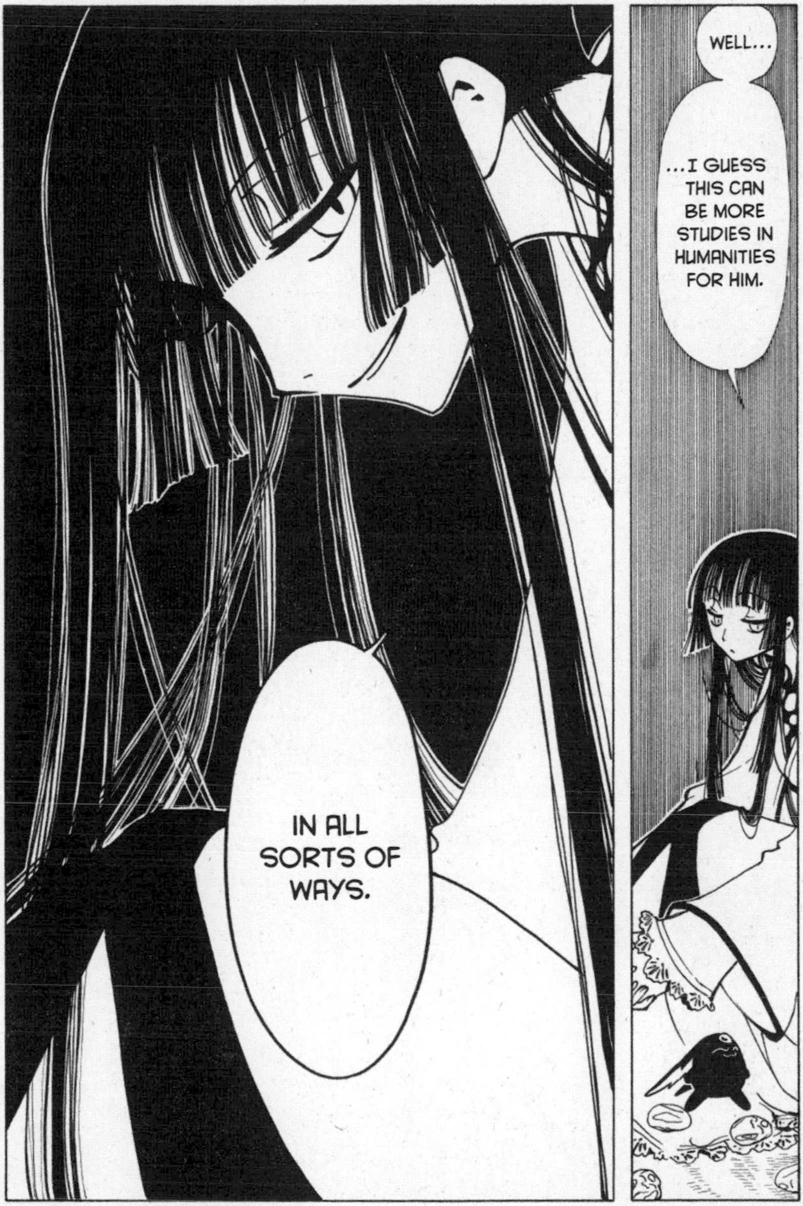
WELL...
...I GUESS THIS CAN BE MORE STUDIES IN HUMANITIES FOR HIM.
IN ALL SORTS OF WAYS.

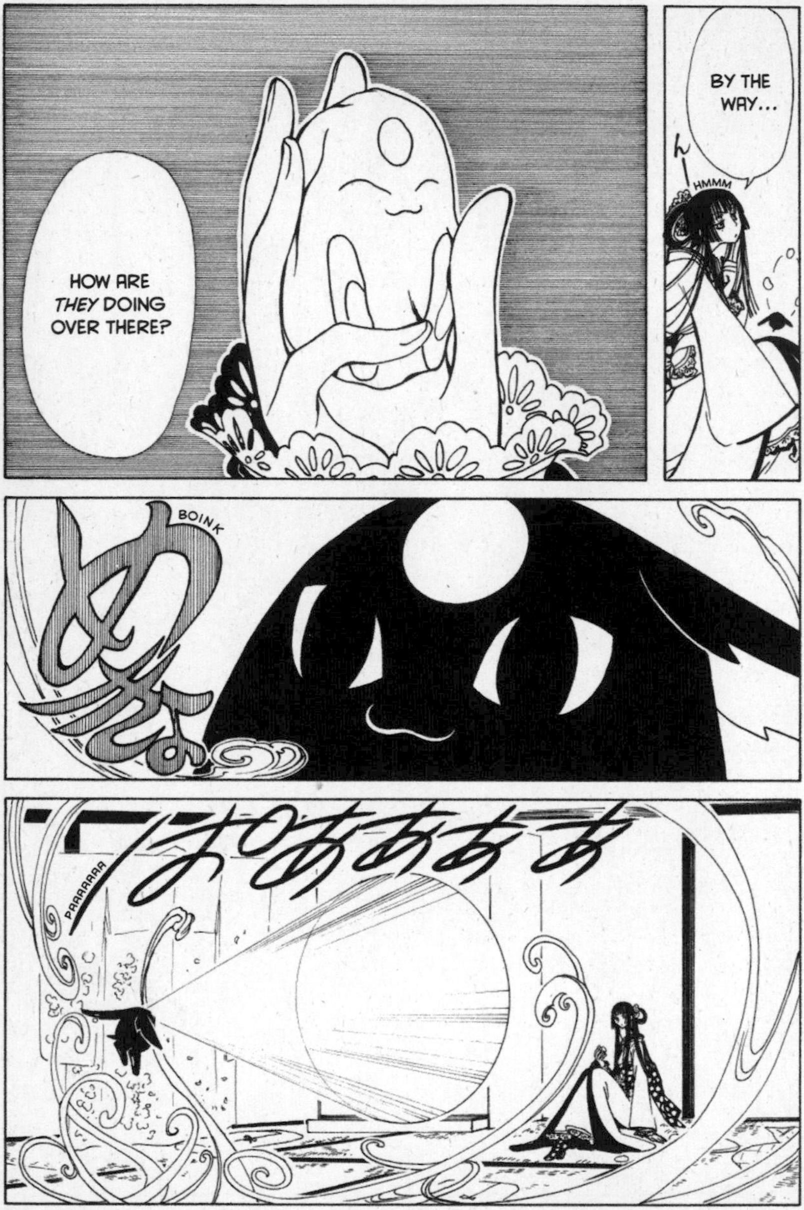

BY THE WAY...
ん
HMMM
HOW ARE *THEY* DOING OVER THERE?
BOINK
PAAAAAAA

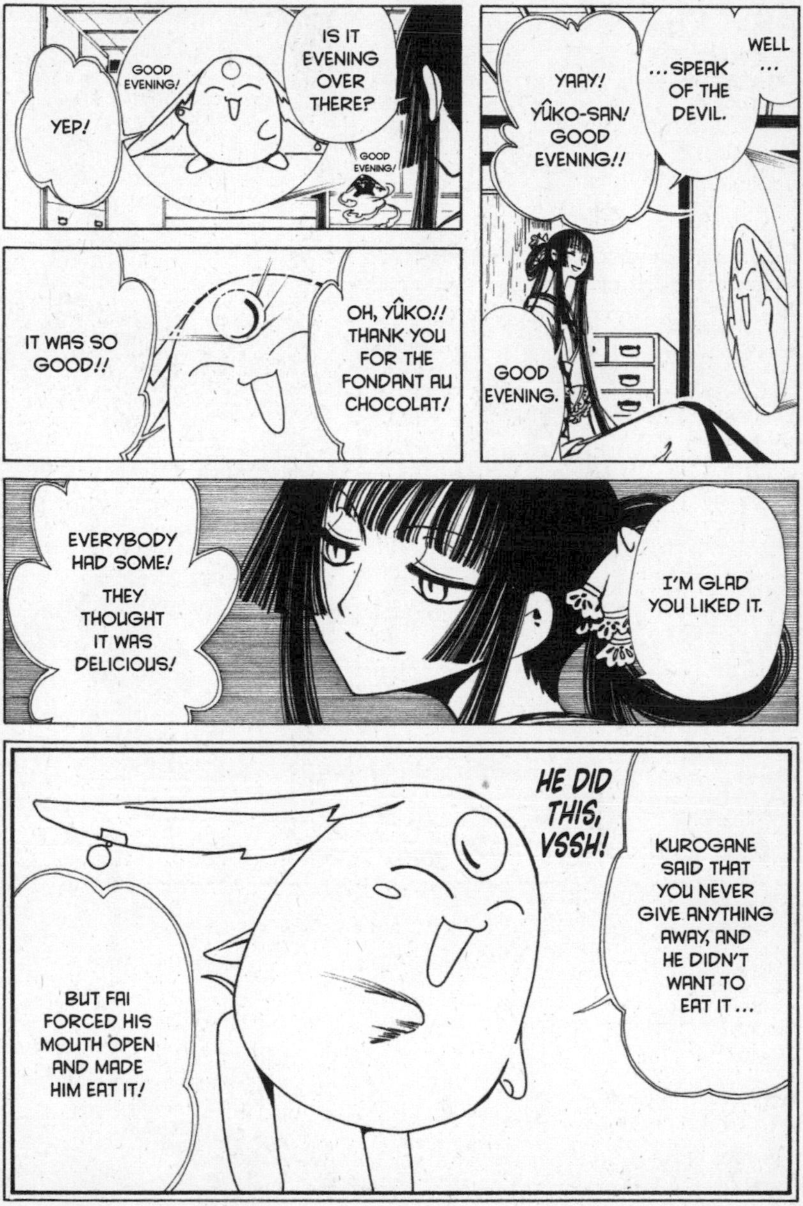
WELL ...
...SPEAK OF THE DEVIL.
YAAY! YÛKO-SAN! GOOD EVENING!!
GOOD EVENING.
IS IT EVENING OVER THERE?
GOOD EVENING!
GOOD EVENING!
YEP!
OH, YÛKO!! THANK YOU FOR THE FONDANT AU CHOCOLAT!
IT WAS SO GOOD!!
I'M GLAD YOU LIKED IT.
EVERYBODY HAD SOME!
THEY THOUGHT IT WAS DELICIOUS!
KUROGANE SAID THAT YOU NEVER GIVE ANYTHING AWAY, AND HE DIDN'T WANT TO EAT IT...
HE DID THIS, VSSH!
BUT FAI FORCED HIS MOUTH OPEN AND MADE HIM EAT IT!

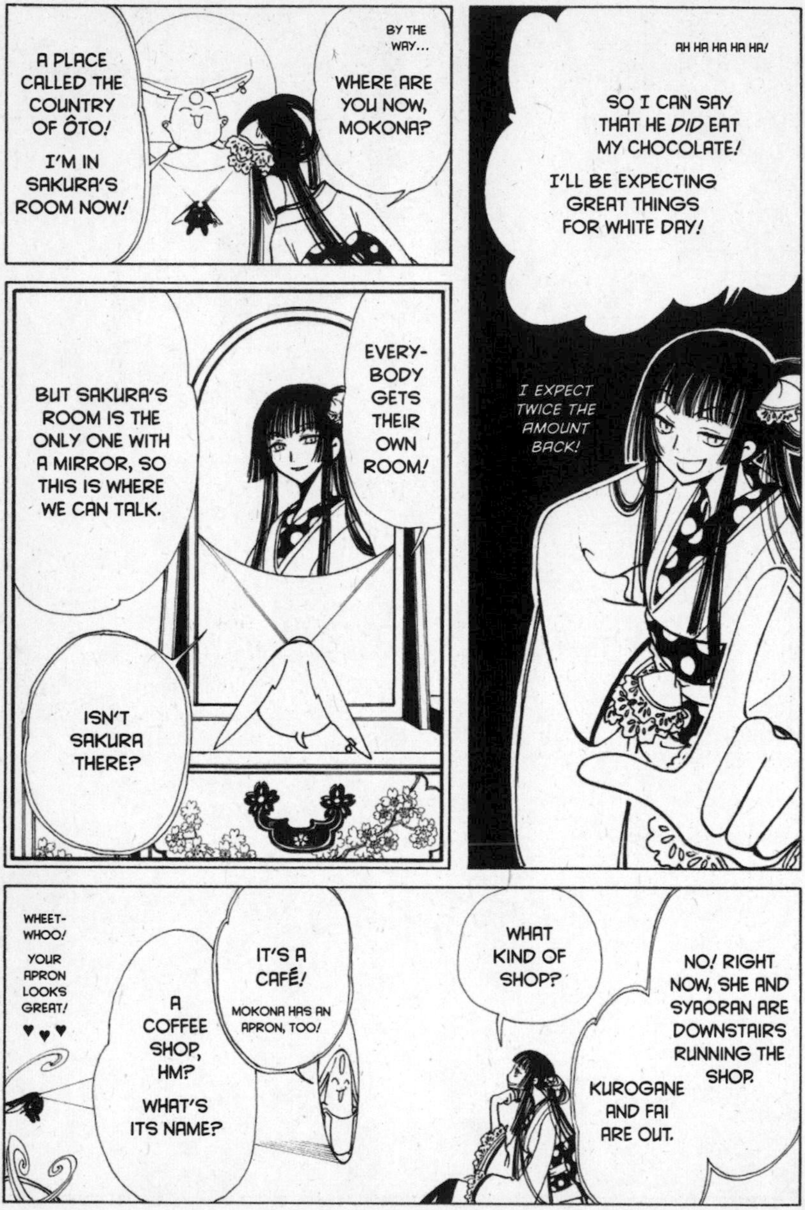
AH HA HA HA HA!
SO I CAN SAY THAT HE *DID* EAT MY CHOCOLATE!
I'LL BE EXPECTING GREAT THINGS FOR WHITE DAY!
I EXPECT TWICE THE AMOUNT BACK!
BY THE WAY...
WHERE ARE YOU NOW, MOKONA?
A PLACE CALLED THE COUNTRY OF ÔTO!
I'M IN SAKURA'S ROOM NOW!
EVERYBODY GETS THEIR OWN ROOM!
BUT SAKURA'S ROOM IS THE ONLY ONE WITH A MIRROR, SO THIS IS WHERE WE CAN TALK.
ISN'T SAKURA THERE?
NO! RIGHT NOW, SHE AND SYAORAN ARE DOWNSTAIRS RUNNING THE SHOP.
KUROGANE AND FAI ARE OUT.
WHAT KIND OF SHOP?
IT'S A CAFÉ!
MOKONA HAS AN APRON, TOO!
A COFFEE SHOP, HM?
WHAT'S ITS NAME?
WHEET-WHOO!
YOUR APRON LOOKS GREAT!
♥♥♥

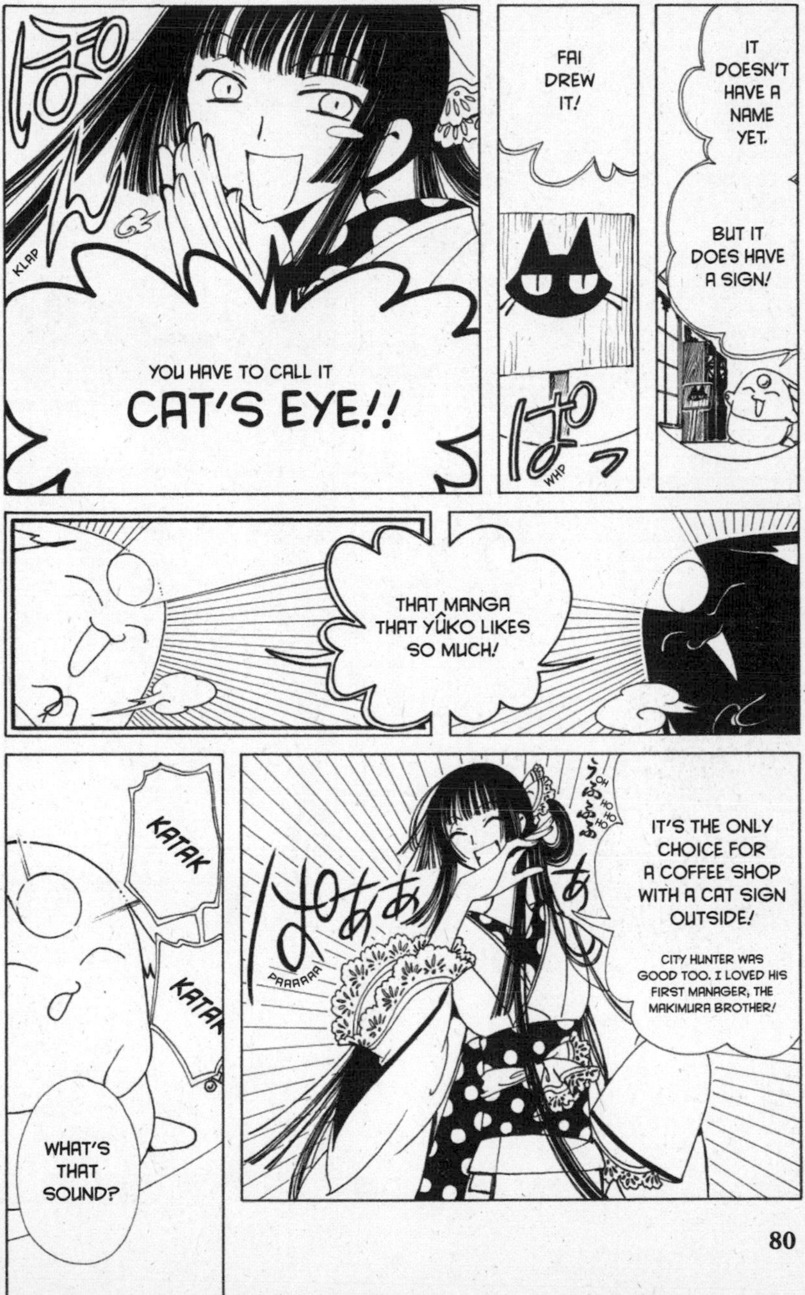
IT DOESN'T HAVE A NAME YET.
BUT IT DOES HAVE A SIGN!
FAI DREW IT!
ぱっ
WHP
ぽん
KLAP
YOU HAVE TO CALL IT
CAT'S EYE!!
THAT MANGA THAT YÛKO LIKES SO MUCH!
うふふふ
OH HO HO HO
IT'S THE ONLY CHOICE FOR A COFFEE SHOP WITH A CAT SIGN OUTSIDE!
CITY HUNTER WAS GOOD TOO. I LOVED HIS FIRST MANAGER, THE MAKIMURA BROTHER!
はあああ
PAAAAAAA
KATAK
KATAK
WHAT'S THAT SOUND?

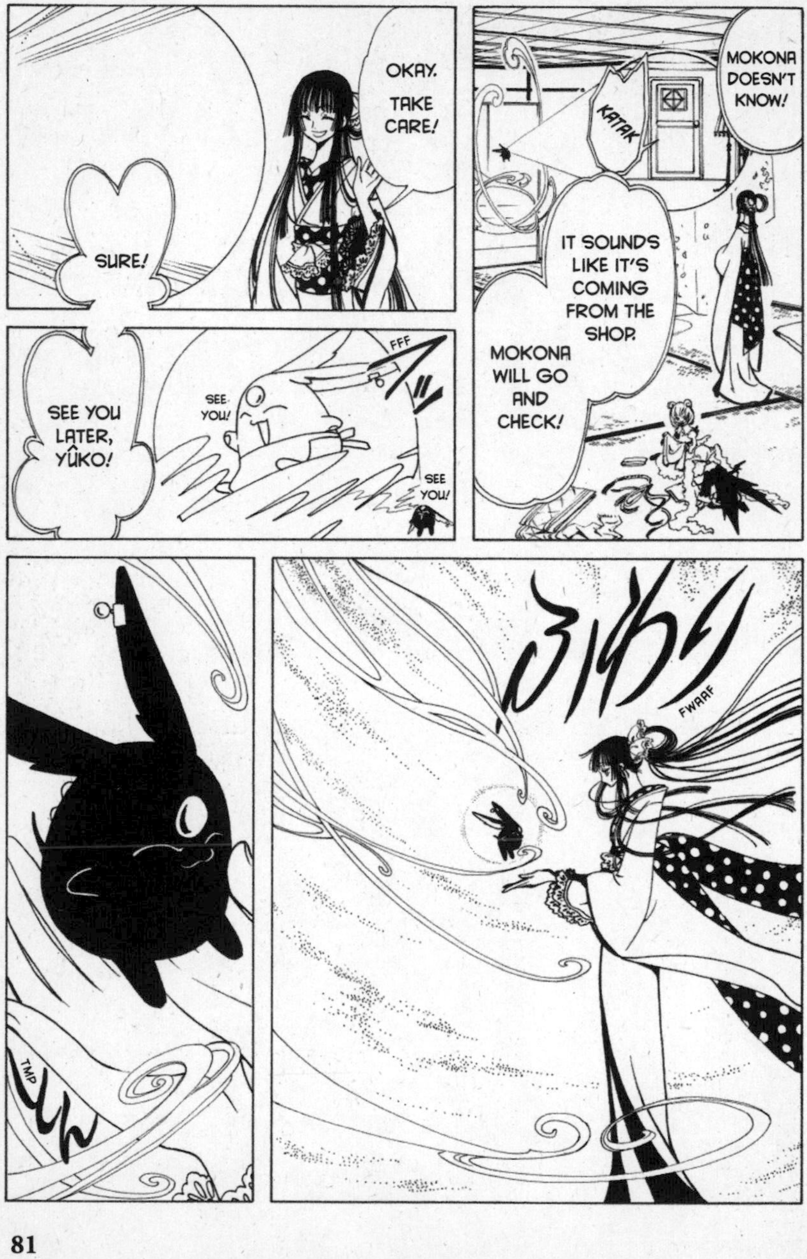

MOKONA DOESN'T KNOW!
KATAK
IT SOUNDS LIKE IT'S COMING FROM THE SHOP.
MOKONA WILL GO AND CHECK!
OKAY. TAKE CARE!
SURE!
FFF
SEE YOU!
SEE YOU!
SEE YOU LATER, YÛKO!
ふわり
FWAAF
TMP

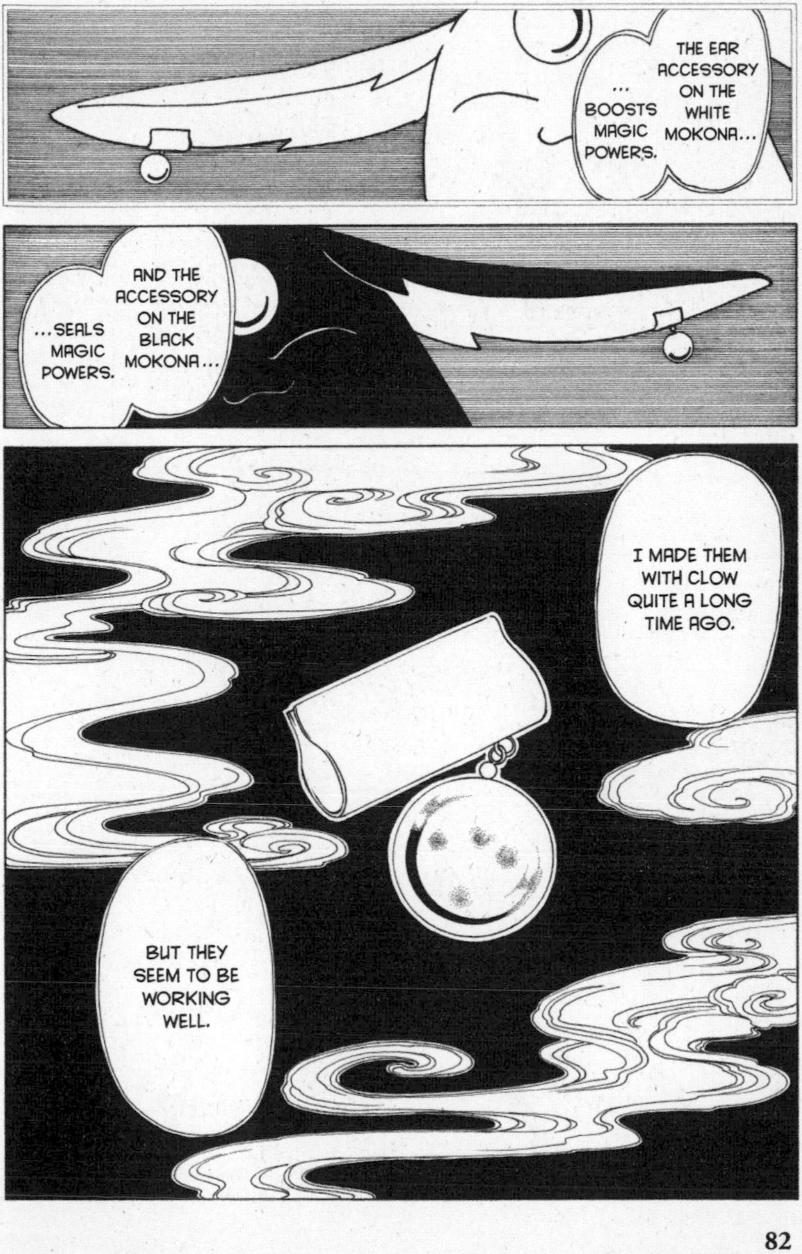
THE EAR ACCESSORY ON THE WHITE MOKONA...
... BOOSTS MAGIC POWERS.
AND THE ACCESSORY ON THE BLACK MOKONA...
...SEALS MAGIC POWERS.
I MADE THEM WITH CLOW QUITE A LONG TIME AGO.
BUT THEY SEEM TO BE WORKING WELL.

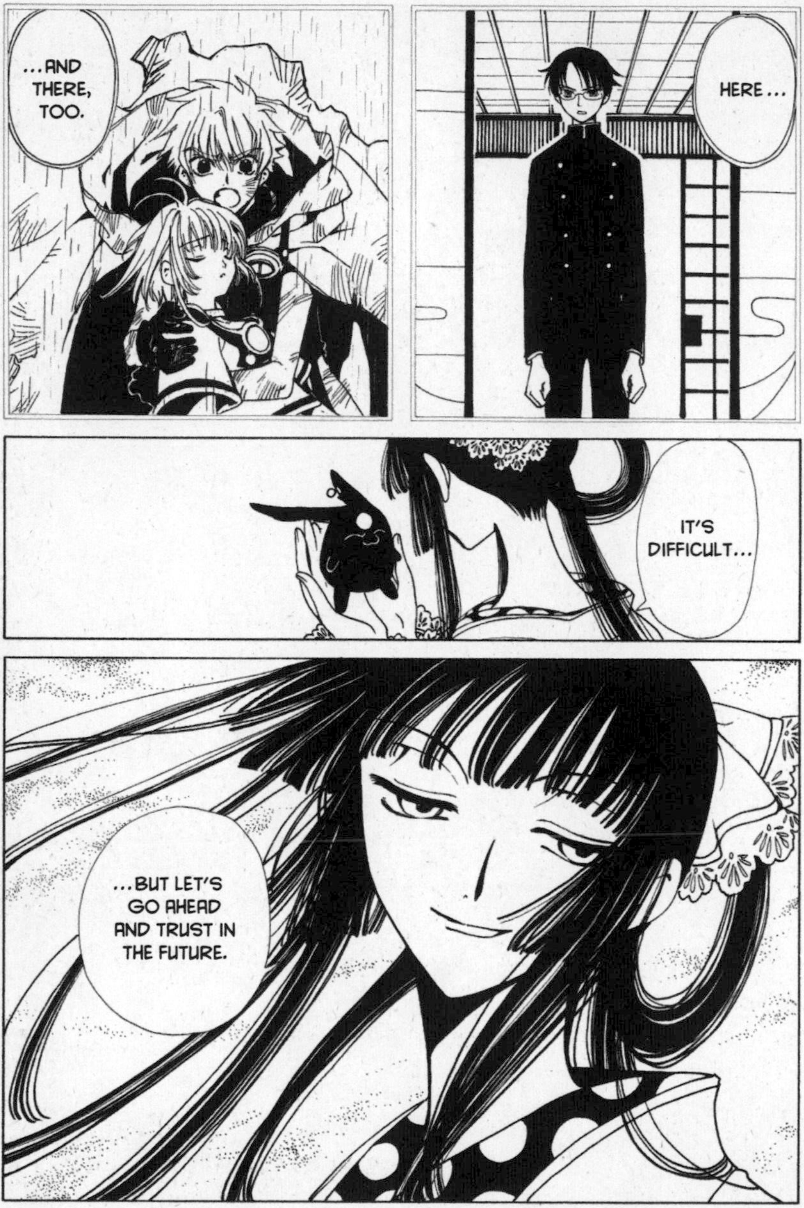
HERE...
...AND THERE, TOO.
IT'S DIFFICULT...
...BUT LET'S GO AHEAD AND TRUST IN THE FUTURE.

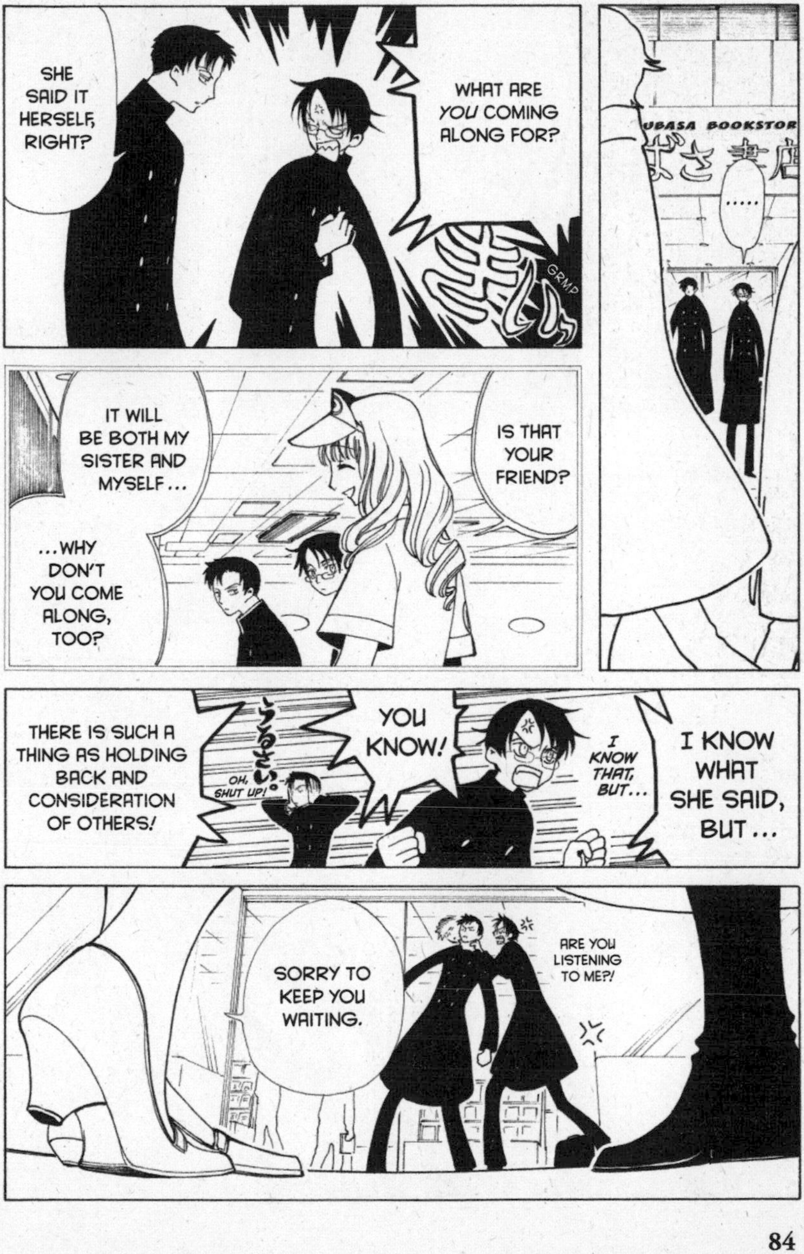
UBASA BOOKSTOR
......
WHAT ARE YOU COMING ALONG FOR?
GRMP
SHE SAID IT HERSELF, RIGHT?
IS THAT YOUR FRIEND?
IT WILL BE BOTH MY SISTER AND MYSELF...
...WHY DON'T YOU COME ALONG, TOO?
I KNOW WHAT SHE SAID, BUT...
I KNOW THAT, BUT...
YOU KNOW!
うるさい。
OH, SHUT UP!
THERE IS SUCH A THING AS HOLDING BACK AND CONSIDERATION OF OTHERS!
ARE YOU LISTENING TO ME?!
SORRY TO KEEP YOU WAITING.

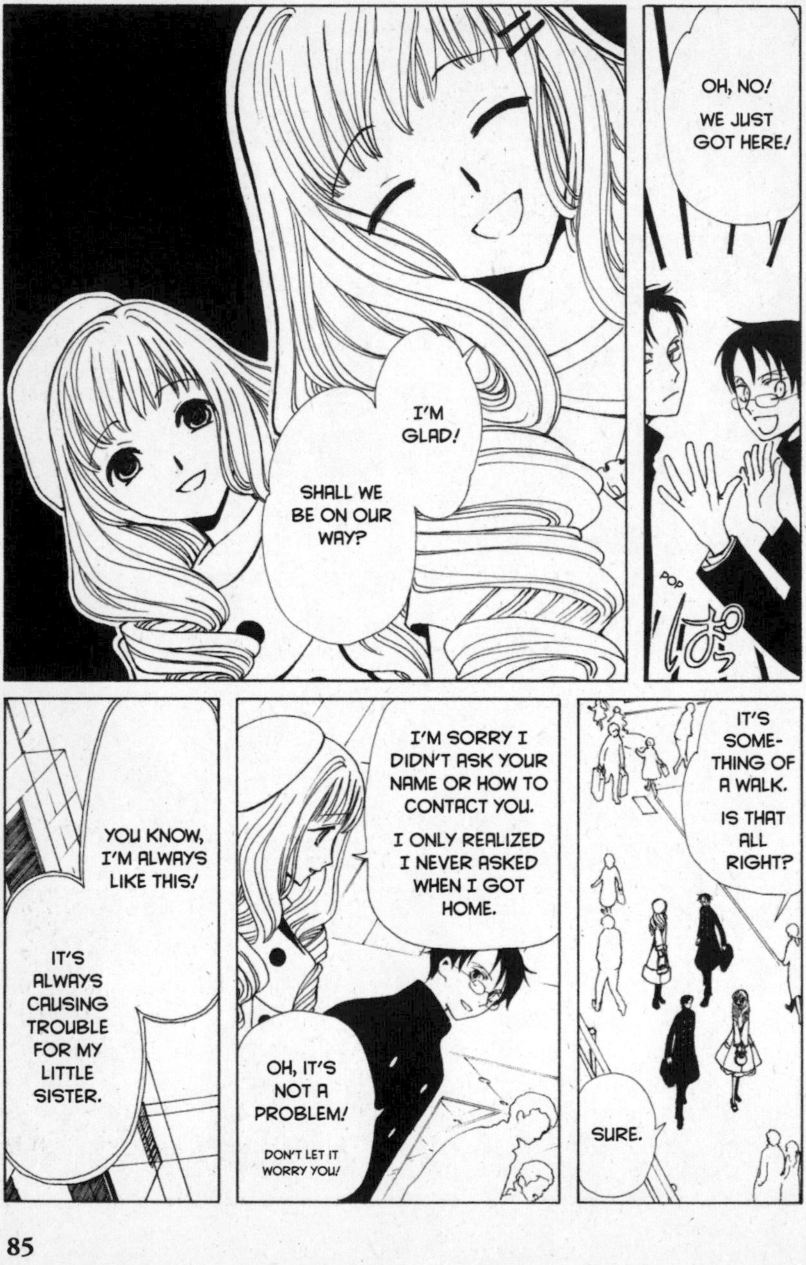
OH, NO!
WE JUST GOT HERE!
POP
I'M GLAD!
SHALL WE BE ON OUR WAY?
IT'S SOME-THING OF A WALK.
IS THAT ALL RIGHT?
SURE.
I'M SORRY I DIDN'T ASK YOUR NAME OR HOW TO CONTACT YOU.
I ONLY REALIZED I NEVER ASKED WHEN I GOT HOME.
OH, IT'S NOT A PROBLEM!
DON'T LET IT WORRY YOU!
YOU KNOW, I'M ALWAYS LIKE THIS!
IT'S ALWAYS CAUSING TROUBLE FOR MY LITTLE SISTER.

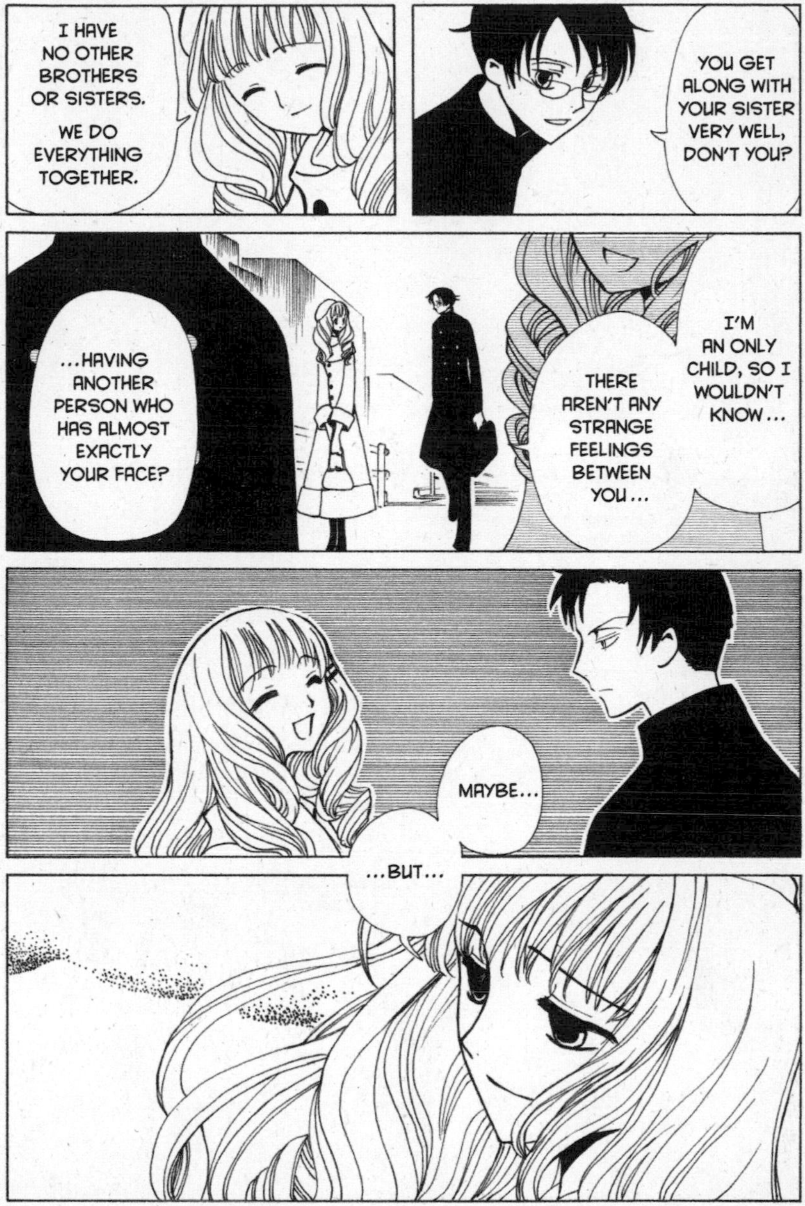
YOU GET ALONG WITH YOUR SISTER VERY WELL, DON'T YOU?
I HAVE NO OTHER BROTHERS OR SISTERS.
WE DO EVERYTHING TOGETHER.
I'M AN ONLY CHILD, SO I WOULDN'T KNOW...
THERE AREN'T ANY STRANGE FEELINGS BETWEEN YOU...
...HAVING ANOTHER PERSON WHO HAS ALMOST EXACTLY YOUR FACE?
MAYBE...
...BUT...

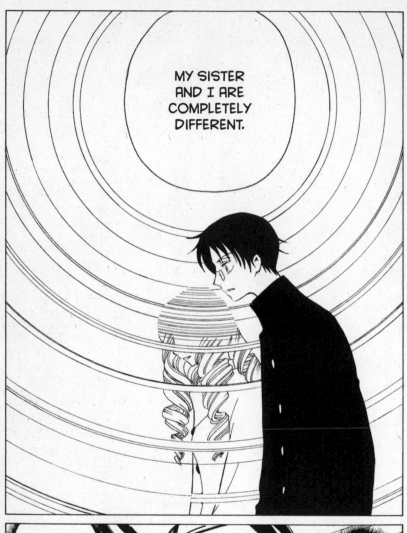

MY SISTER
AND I ARE
COMPLETELY
DIFFERENT.

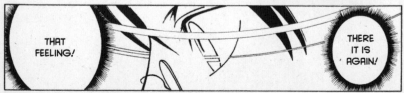

THAT
FEELING!

THERE
IT IS
AGAIN!

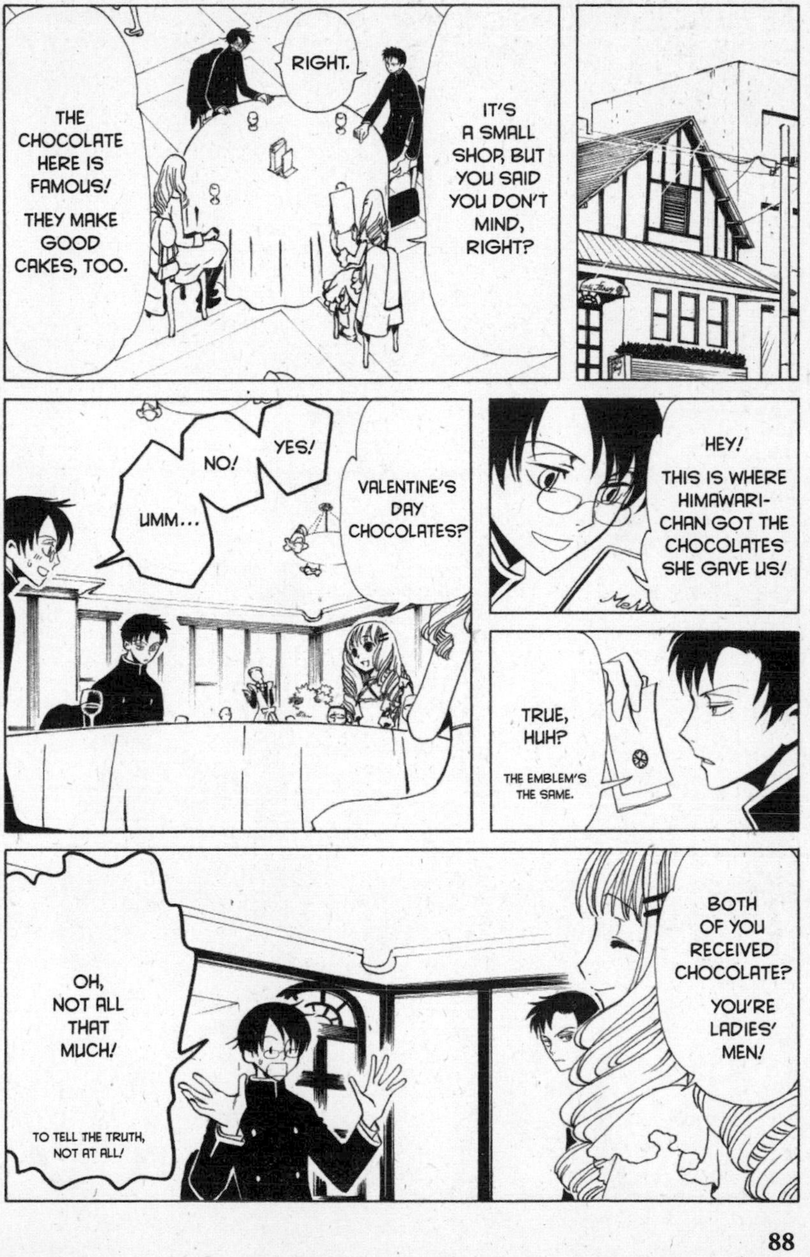
IT'S A SMALL SHOP, BUT YOU SAID YOU DON'T MIND, RIGHT?
RIGHT.
THE CHOCOLATE HERE IS FAMOUS!
THEY MAKE GOOD CAKES, TOO.
HEY!
THIS IS WHERE HIMAWARI-CHAN GOT THE CHOCOLATES SHE GAVE US!
TRUE, HUH?
THE EMBLEM'S THE SAME.
VALENTINE'S DAY CHOCOLATES?
YES!
NO!
UMM...
BOTH OF YOU RECEIVED CHOCOLATE?
YOU'RE LADIES' MEN!
OH, NOT ALL THAT MUCH!
TO TELL THE TRUTH, NOT AT ALL!

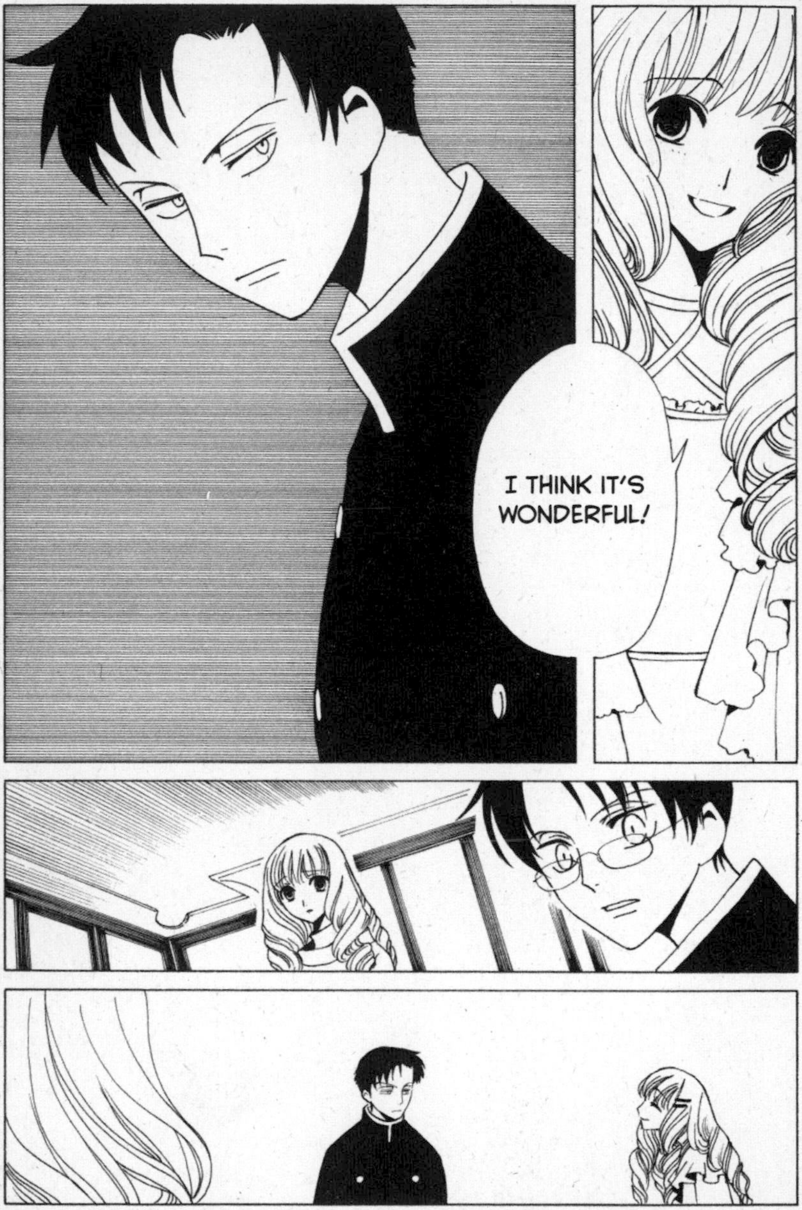
I THINK IT'S WONDERFUL!

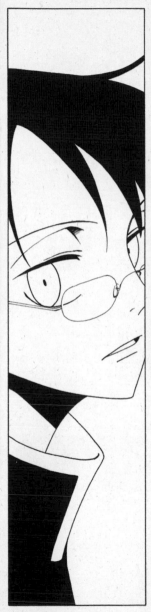
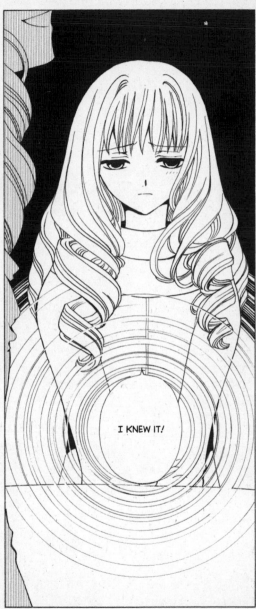

I KNEW IT!

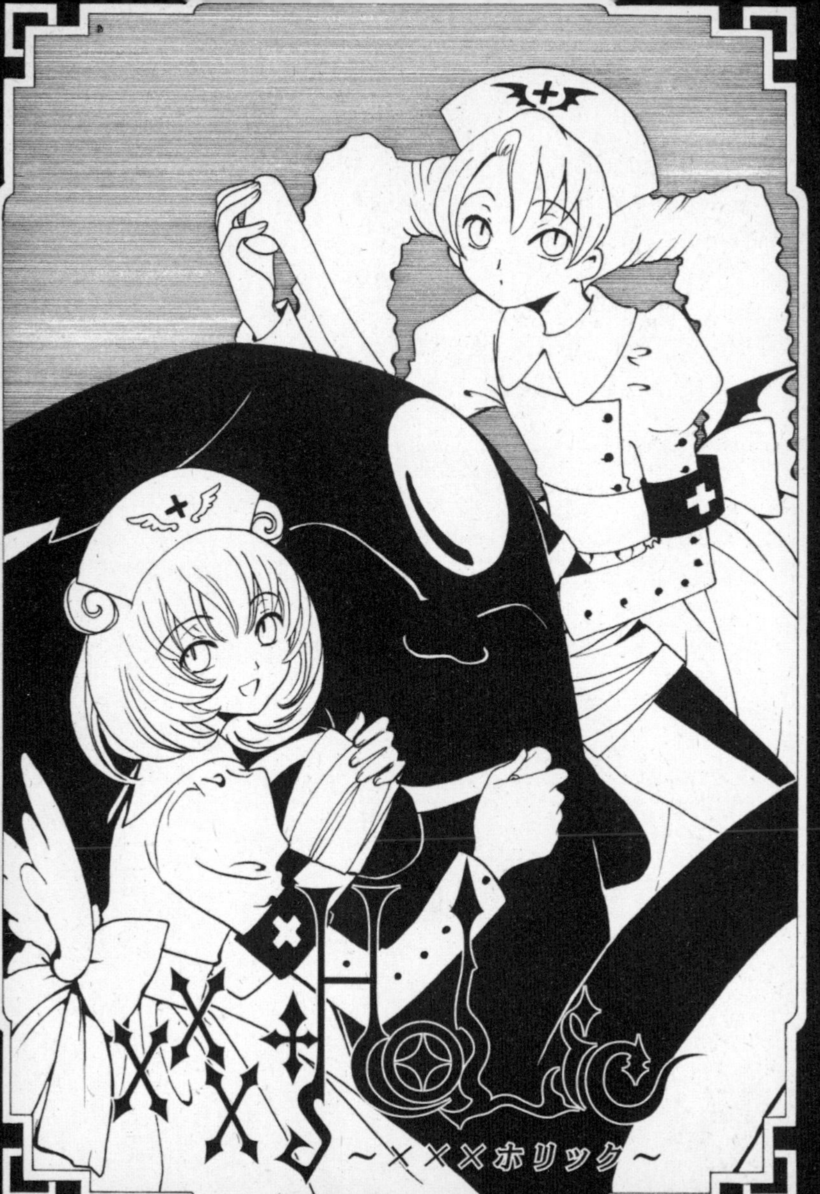
xxxHOLiC
~×××ホリック~

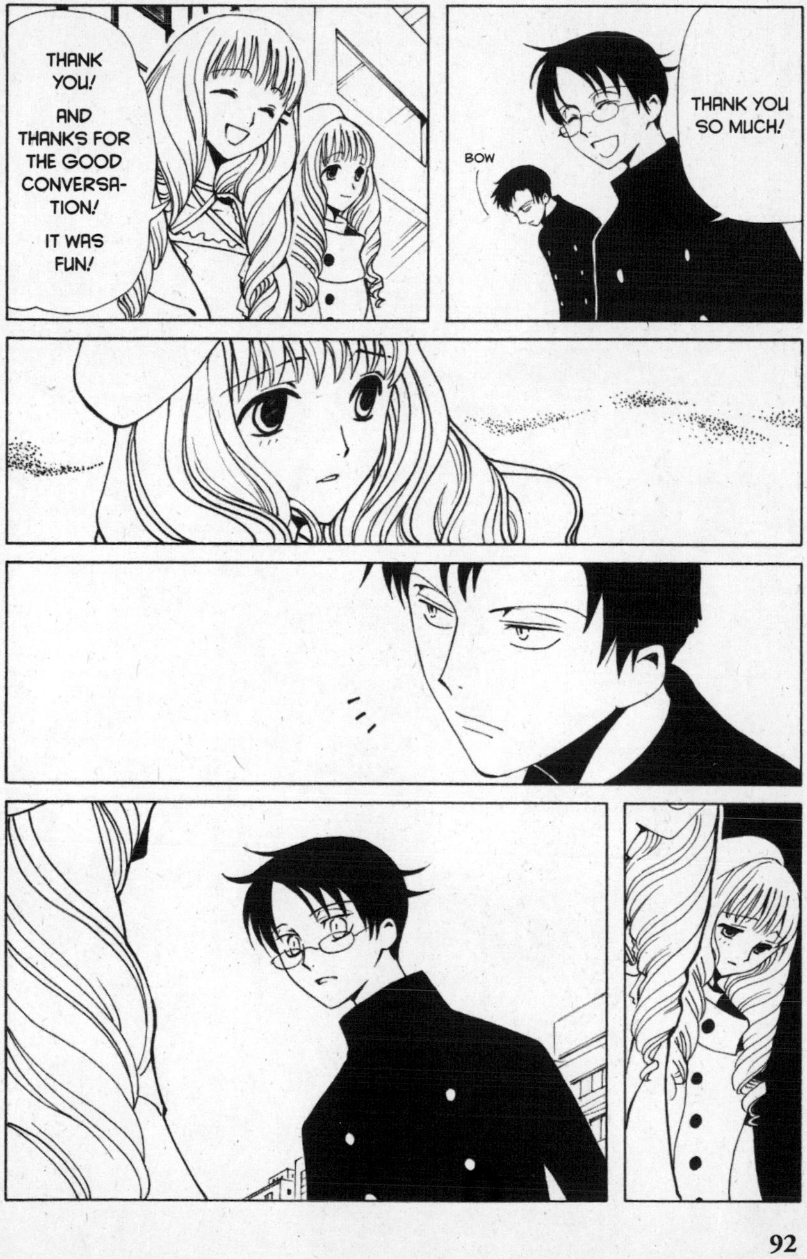
THANK YOU SO MUCH!
BOW
THANK YOU!
AND THANKS FOR THE GOOD CONVERSA-TION!
IT WAS FUN!

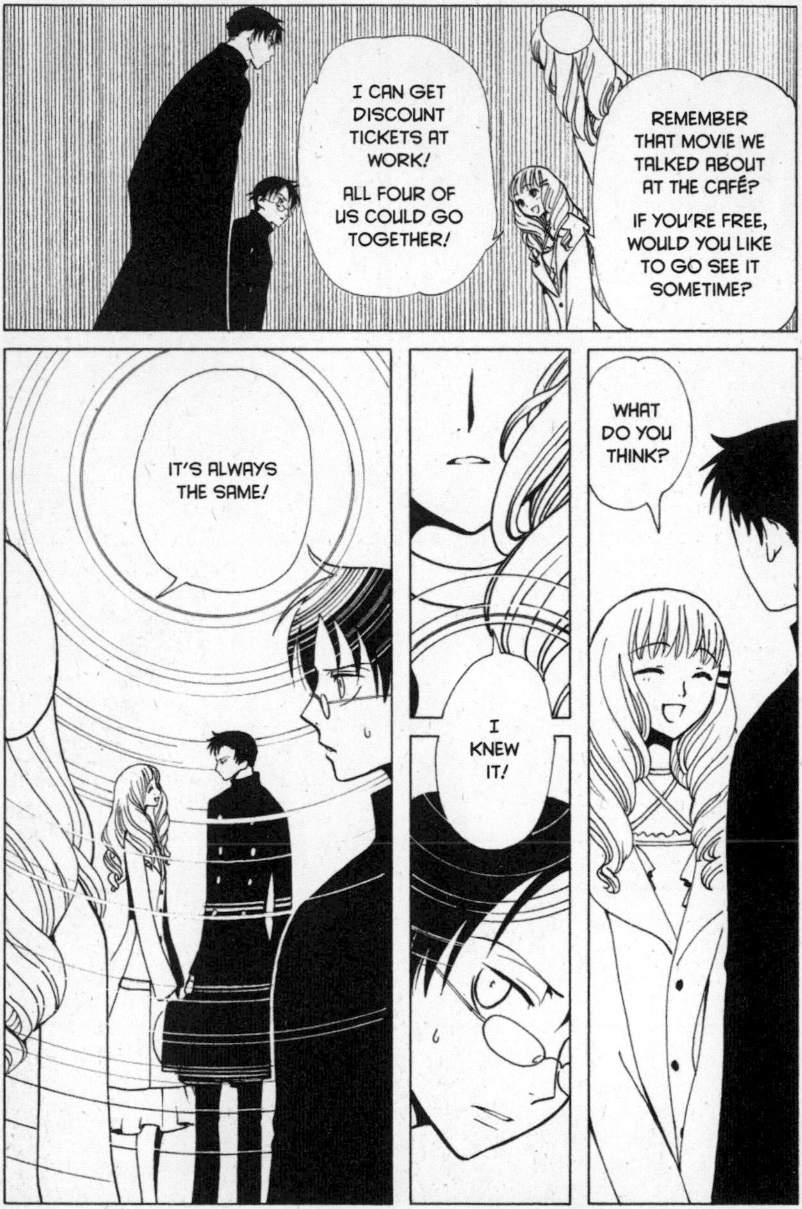
REMEMBER THAT MOVIE WE TALKED ABOUT AT THE CAFÉ?
IF YOU'RE FREE, WOULD YOU LIKE TO GO SEE IT SOMETIME?
I CAN GET DISCOUNT TICKETS AT WORK!
ALL FOUR OF US COULD GO TOGETHER!
WHAT DO YOU THINK?
I KNEW IT!
IT'S ALWAYS THE SAME!

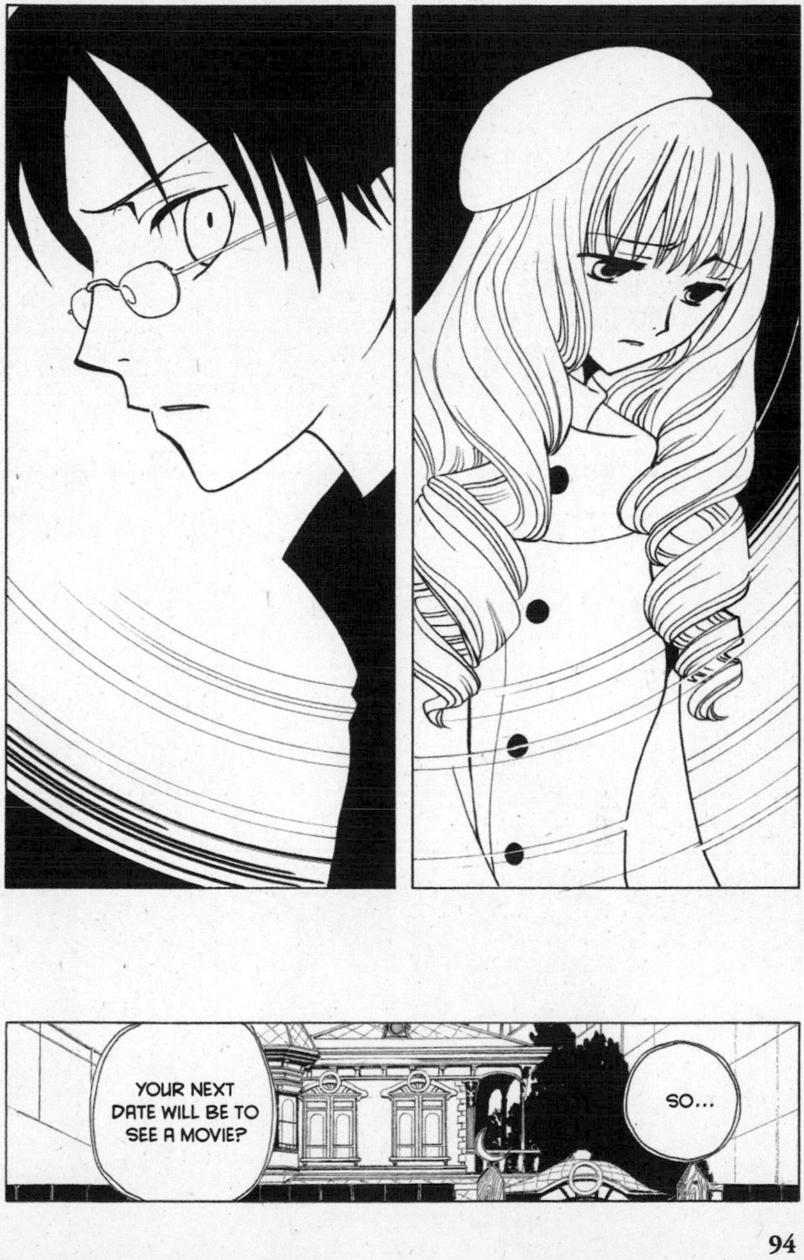
SO...
YOUR NEXT DATE WILL BE TO SEE A MOVIE?

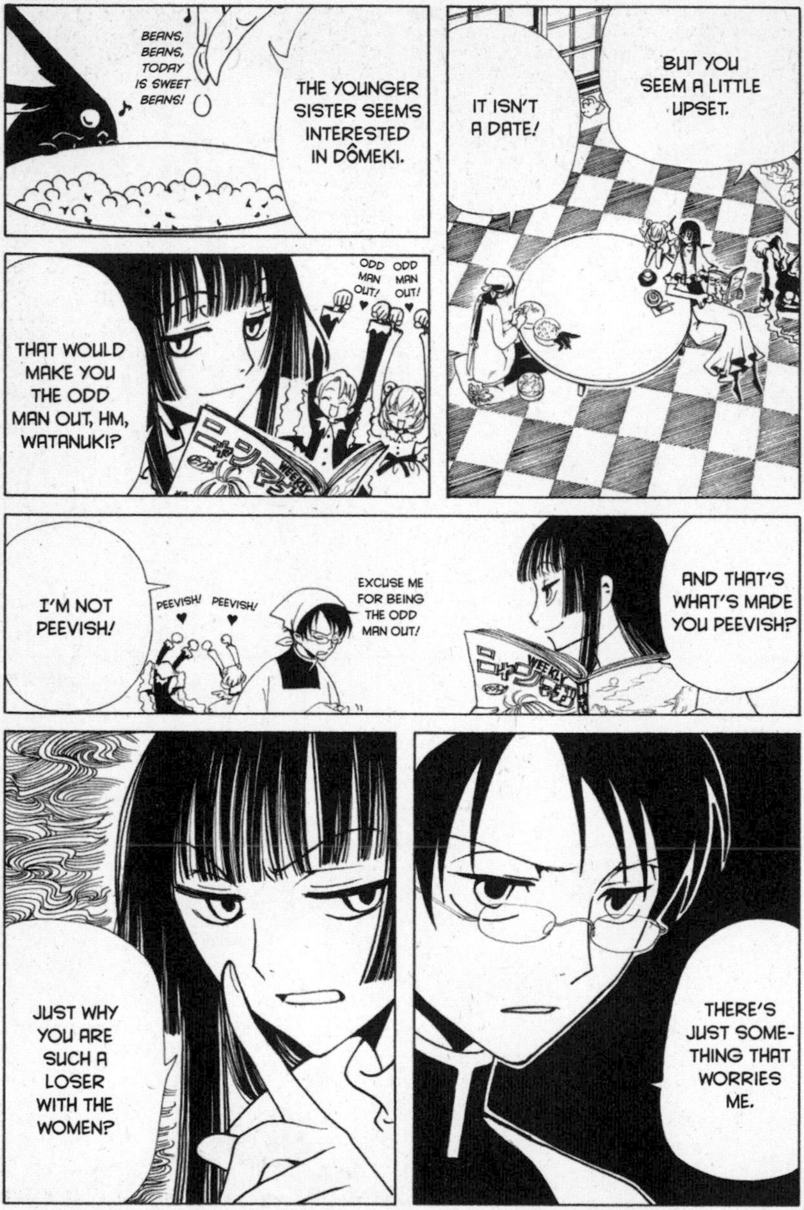
BUT YOU SEEM A LITTLE UPSET.
IT ISN'T A DATE!
THE YOUNGER SISTER SEEMS INTERESTED IN DÔMEKI.
BEANS, BEANS, TODAY IS SWEET BEANS!
ODD MAN OUT!
ODD MAN OUT!
THAT WOULD MAKE YOU THE ODD MAN OUT, HM, WATANUKI?
AND THAT'S WHAT'S MADE YOU PEEVISH?
WEEKLY
EXCUSE ME FOR BEING THE ODD MAN OUT!
PEEVISH!
PEEVISH!
I'M NOT PEEVISH!
THERE'S JUST SOME-THING THAT WORRIES ME.
JUST WHY YOU ARE SUCH A LOSER WITH THE WOMEN?

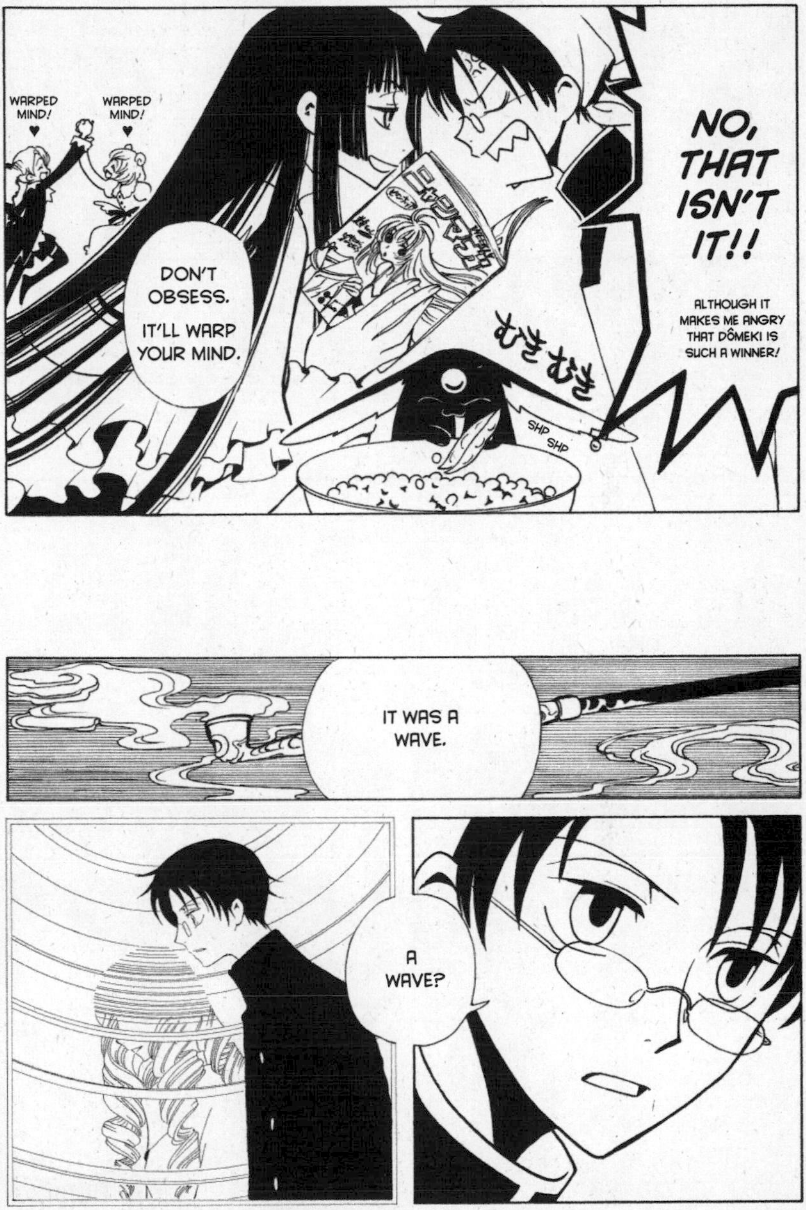
NO, THAT ISN'T IT!!
ALTHOUGH IT MAKES ME ANGRY THAT DÔMEKI IS SUCH A WINNER!
むきむき
SHP SHP
DON'T OBSESS.
IT'LL WARP YOUR MIND.
WARPED MIND! ♥
WARPED MIND! ♥
IT WAS A WAVE.
A WAVE?

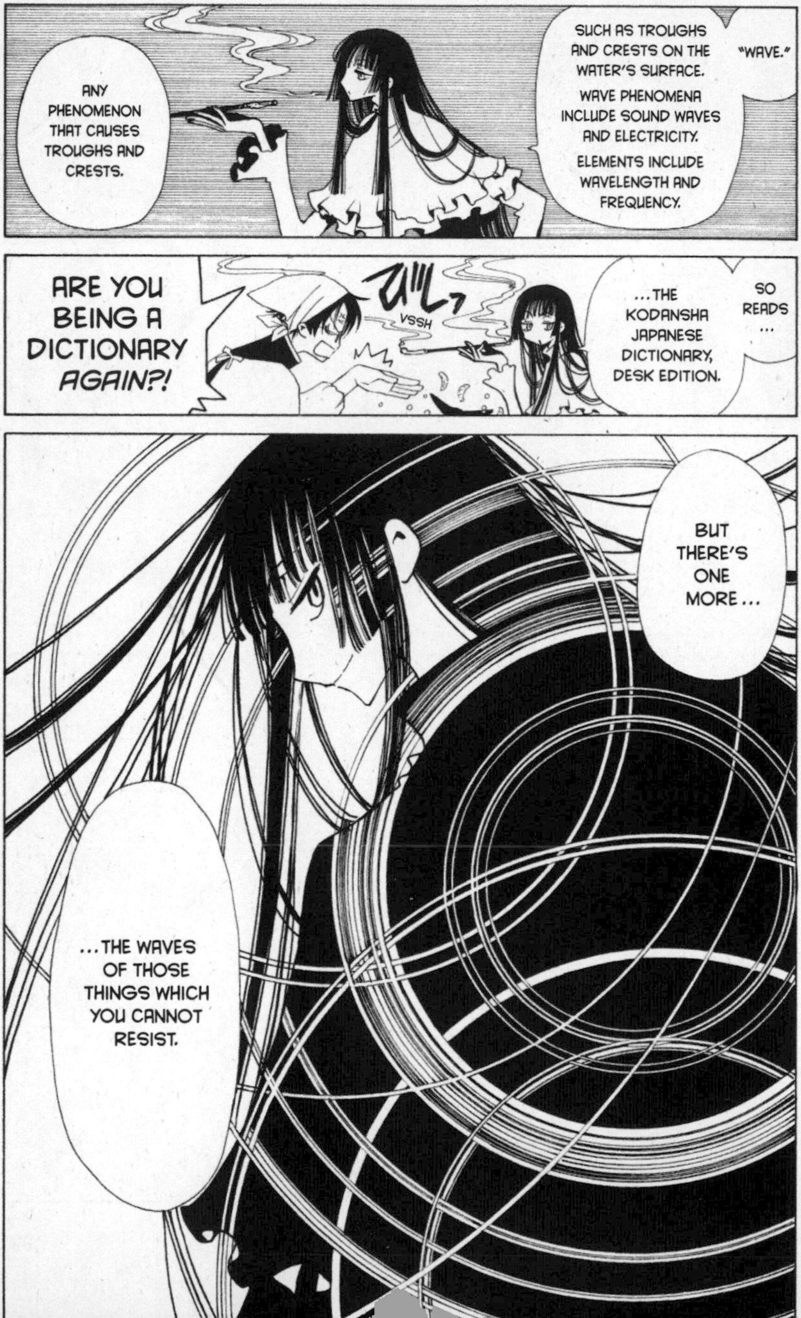
"WAVE."
SUCH AS TROUGHS AND CRESTS ON THE WATER'S SURFACE. WAVE PHENOMENA INCLUDE SOUND WAVES AND ELECTRICITY. ELEMENTS INCLUDE WAVELENGTH AND FREQUENCY.
ANY PHENOMENON THAT CAUSES TROUGHS AND CRESTS.
SO READS ...
...THE KODANSHA JAPANESE DICTIONARY, DESK EDITION.
VSSH
ARE YOU BEING A DICTIONARY AGAIN?!
BUT THERE'S ONE MORE...
...THE WAVES OF THOSE THINGS WHICH YOU CANNOT RESIST.

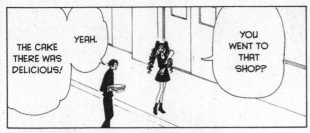

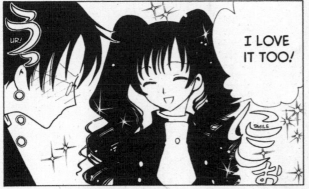

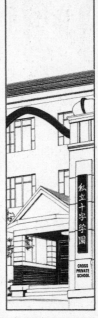

私立十字学園
CROSS PRIVATE SCHOOL
YOU WENT TO THAT SHOP?
YEAH.
THE CAKE THERE WAS DELICIOUS!
I LOVE IT TOO!
SMILE
UR!
HIMAWARI-CHAN IS TOO CUTE!!
?
?
KLUTCH
ARE YOU ALL RIGHT?
MAYBE I SHOULD CARRY THE PRINTOUTS.
SHAKE SHAKE
I'M JUST FINE!!

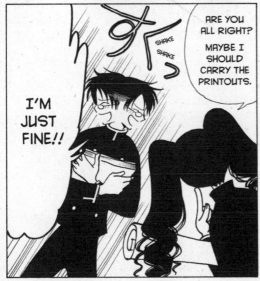

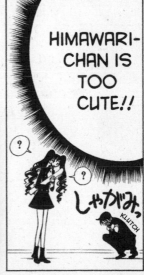

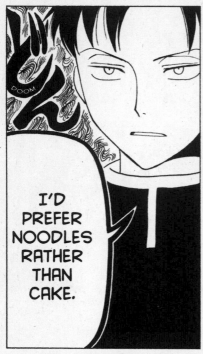

PAK
UM... WHY DON'T WE GO FOR CAKE?!
DOOM
I'D PREFER NOODLES RATHER THAN CAKE.
YOU'RE HERE ON TEACHER BUSINESS TOO, DÔMEKI-KUN?
YEAH.
FWAAM
WHY IS DÔMEKI ALWAYS APPEARING?!
GLOOOM
IS THIS WHAT THAT FORTUNE TELLER OLD LADY TOLD ME ABOUT A GUY I ALWAYS FIGHT WITH, AND HOW WE'LL BE THROWN TOGETHER?
AH!

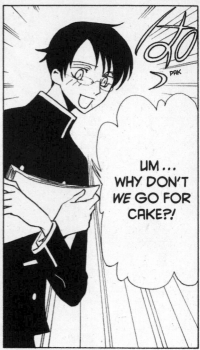

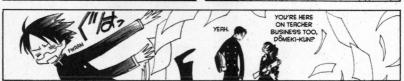

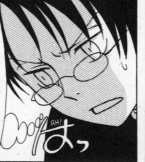

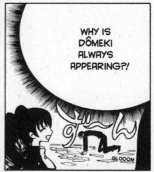

いやあああ!!
NOOOOO!!!
WATANUKI ALWAYS HAS SO MUCH ENERGY!
MOST IDIOTS DO.
WHO ARE YOU CALLING AN IDIOT?!
YOU CAN HEAR THAT?
SENSITIVE EARS.
TODAY, WHEN CLASSES ARE OVER, STAY IN YOUR CLASSROOM.
WE'LL LEAVE FROM THERE.
GOT IT.
ARE YOU GOING SOME-WHERE?
NO!
UM...
A MOVIE.
THE TWO OF YOU?
FOUR, ACTUALLY.
A COUPLE OF COLLEGE STUDENTS SAID THEY COULD GET DISCOUNT PASSES...
OH, COLLEGE CO-EDS, HUH?
NO!
IT'S NOT...
THAT'S WRONG...
HIMAWARI-CHAN!!
うわーっ
GLOOMM

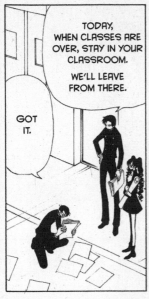

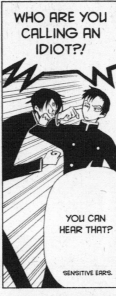

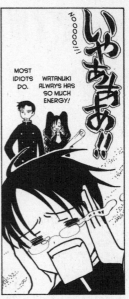

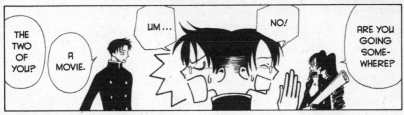

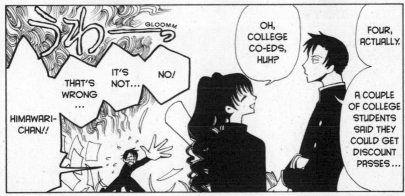

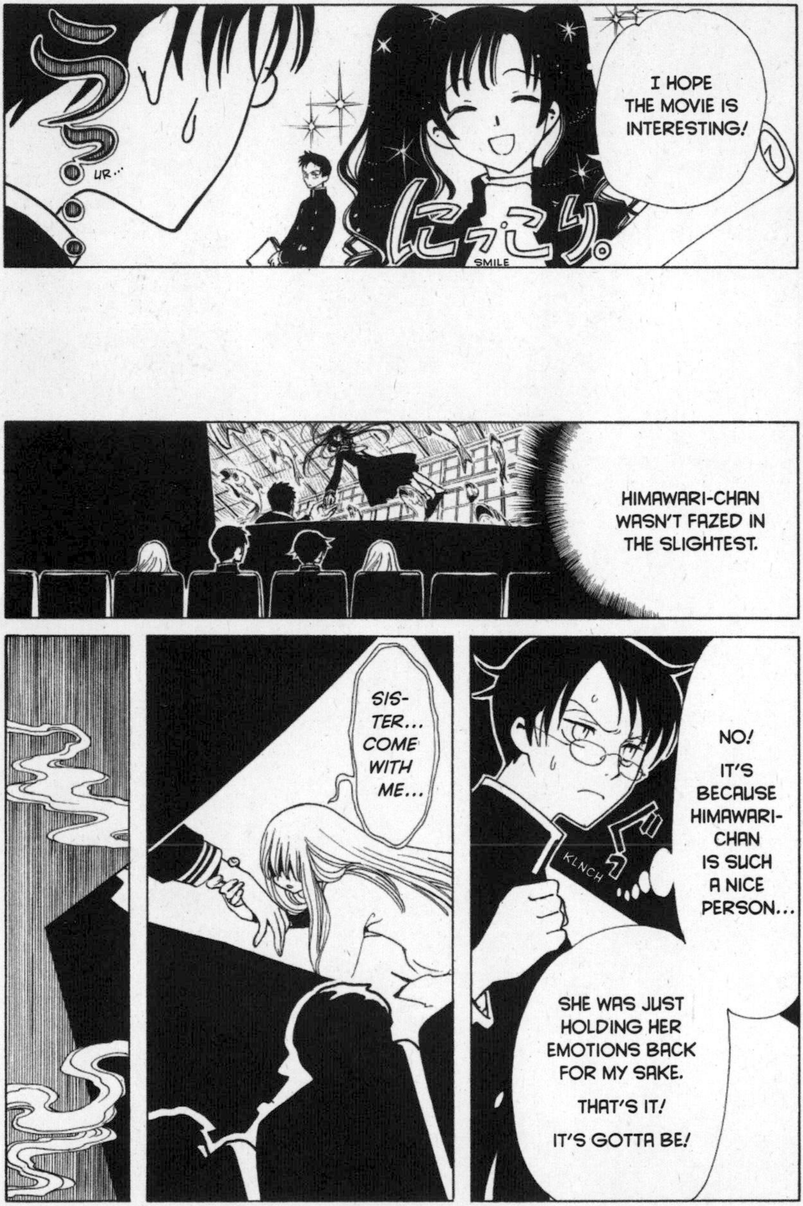
I HOPE THE MOVIE IS INTERESTING!
にっこり。
SMILE
UR...
HIMAWARI-CHAN WASN'T FAZED IN THE SLIGHTEST.
NO! IT'S BECAUSE HIMAWARI-CHAN IS SUCH A NICE PERSON...
KLNCH
SHE WAS JUST HOLDING HER EMOTIONS BACK FOR MY SAKE.
THAT'S IT!
IT'S GOTTA BE!
SIS-TER... COME WITH ME...

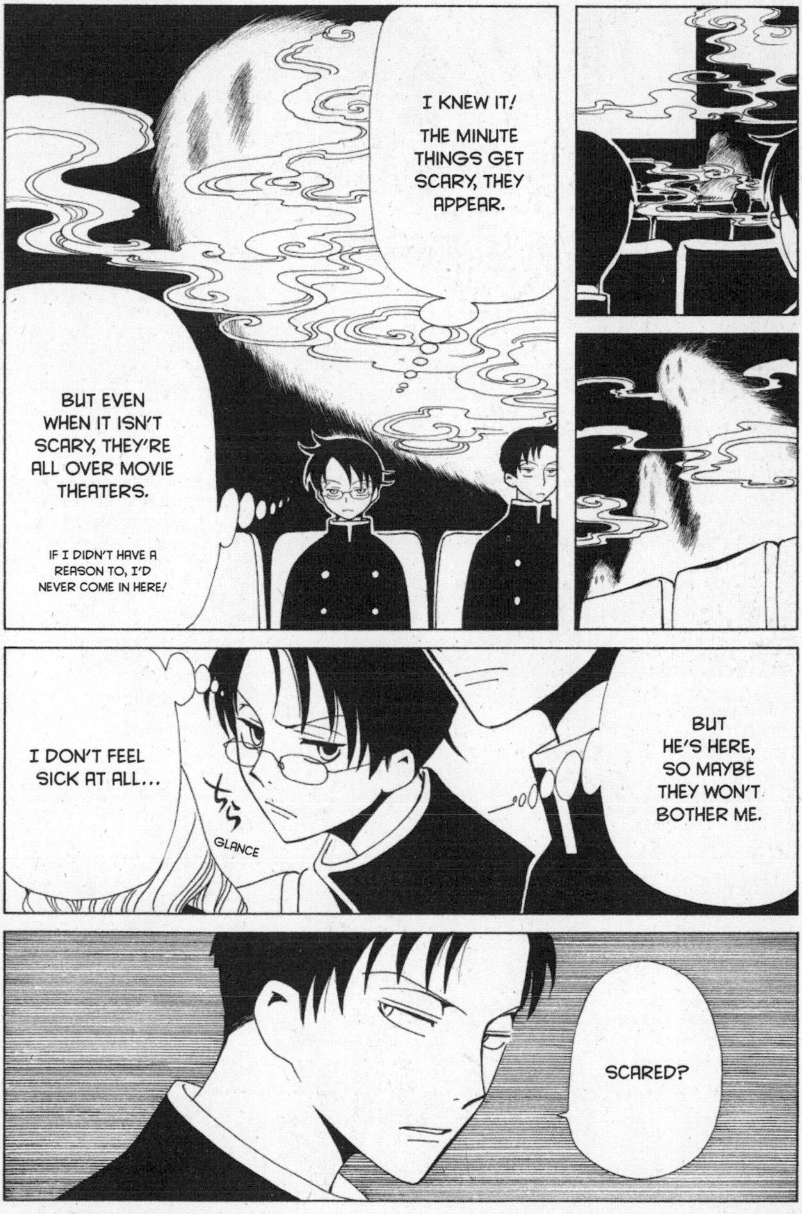
I KNEW IT!
THE MINUTE THINGS GET SCARY, THEY APPEAR.
BUT EVEN WHEN IT ISN'T SCARY, THEY'RE ALL OVER MOVIE THEATERS.
IF I DIDN'T HAVE A REASON TO, I'D NEVER COME IN HERE!
BUT HE'S HERE, SO MAYBE THEY WON'T BOTHER ME.
I DON'T FEEL SICK AT ALL...
GLANCE
SCARED?

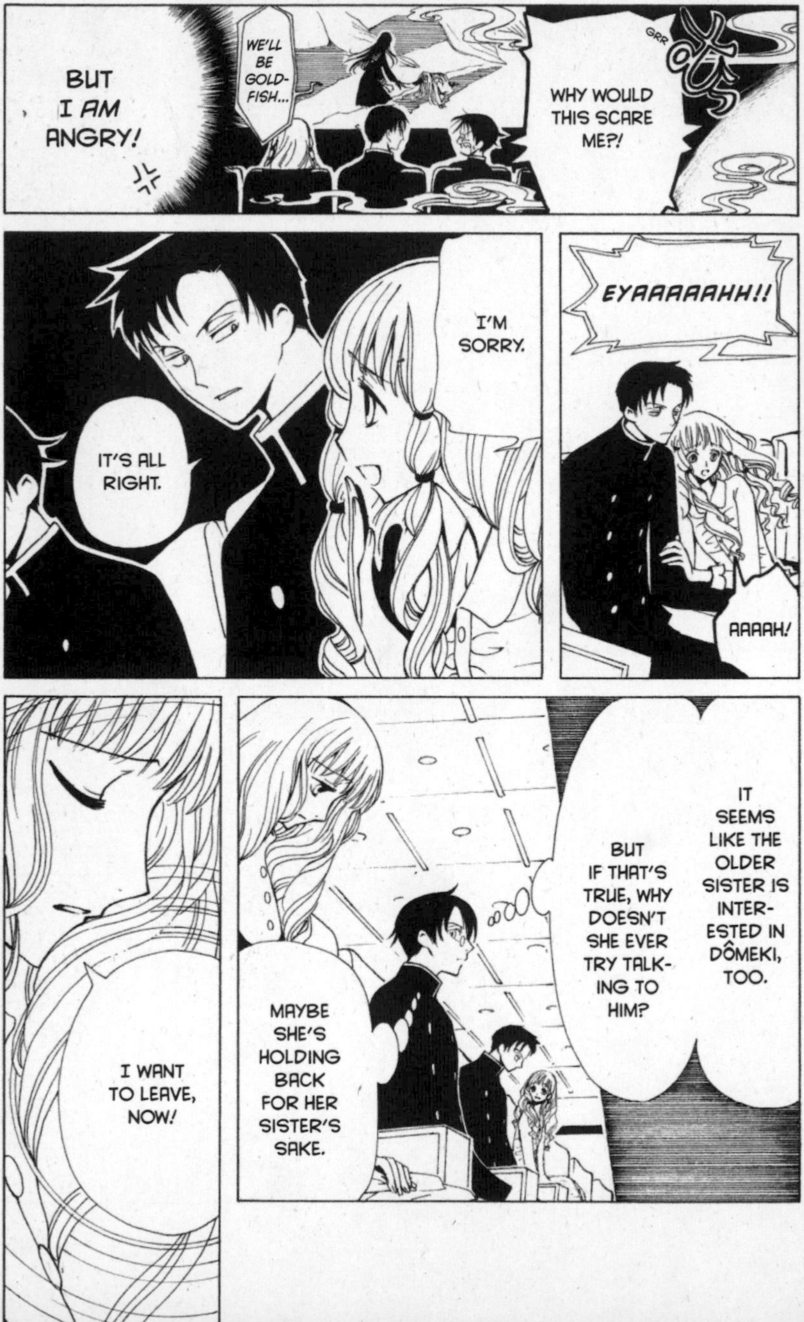
GRR
WHY WOULD THIS SCARE ME?!
WE'LL BE GOLD-FISH...
BUT I AM ANGRY!
EYAAAAAHH!!
AAAAH!
I'M SORRY.
IT'S ALL RIGHT.
IT SEEMS LIKE THE OLDER SISTER IS INTER-ESTED IN DÔMEKI, TOO.
BUT IF THAT'S TRUE, WHY DOESN'T SHE EVER TRY TALK-ING TO HIM?
MAYBE SHE'S HOLDING BACK FOR HER SISTER'S SAKE.
I WANT TO LEAVE, NOW!

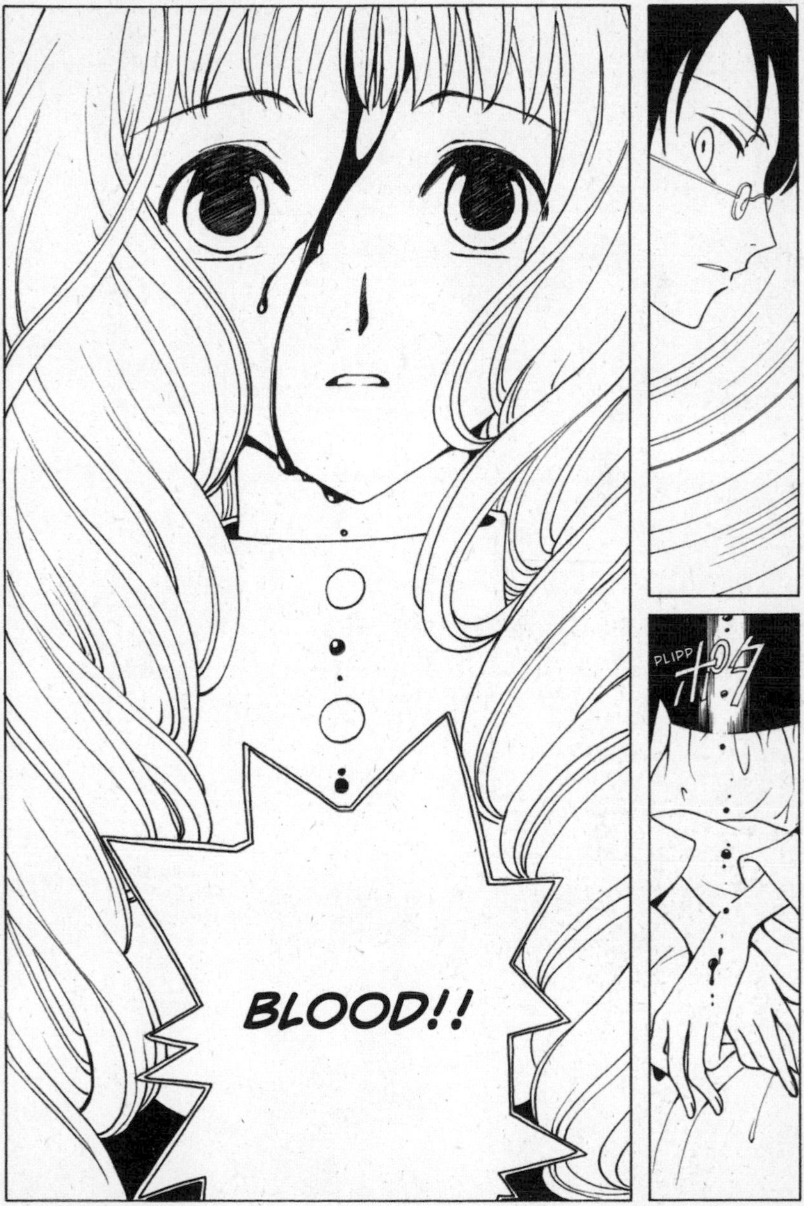
PLIPP
BLOOD!!

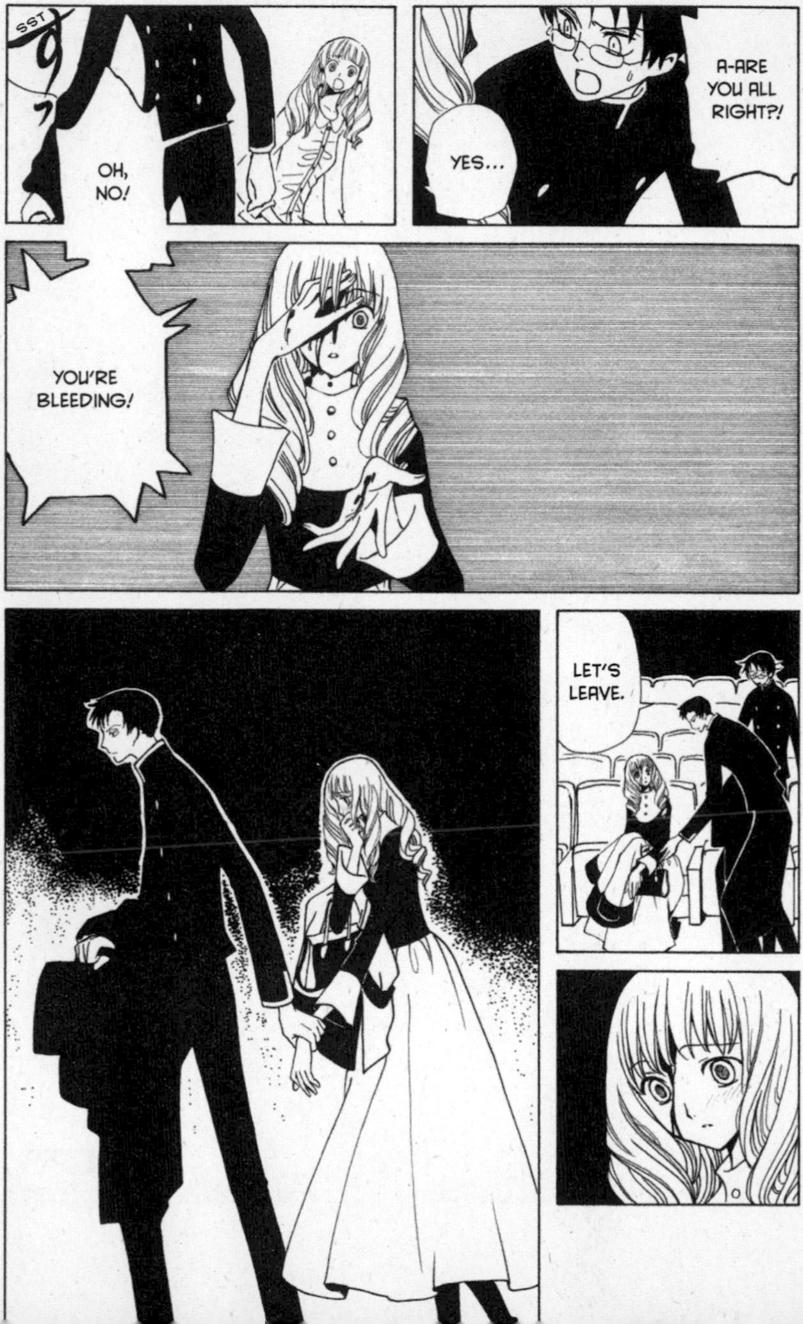
A-ARE YOU ALL RIGHT?!
YES...
SST
OH, NO!
YOU'RE BLEEDING!
LET'S LEAVE.

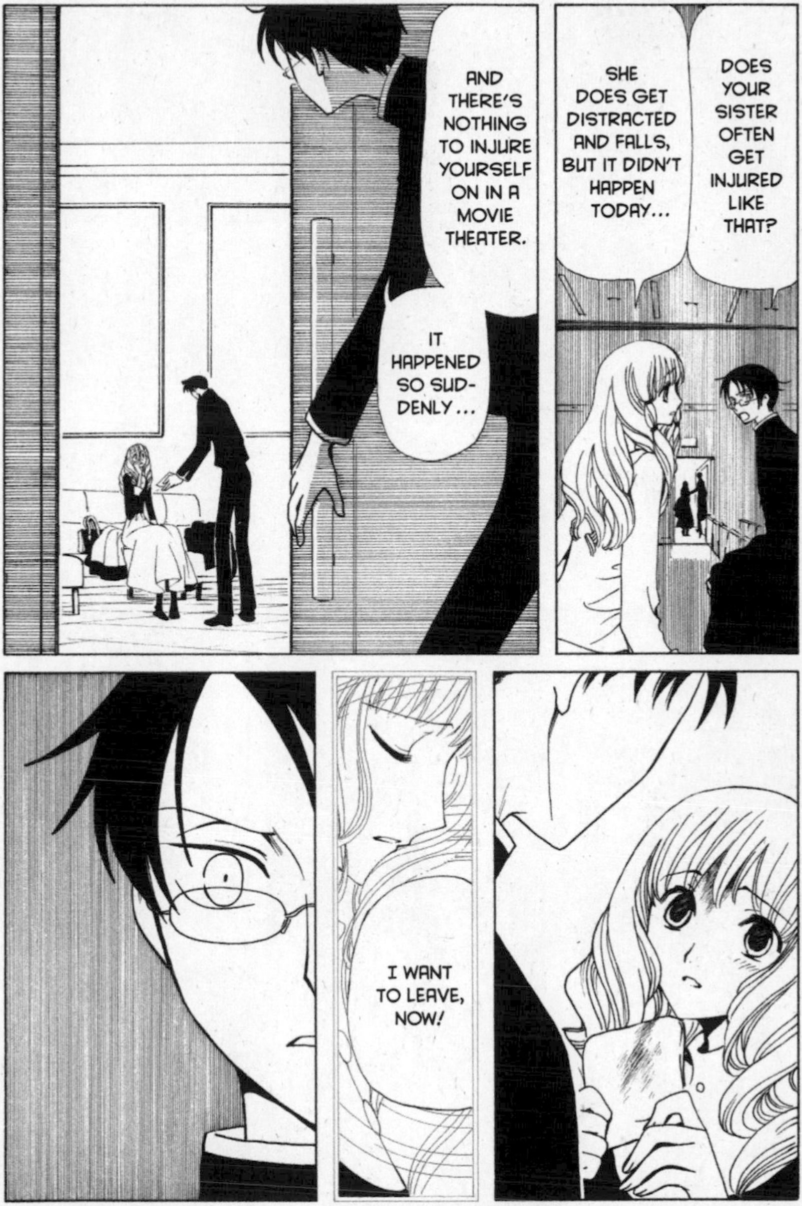
DOES YOUR SISTER OFTEN GET INJURED LIKE THAT?
SHE DOES GET DISTRACTED AND FALLS, BUT IT DIDN'T HAPPEN TODAY...
AND THERE'S NOTHING TO INJURE YOURSELF ON IN A MOVIE THEATER.
IT HAPPENED SO SUD-DENLY...
I WANT TO LEAVE, NOW!

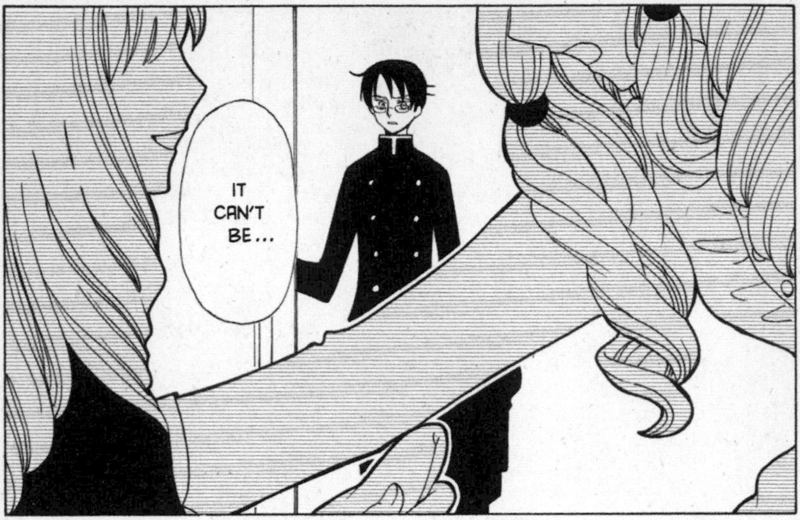
IT CAN'T BE...

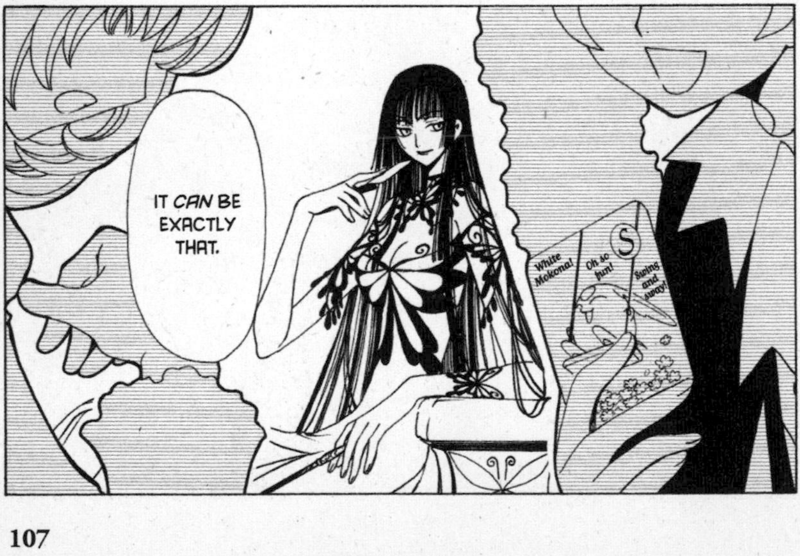
IT *CAN* BE EXACTLY THAT.
White Mokona!
Oh so fun!
S
Swing and away!

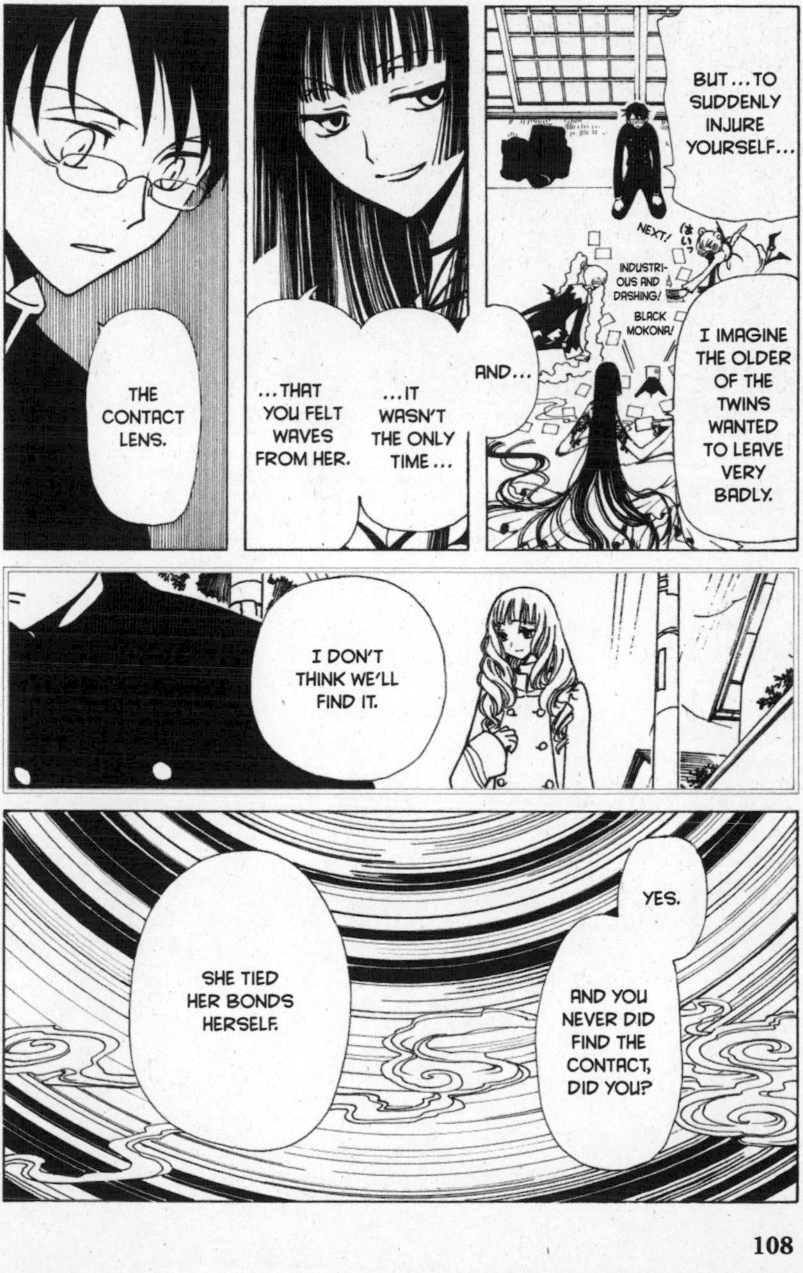
BUT...TO SUDDENLY INJURE YOURSELF...
NEXT!
はいっ
INDUSTRIOUS AND DASHING!
BLACK MOKONA!
I IMAGINE THE OLDER OF THE TWINS WANTED TO LEAVE VERY BADLY.
AND...
...IT WASN'T THE ONLY TIME...
...THAT YOU FELT WAVES FROM HER.
THE CONTACT LENS.
I DON'T THINK WE'LL FIND IT.
YES.
AND YOU NEVER DID FIND THE CONTACT, DID YOU?
SHE TIED HER BONDS HERSELF.

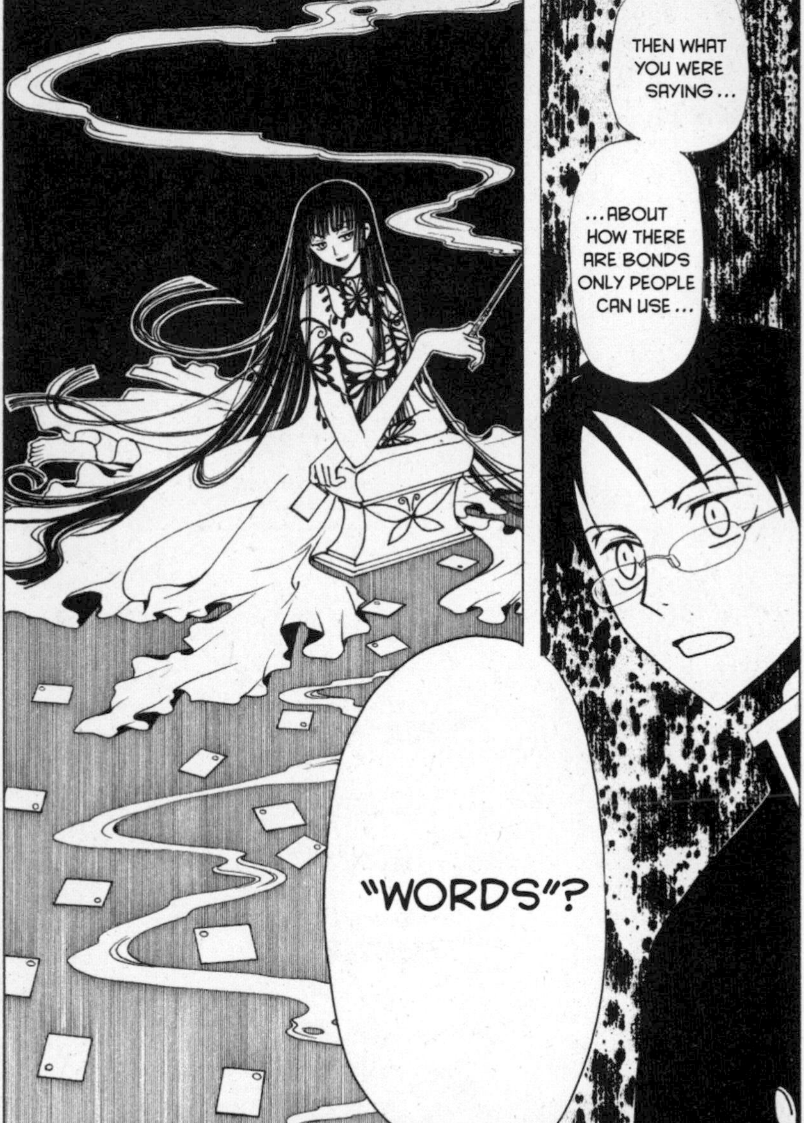
THEN WHAT YOU WERE SAYING...
...ABOUT HOW THERE ARE BONDS ONLY PEOPLE CAN USE...
"WORDS"?

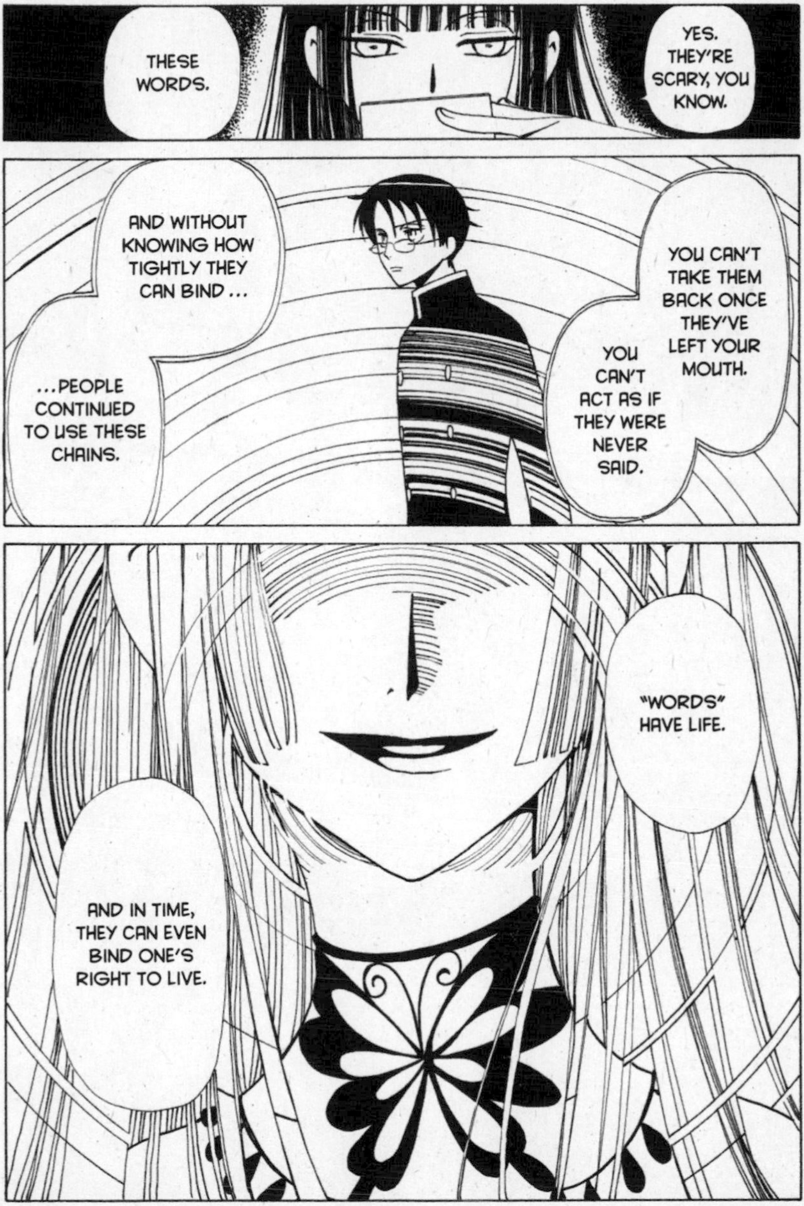
YES. THEY'RE SCARY, YOU KNOW.
THESE WORDS.
YOU CAN'T TAKE THEM BACK ONCE THEY'VE LEFT YOUR MOUTH.
YOU CAN'T ACT AS IF THEY WERE NEVER SAID.
AND WITHOUT KNOWING HOW TIGHTLY THEY CAN BIND ...
...PEOPLE CONTINUED TO USE THESE CHAINS.
"WORDS" HAVE LIFE.
AND IN TIME, THEY CAN EVEN BIND ONE'S RIGHT TO LIVE.

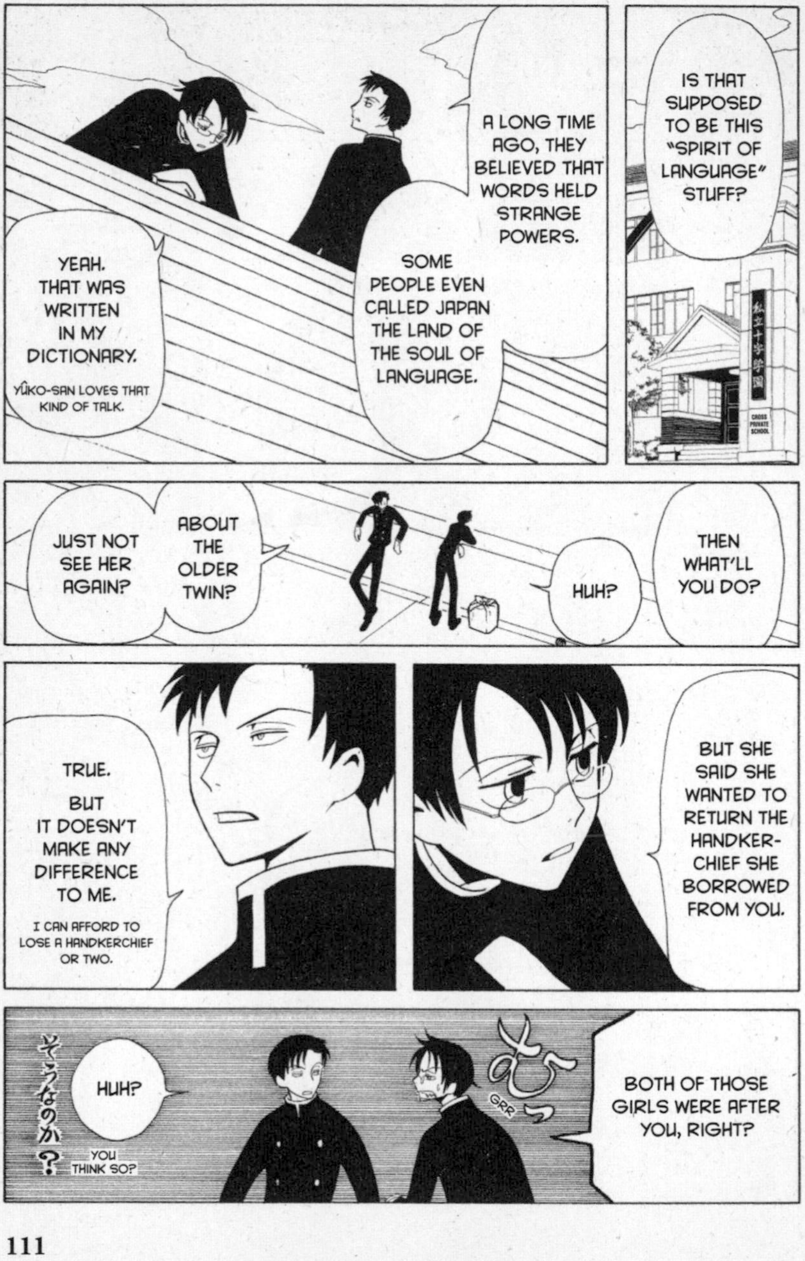
IS THAT SUPPOSED TO BE THIS "SPIRIT OF LANGUAGE" STUFF?
CROSS PRIVATE SCHOOL
A LONG TIME AGO, THEY BELIEVED THAT WORDS HELD STRANGE POWERS.
SOME PEOPLE EVEN CALLED JAPAN THE LAND OF THE SOUL OF LANGUAGE.
YEAH. THAT WAS WRITTEN IN MY DICTIONARY.
YÛKO-SAN LOVES THAT KIND OF TALK.
THEN WHAT'LL YOU DO?
HUH?
ABOUT THE OLDER TWIN?
JUST NOT SEE HER AGAIN?
BUT SHE SAID SHE WANTED TO RETURN THE HANDKER-CHIEF SHE BORROWED FROM YOU.
TRUE.
BUT IT DOESN'T MAKE ANY DIFFERENCE TO ME.
I CAN AFFORD TO LOSE A HANDKERCHIEF OR TWO.
BOTH OF THOSE GIRLS WERE AFTER YOU, RIGHT?
むぅ
GRR
HUH?
そうなのか？
YOU THINK SO?

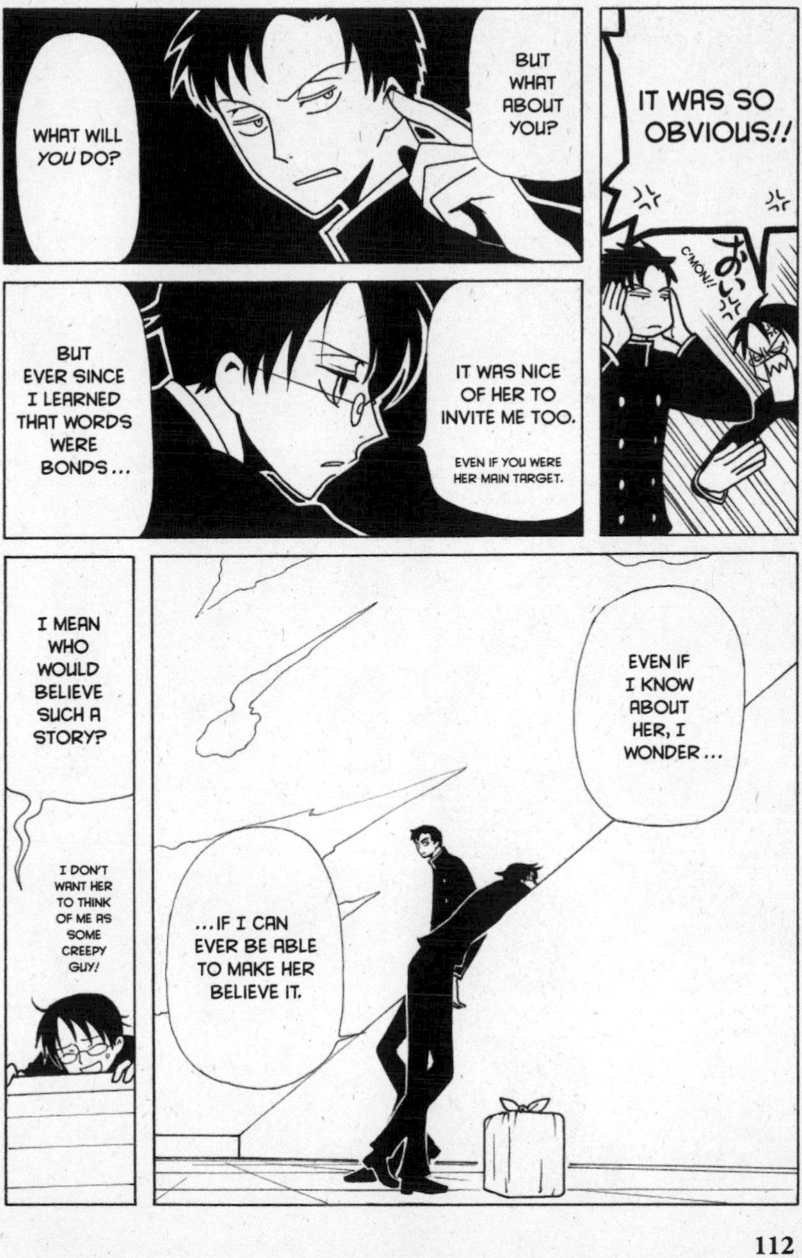

IT WAS SO OBVIOUS!!
おい
C'MON!!
BUT WHAT ABOUT YOU?
WHAT WILL *YOU* DO?
IT WAS NICE OF HER TO INVITE ME TOO.
EVEN IF YOU WERE HER MAIN TARGET.
BUT EVER SINCE I LEARNED THAT WORDS WERE BONDS...
EVEN IF I KNOW ABOUT HER, I WONDER...
...IF I CAN EVER BE ABLE TO MAKE HER BELIEVE IT.
I MEAN WHO WOULD BELIEVE SUCH A STORY?
I DON'T WANT HER TO THINK OF ME AS SOME CREEPY GUY!

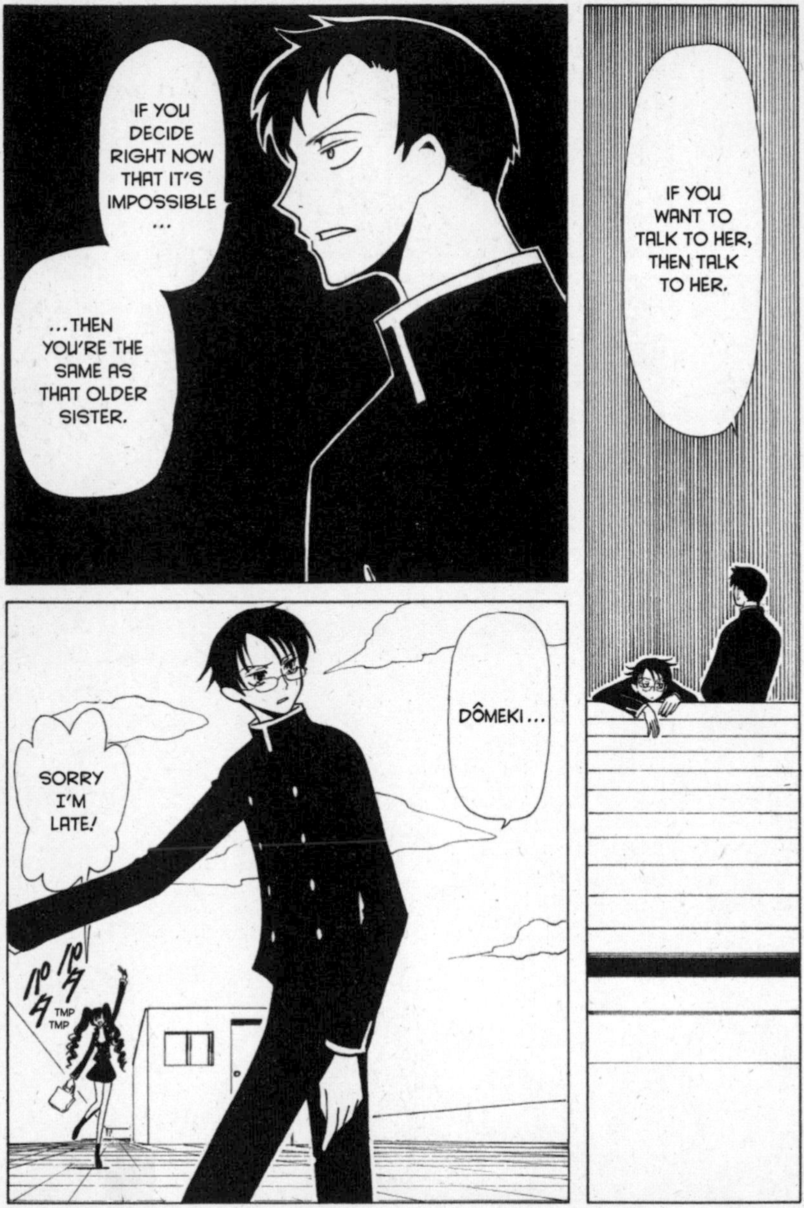
IF YOU WANT TO TALK TO HER, THEN TALK TO HER.
IF YOU DECIDE RIGHT NOW THAT IT'S IMPOSSIBLE ...
...THEN YOU'RE THE SAME AS THAT OLDER SISTER.
DÔMEKI...
SORRY I'M LATE!
パタパタ
TMP TMP

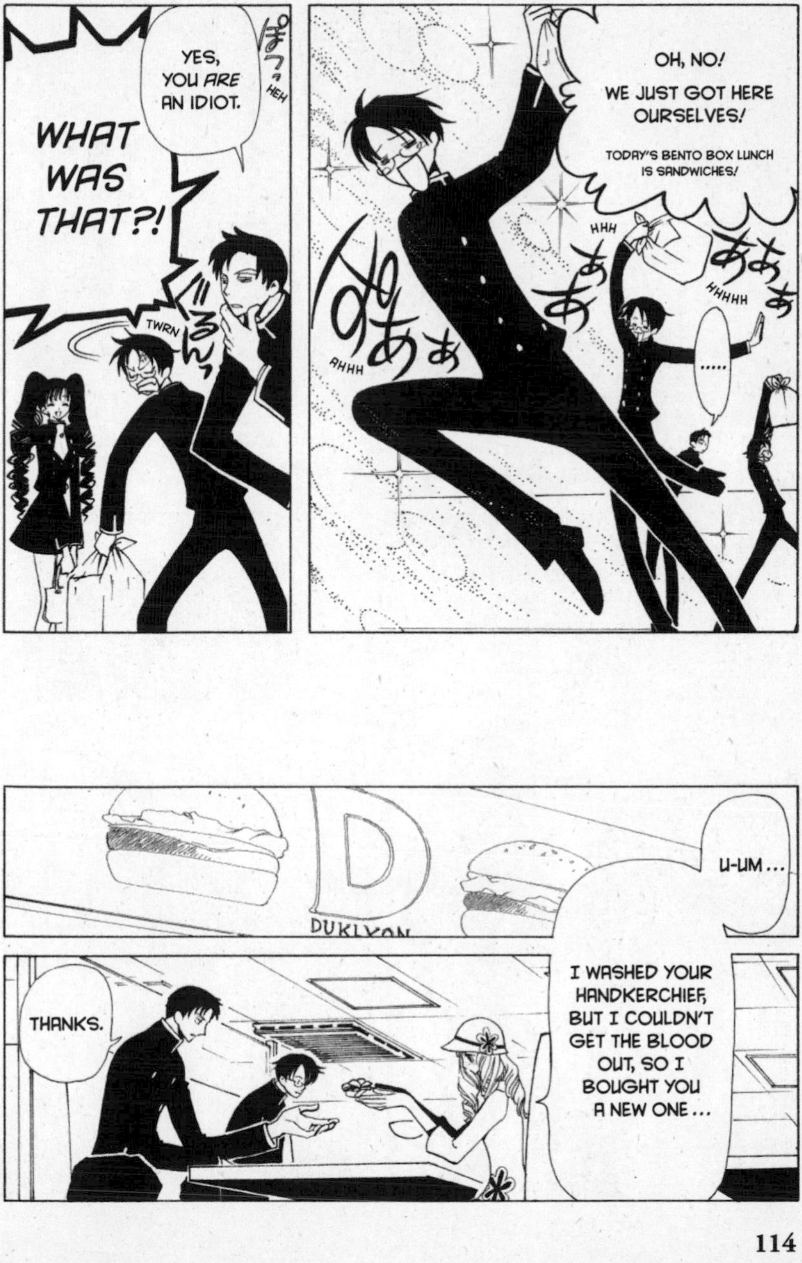
OH, NO!
WE JUST GOT HERE OURSELVES!
TODAY'S BENTO BOX LUNCH IS SANDWICHES!
HHH
HHHHH
......
AHHH
HEH
YES, YOU ARE AN IDIOT.
WHAT WAS THAT?!
TWRN
U-UM...
DUKLYON
I WASHED YOUR HANDKERCHIEF, BUT I COULDN'T GET THE BLOOD OUT, SO I BOUGHT YOU A NEW ONE...
THANKS.

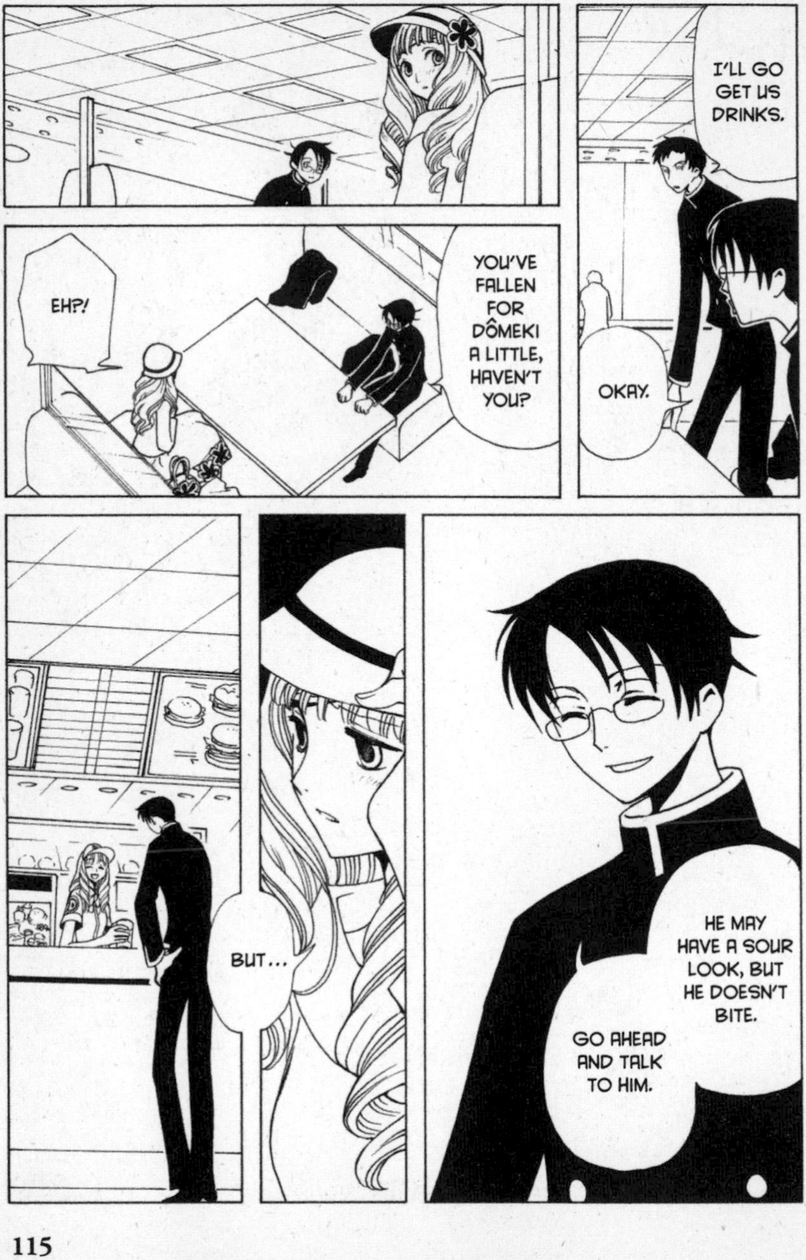
I'LL GO GET US DRINKS.
OKAY.
YOU'VE FALLEN FOR DÔMEKI A LITTLE, HAVEN'T YOU?
EH?!
HE MAY HAVE A SOUR LOOK, BUT HE DOESN'T BITE.
GO AHEAD AND TALK TO HIM.
BUT...

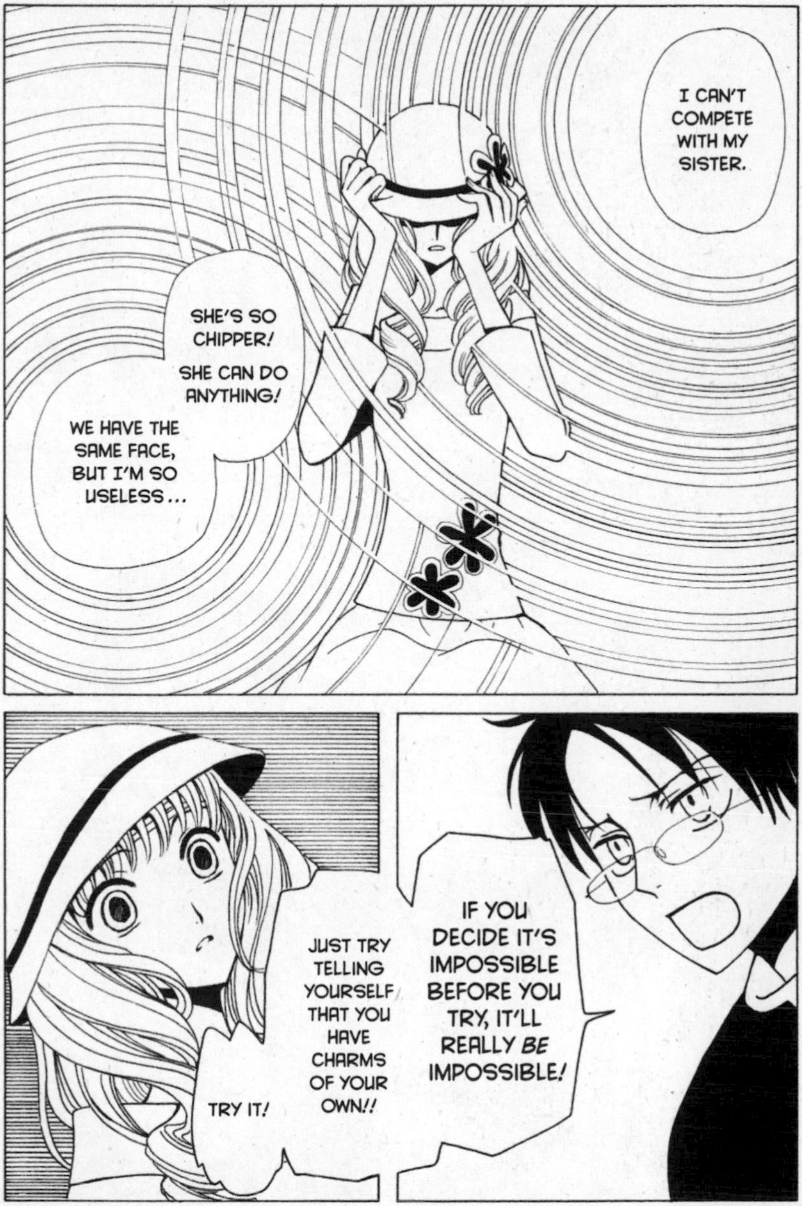
I CAN'T COMPETE WITH MY SISTER.
SHE'S SO CHIPPER! SHE CAN DO ANYTHING!
WE HAVE THE SAME FACE, BUT I'M SO USELESS...
IF YOU DECIDE IT'S IMPOSSIBLE BEFORE YOU TRY, IT'LL REALLY *BE* IMPOSSIBLE!
JUST TRY TELLING YOURSELF THAT YOU HAVE CHARMS OF YOUR OWN!!
TRY IT!

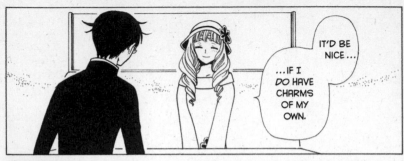

IT'D BE NICE...

...IF I *DO* HAVE CHARMS OF MY OWN.

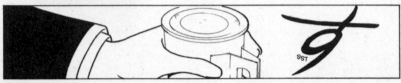

SST

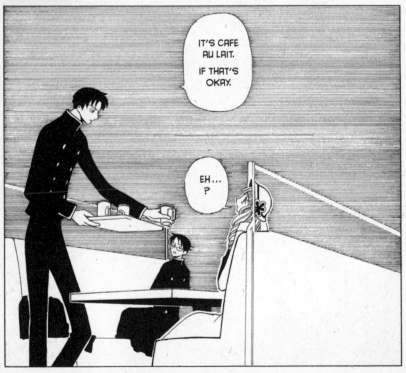

IT'S CAFE AU LAIT.

IF THAT'S OKAY.

EH...?

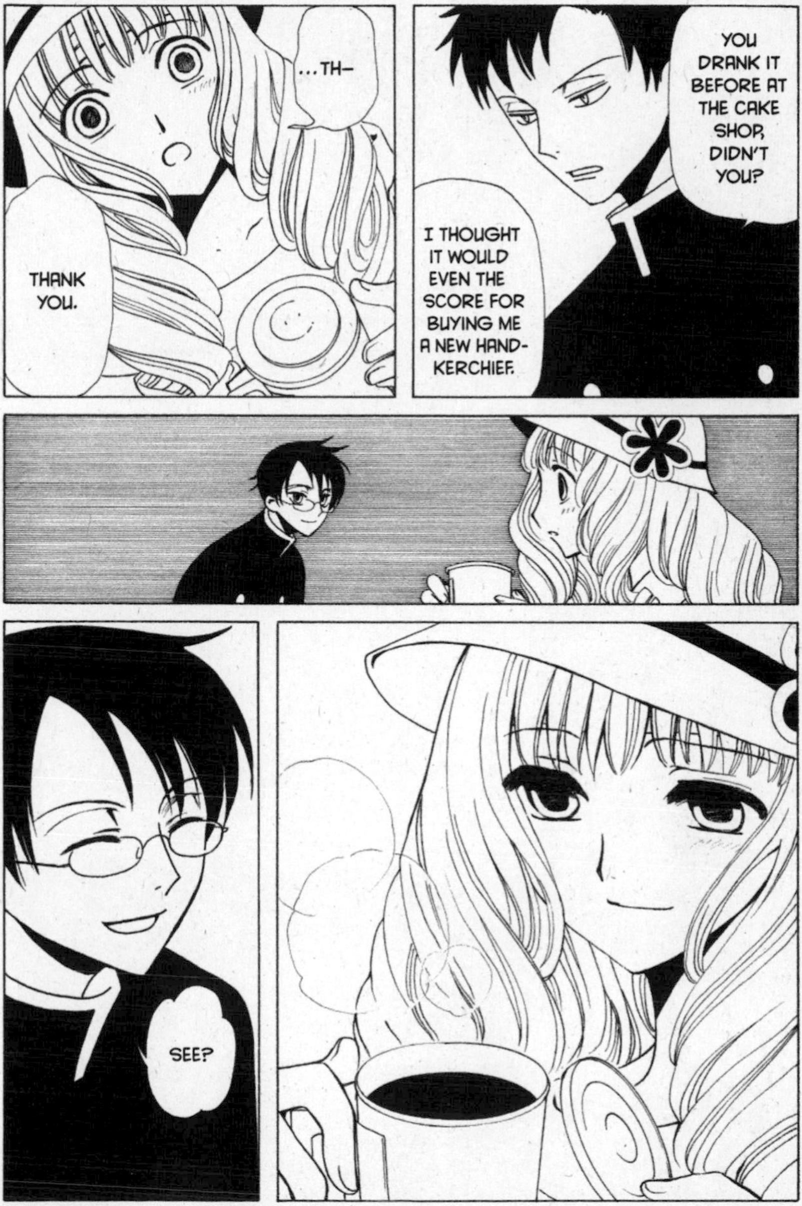
YOU DRANK IT BEFORE AT THE CAKE SHOP, DIDN'T YOU?
I THOUGHT IT WOULD EVEN THE SCORE FOR BUYING ME A NEW HAND-KERCHIEF.
...TH-
THANK YOU.
SEE?

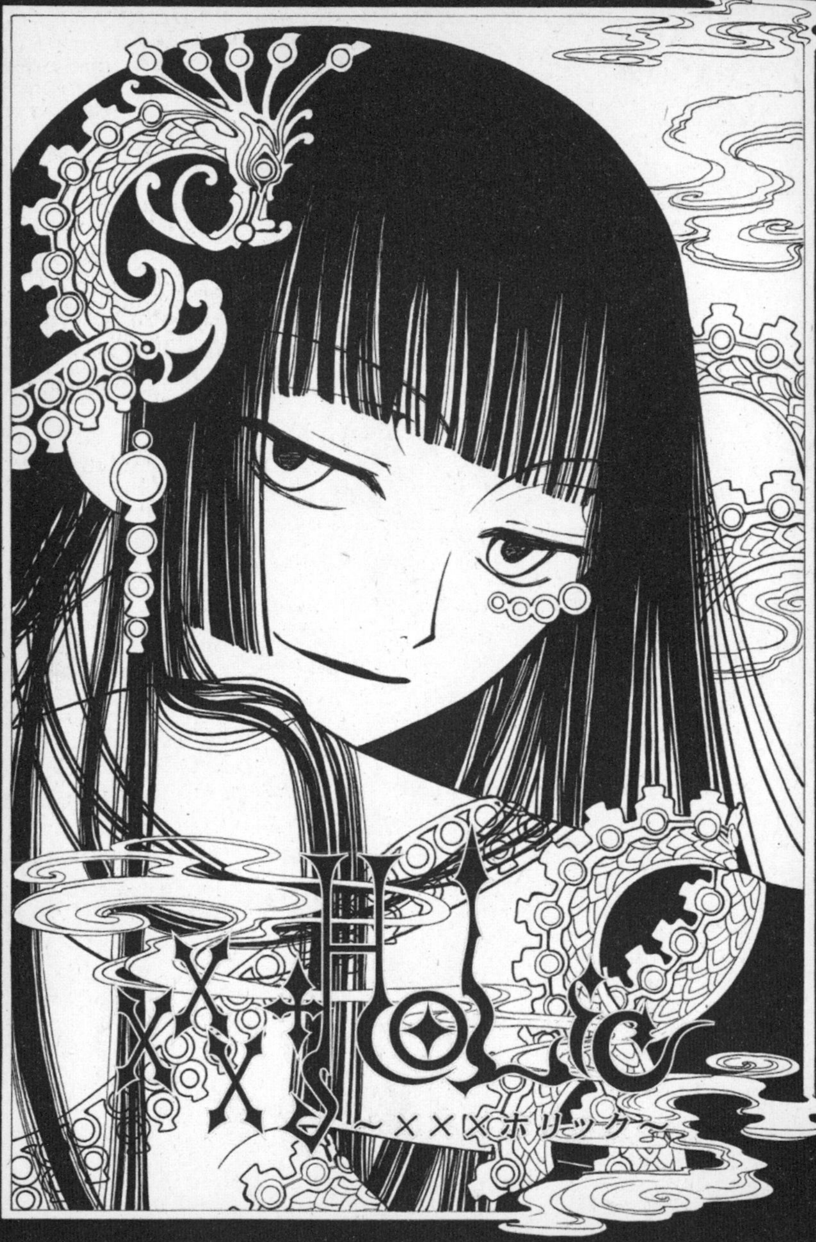
xxxHOLiC
～×××ホリック～

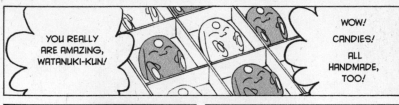

WOW! CANDIES! ALL HANDMADE, TOO!
YOU REALLY ARE AMAZING, WATANUKI-KUN!
I TRIED TO THINK OF WHAT TO DO FOR WHITE DAY, AND I THOUGHT CANDIES MIGHT BE OKAY.
てれてれ
WORRY WORRY
WELL, I JUST LOVE DOUGHY CANDIES!
ひょいっ
PO IT
ぱくっ
CHOMP

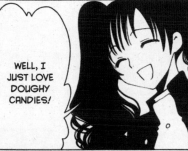

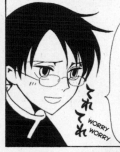

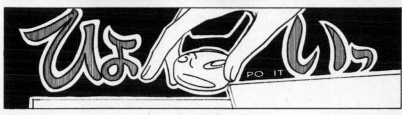

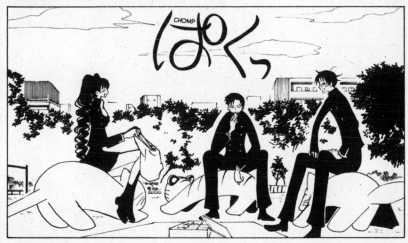

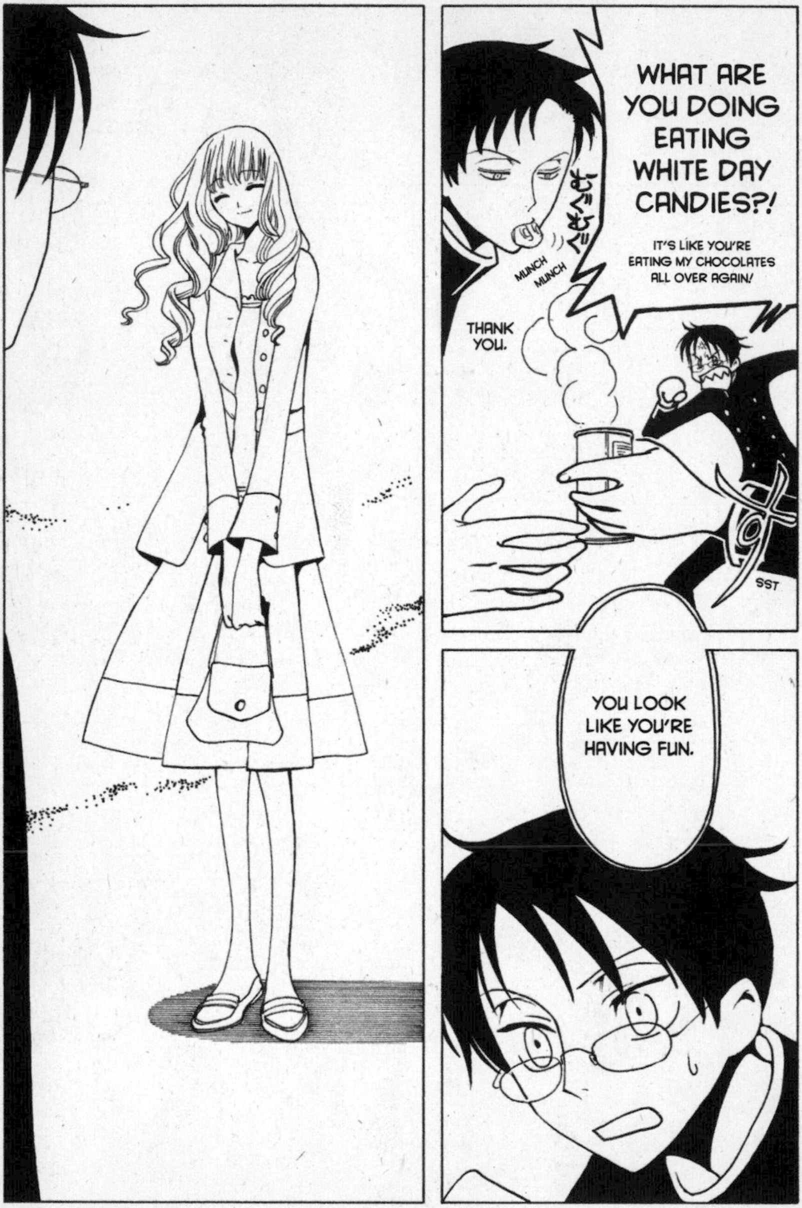
WHAT ARE YOU DOING EATING WHITE DAY CANDIES?!
IT'S LIKE YOU'RE EATING MY CHOCOLATES ALL OVER AGAIN!
MUNCH MUNCH
THANK YOU.
SST
YOU LOOK LIKE YOU'RE HAVING FUN.

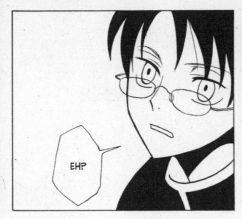

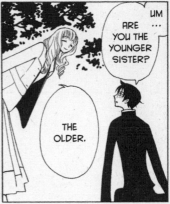

UM ... ARE YOU THE YOUNGER SISTER?
THE OLDER.
EH?
I'M SORRY, I MISTOOK YOU...
OH, DON'T WORRY ABOUT IT.
THERE ARE A LOT OF PEOPLE MISTAKING ME FOR MY SISTER THESE DAYS.
I CAN UNDER-STAND WHY. IT'S THAT...
I'M MORE CHIPPER?
RIGHT.

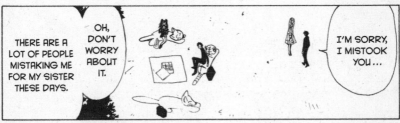

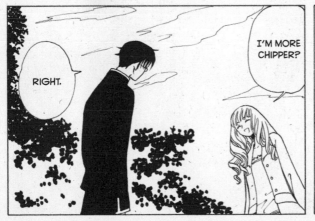

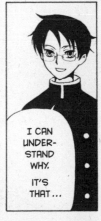

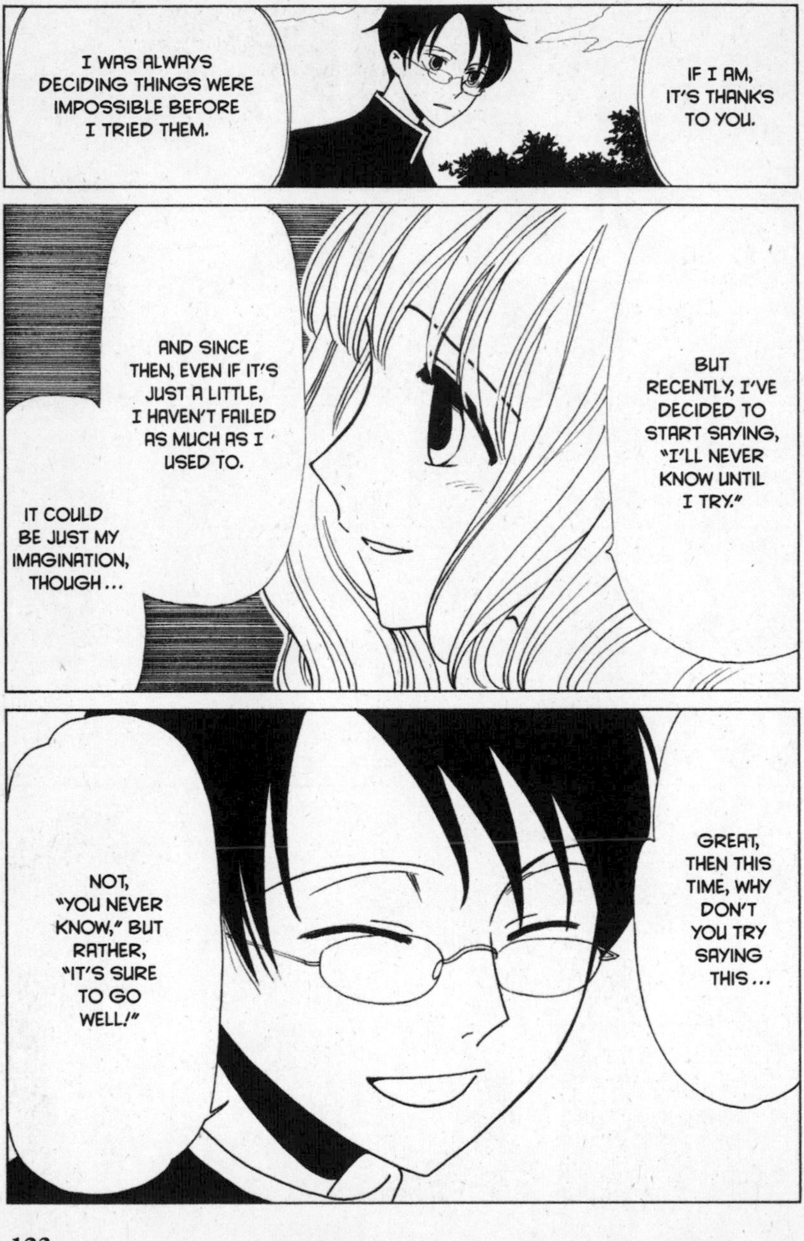
IF I AM, IT'S THANKS TO YOU.
I WAS ALWAYS DECIDING THINGS WERE IMPOSSIBLE BEFORE I TRIED THEM.
BUT RECENTLY, I'VE DECIDED TO START SAYING, "I'LL NEVER KNOW UNTIL I TRY."
AND SINCE THEN, EVEN IF IT'S JUST A LITTLE, I HAVEN'T FAILED AS MUCH AS I USED TO.
IT COULD BE JUST MY IMAGINATION, THOUGH...
GREAT, THEN THIS TIME, WHY DON'T YOU TRY SAYING THIS...
NOT, "YOU NEVER KNOW," BUT RATHER, "IT'S SURE TO GO WELL!"

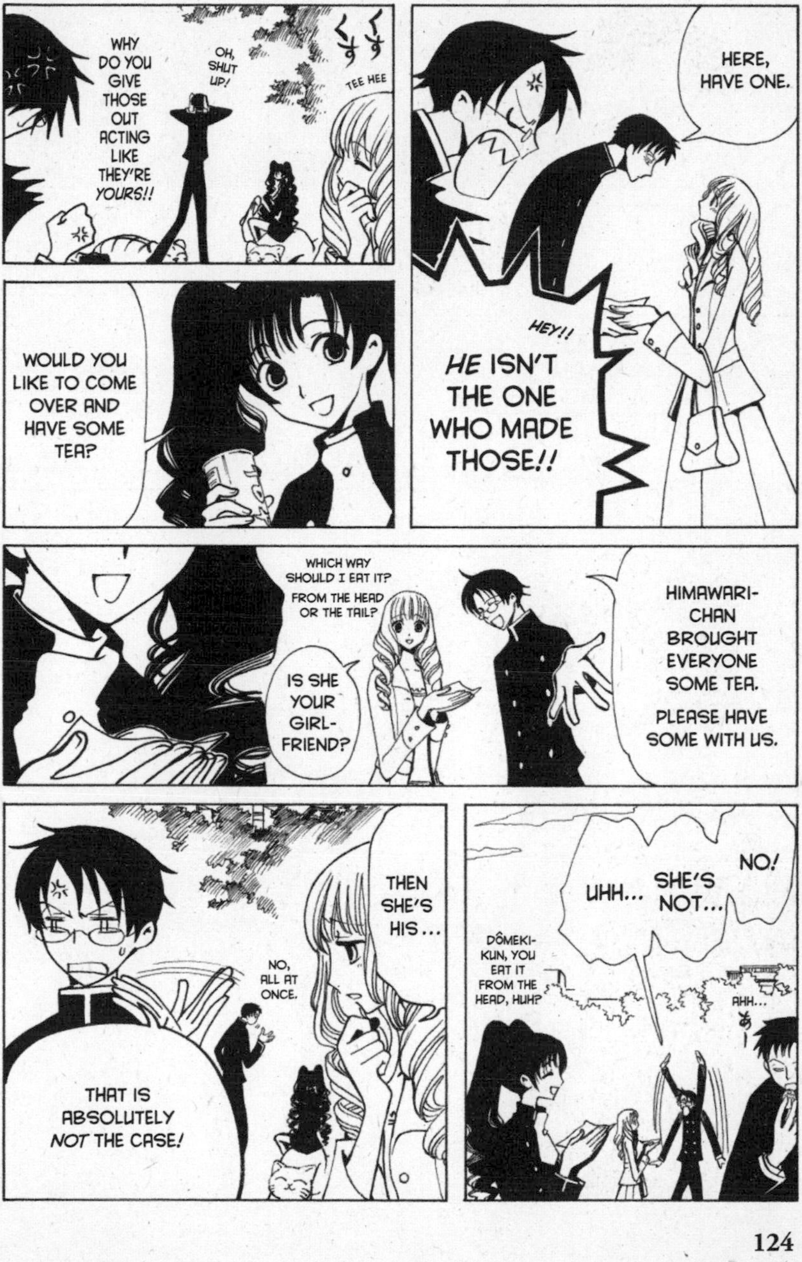
HERE, HAVE ONE.
HEY!!
HE ISN'T THE ONE WHO MADE THOSE!!
くすくす
TEE HEE
OH, SHUT UP!
WHY DO YOU GIVE THOSE OUT ACTING LIKE THEY'RE YOURS!!
WOULD YOU LIKE TO COME OVER AND HAVE SOME TEA?
HIMAWARI-CHAN BROUGHT EVERYONE SOME TEA.
PLEASE HAVE SOME WITH US.
WHICH WAY SHOULD I EAT IT?
FROM THE HEAD OR THE TAIL?
IS SHE YOUR GIRL-FRIEND?
NO!
SHE'S NOT...
UHH...
AHH... あー
DÔMEKI-KUN, YOU EAT IT FROM THE HEAD, HUH?
THEN SHE'S HIS...
NO, ALL AT ONCE.
THAT IS ABSOLUTELY NOT THE CASE!

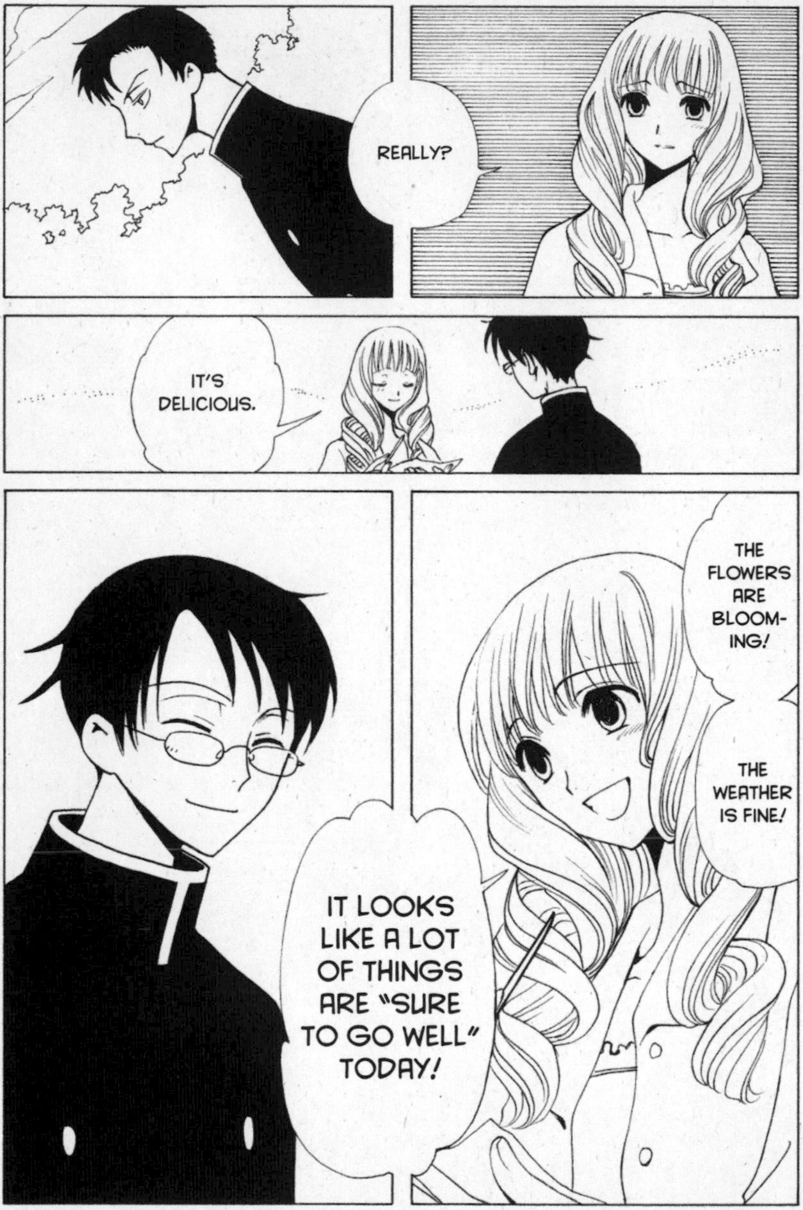
REALLY?
IT'S DELICIOUS.
THE FLOWERS ARE BLOOMING!
THE WEATHER IS FINE!
IT LOOKS LIKE A LOT OF THINGS ARE "SURE TO GO WELL" TODAY!

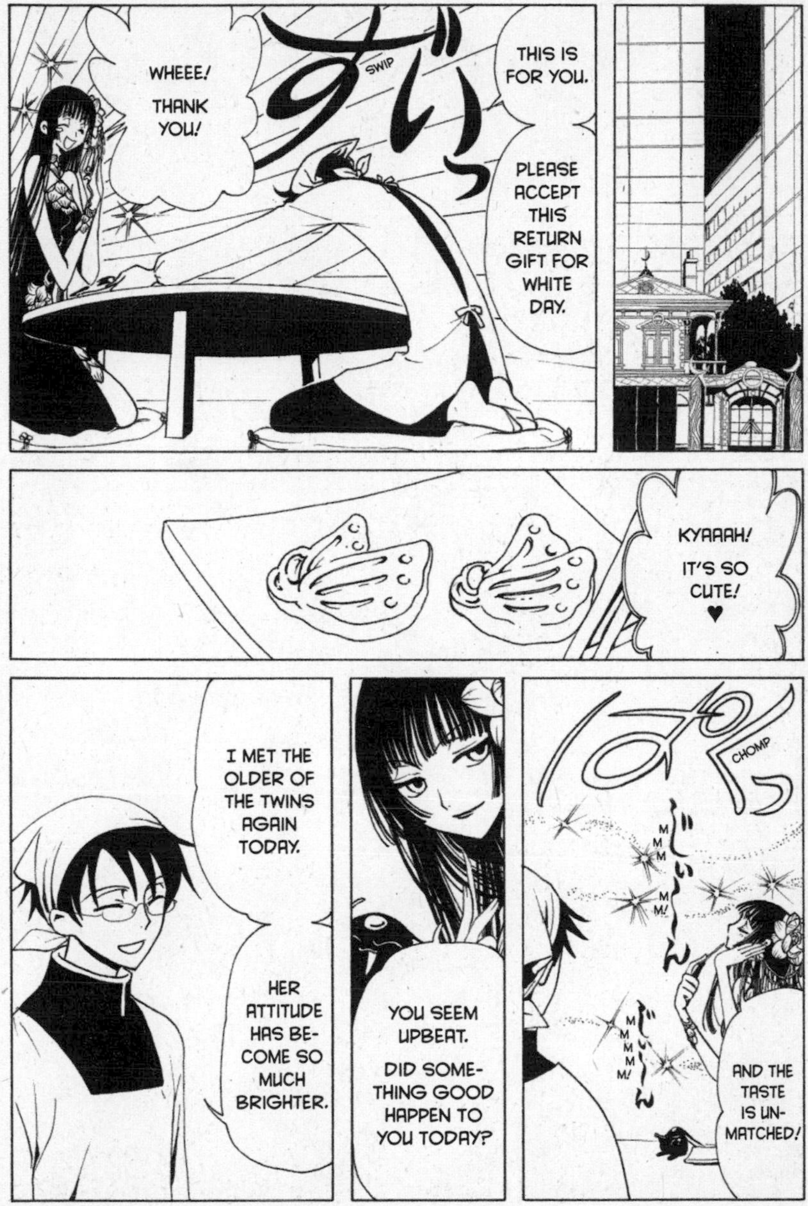
THIS IS FOR YOU.
PLEASE ACCEPT THIS RETURN GIFT FOR WHITE DAY.
SWIP
WHEEE!
THANK YOU!
KYAAAH!
IT'S SO CUTE! ♥
CHOMP
MMM
MM!
MMMMM!
AND THE TASTE IS UN-MATCHED!
YOU SEEM UPBEAT.
DID SOME-THING GOOD HAPPEN TO YOU TODAY?
I MET THE OLDER OF THE TWINS AGAIN TODAY.
HER ATTITUDE HAS BE-COME SO MUCH BRIGHTER.

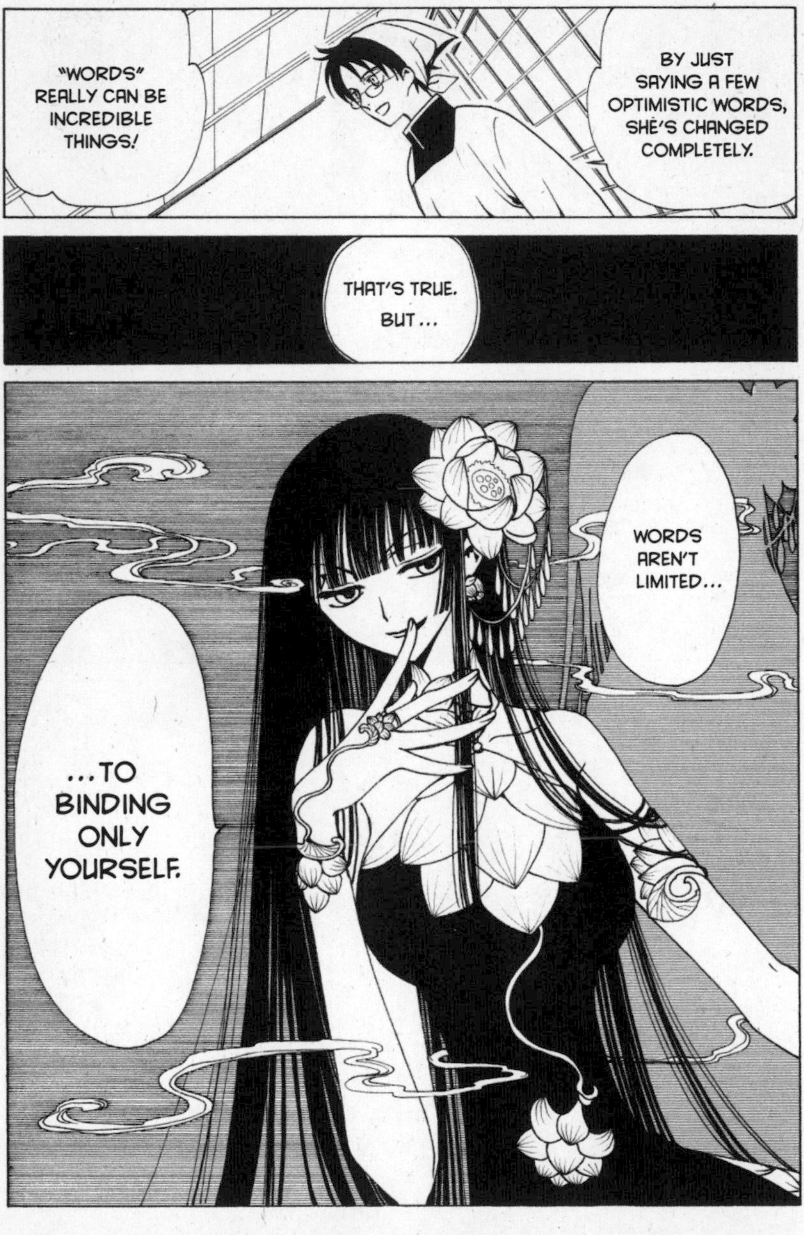
BY JUST SAYING A FEW OPTIMISTIC WORDS, SHE'S CHANGED COMPLETELY.
"WORDS" REALLY CAN BE INCREDIBLE THINGS!
THAT'S TRUE. BUT...
WORDS AREN'T LIMITED...
...TO BINDING ONLY YOURSELF.

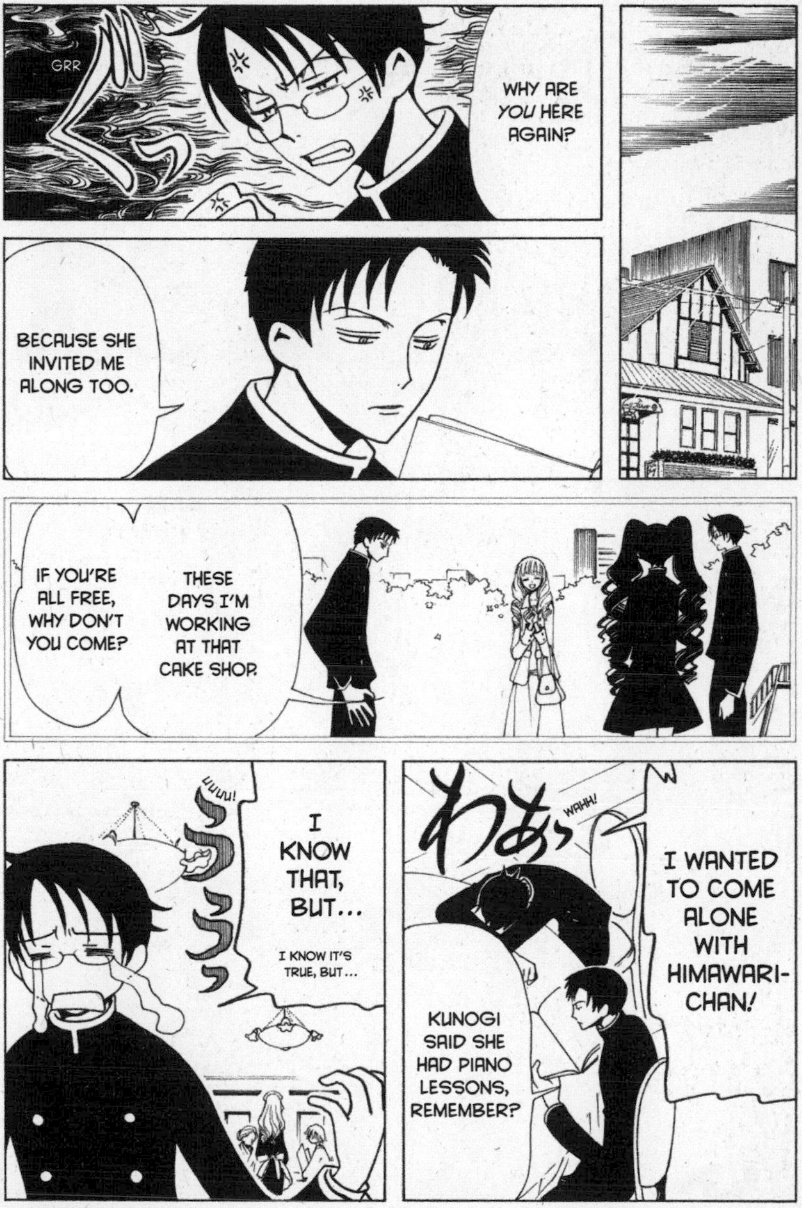
GRR
WHY ARE *YOU* HERE AGAIN?
BECAUSE SHE INVITED ME ALONG TOO.
THESE DAYS I'M WORKING AT THAT CAKE SHOP.
IF YOU'RE ALL FREE, WHY DON'T YOU COME?
WAHH!
I WANTED TO COME ALONE WITH HIMAWARI-CHAN!
KUNOGI SAID SHE HAD PIANO LESSONS, REMEMBER?
UUUU!
I KNOW THAT, BUT...
I KNOW IT'S TRUE, BUT...

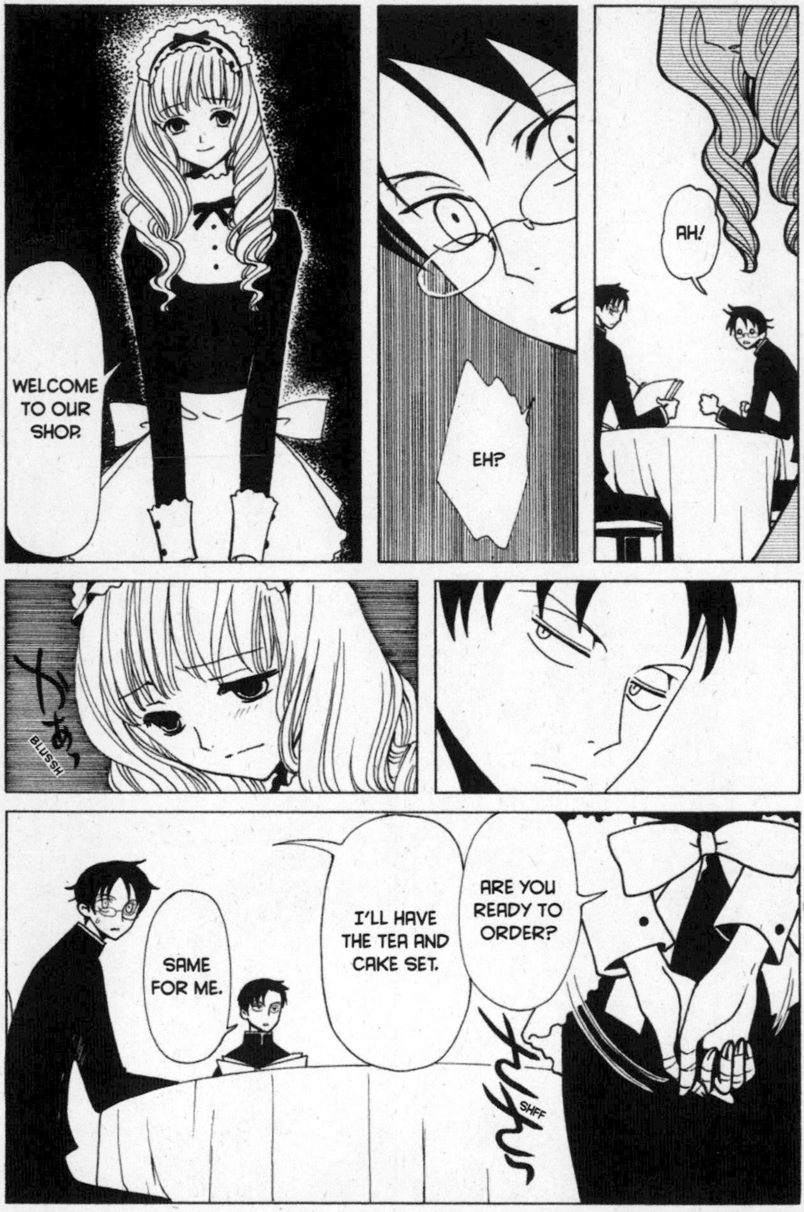
AH!
EH?
WELCOME TO OUR SHOP.
BLUSSH
ARE YOU READY TO ORDER?
I'LL HAVE THE TEA AND CAKE SET.
SHFF
SAME FOR ME.

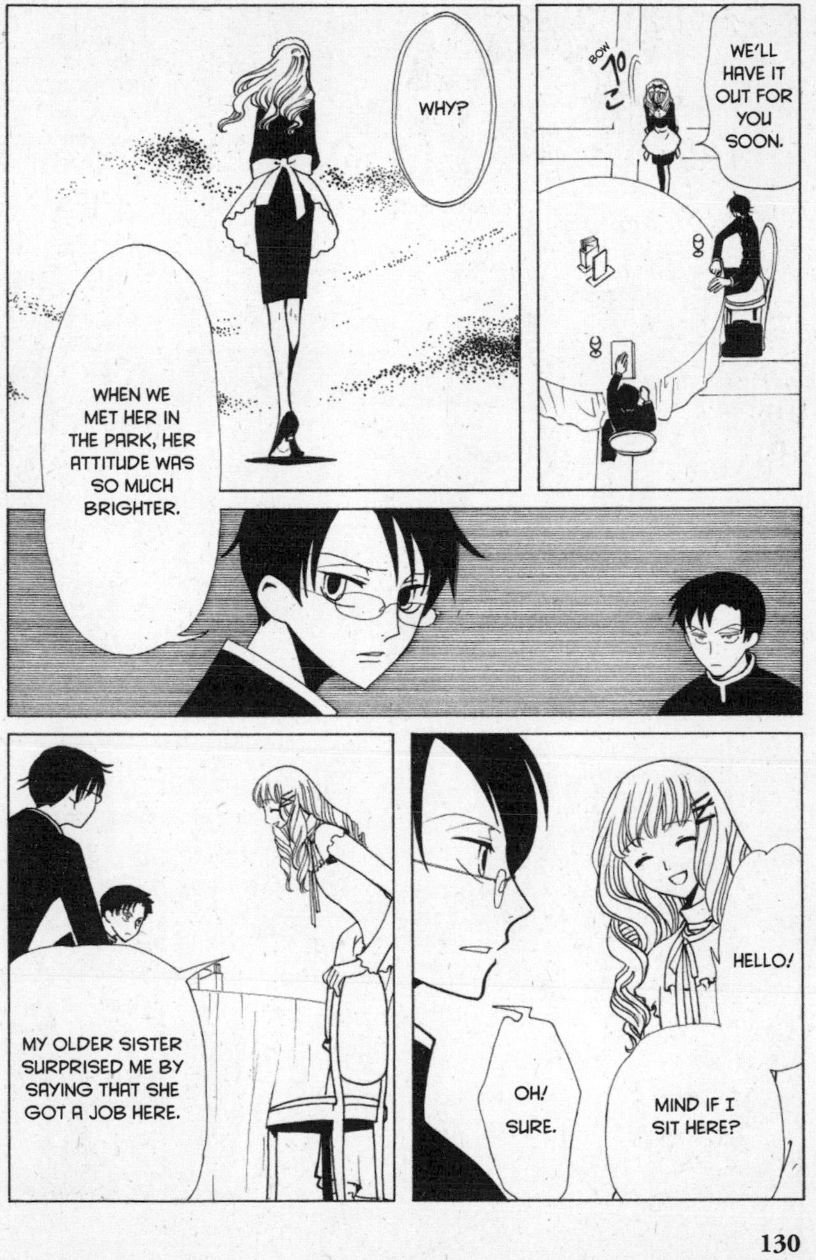
BOW
WE'LL HAVE IT OUT FOR YOU SOON.
WHY?
WHEN WE MET HER IN THE PARK, HER ATTITUDE WAS SO MUCH BRIGHTER.
HELLO!
MIND IF I SIT HERE?
OH! SURE.
MY OLDER SISTER SURPRISED ME BY SAYING THAT SHE GOT A JOB HERE.

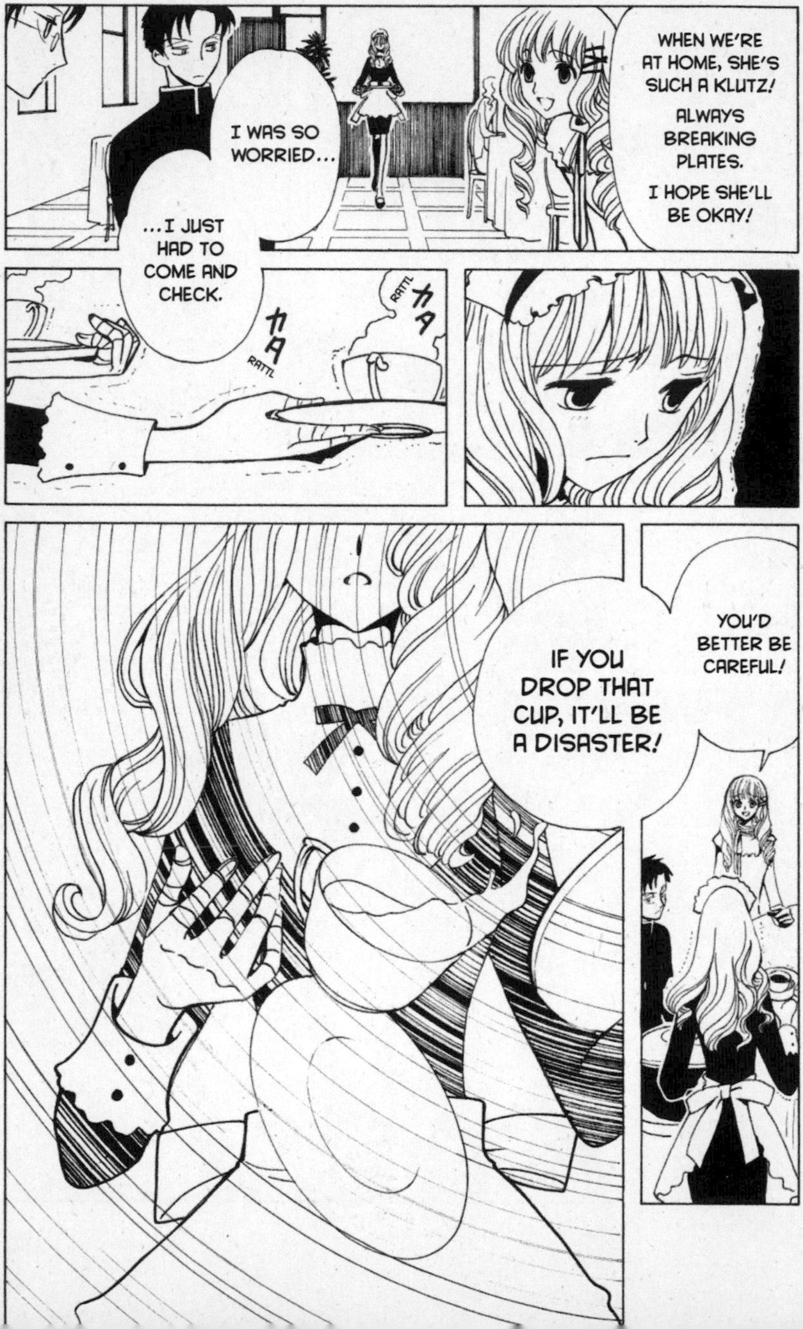
WHEN WE'RE AT HOME, SHE'S SUCH A KLUTZ!
ALWAYS BREAKING PLATES.
I HOPE SHE'LL BE OKAY!
I WAS SO WORRIED...
...I JUST HAD TO COME AND CHECK.
カタ
RATTL
カタ
RATTL
YOU'D BETTER BE CAREFUL!
IF YOU DROP THAT CUP, IT'LL BE A DISASTER!

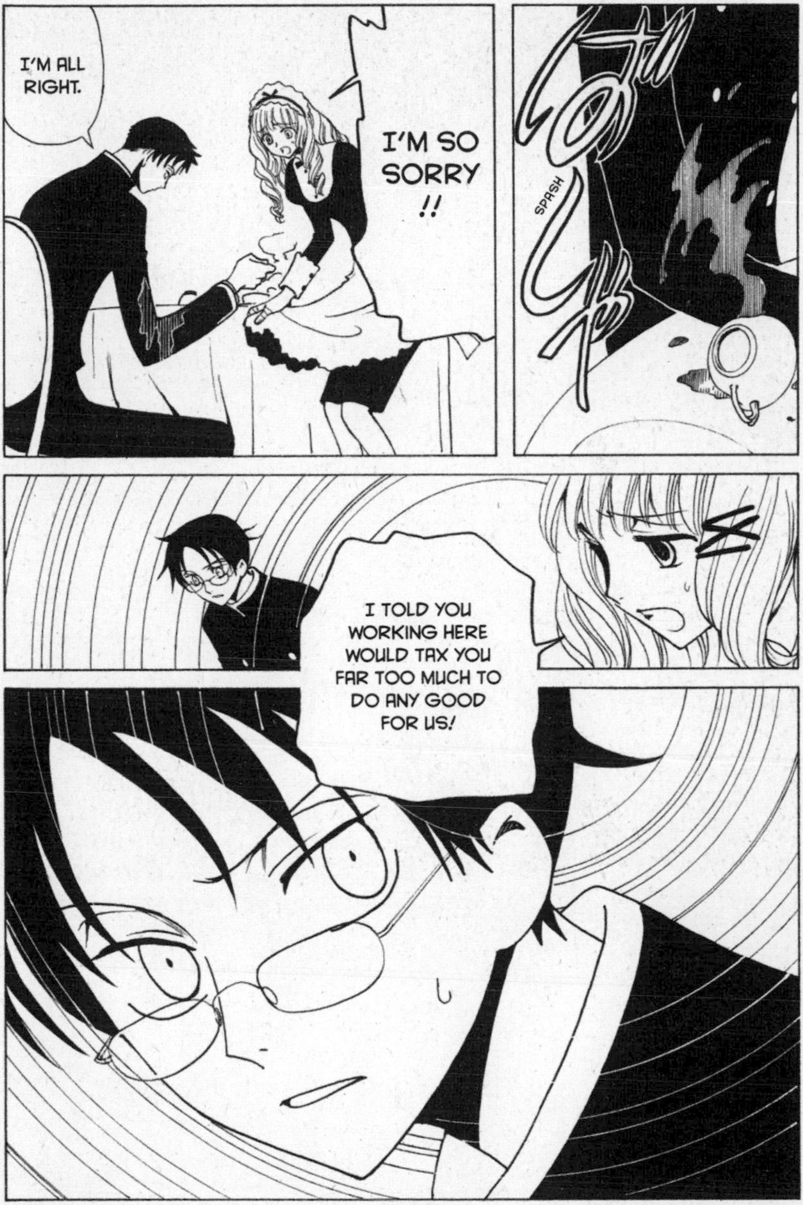
SPASH
I'M SO SORRY !!
I'M ALL RIGHT.
I TOLD YOU WORKING HERE WOULD TAX YOU FAR TOO MUCH TO DO ANY GOOD FOR US!

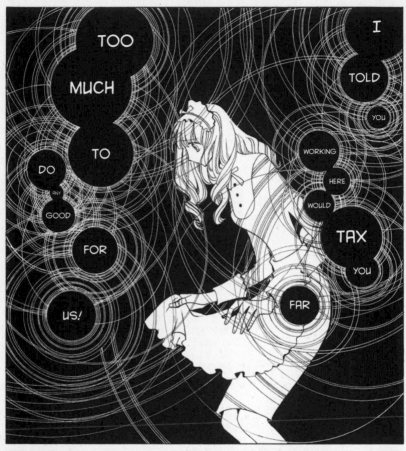

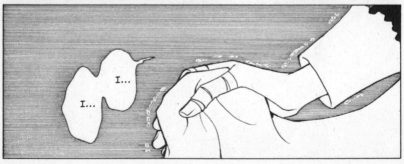

133

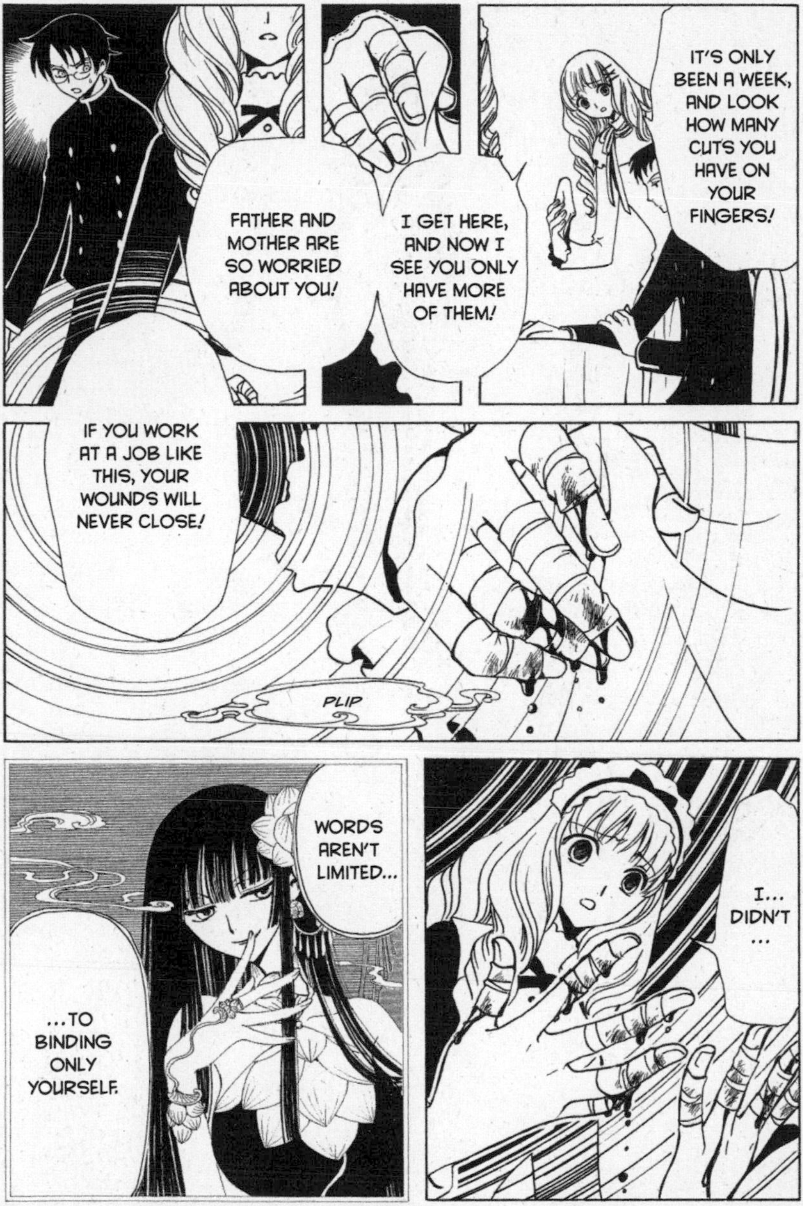
IT'S ONLY BEEN A WEEK, AND LOOK HOW MANY CUTS YOU HAVE ON YOUR FINGERS!
I GET HERE, AND NOW I SEE YOU ONLY HAVE MORE OF THEM!
FATHER AND MOTHER ARE SO WORRIED ABOUT YOU!
IF YOU WORK AT A JOB LIKE THIS, YOUR WOUNDS WILL NEVER CLOSE!
PLIP
I... DIDN'T ...
WORDS AREN'T LIMITED...
...TO BINDING ONLY YOURSELF.

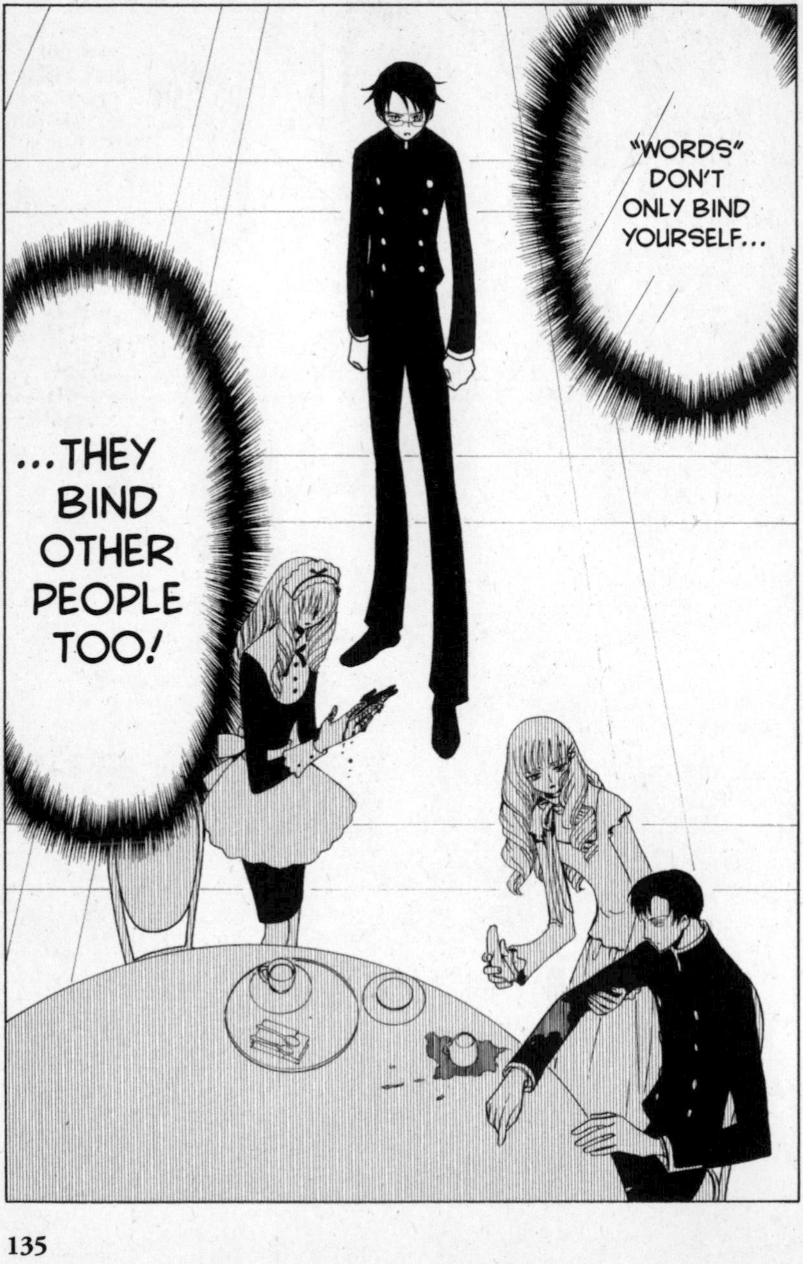
"WORDS" DON'T ONLY BIND YOURSELF...
...THEY BIND OTHER PEOPLE TOO!

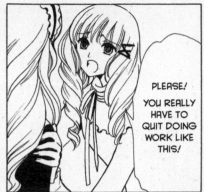

はっ
GASP
WHAT HAPPENED?
DID YOU HURT YOURSELF AGAIN?
PLEASE!
YOU REALLY HAVE TO QUIT DOING WORK LIKE THIS!
YOU'RE BAD AT TALKING TO STRANGERS!
WHO CAN EXPECT YOU TO TAKE ORDERS?
AND REMEMBER WHEN WE WERE AT THAT COFFEE SHOP, AND YOU BURNED YOUR LEG WITH THE COFFEE?
IF YOU WERE TO DO THAT AGAIN...
...IT'LL CAUSE A SCAR THIS TIME!
かくん
SHUMP
ざわ
CHATTR
ざわ
CHATTR
ざわ
CHATTR

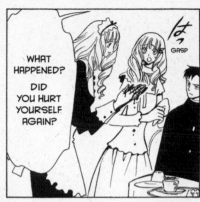

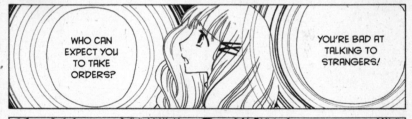

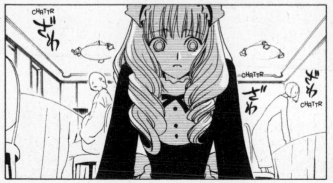

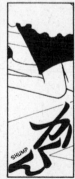

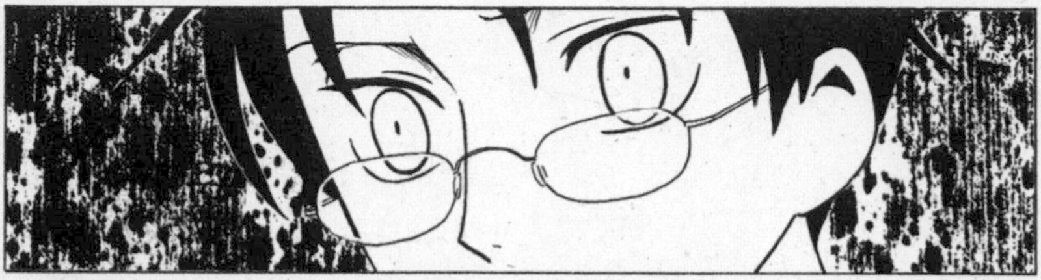
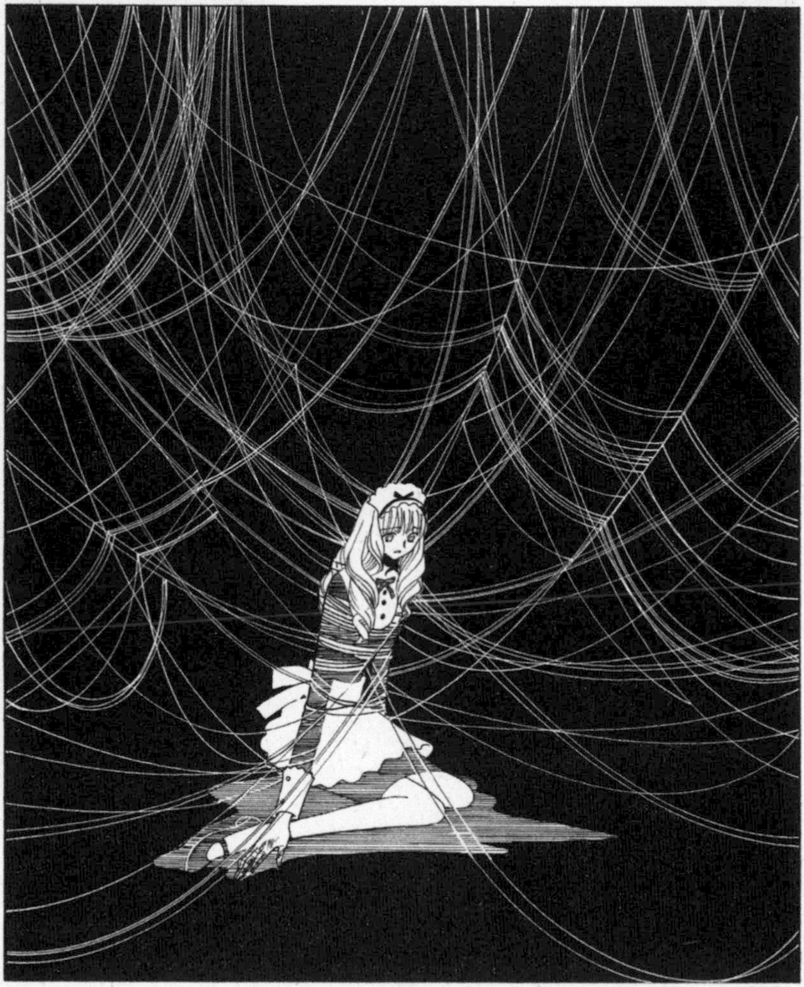

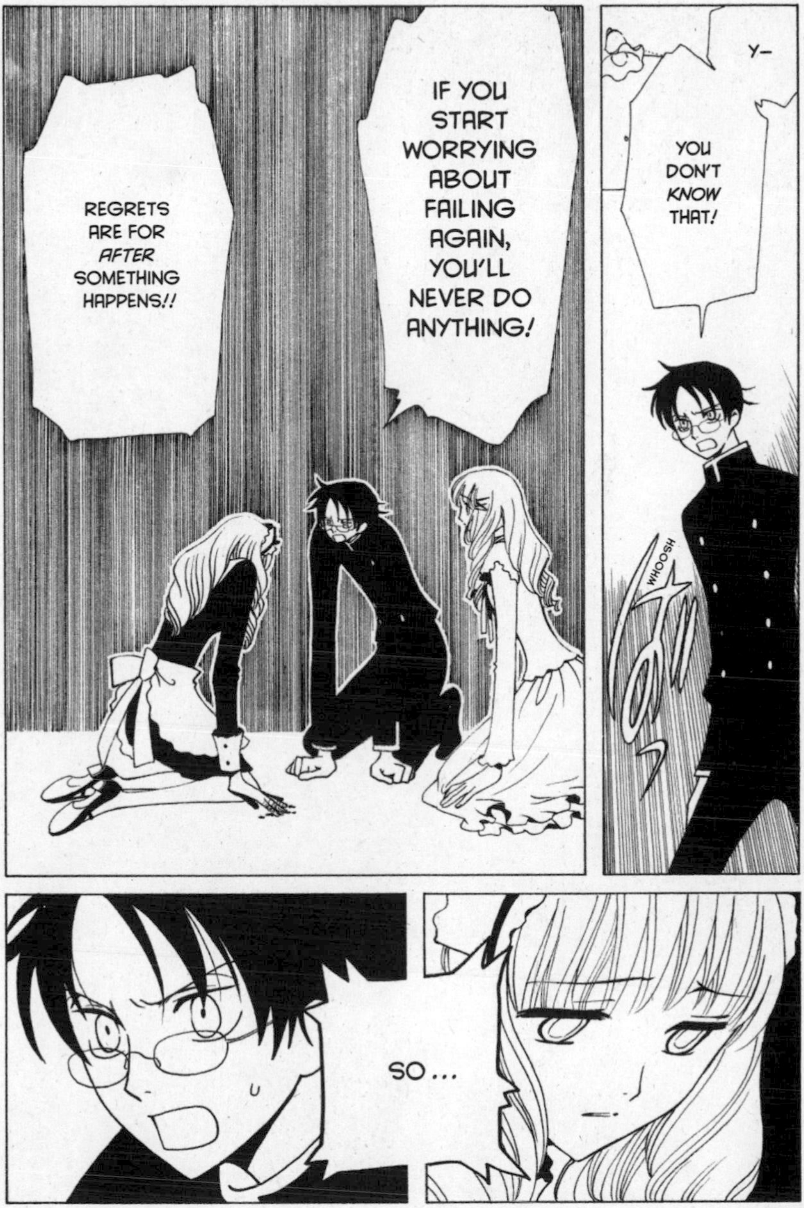
Y–
YOU DON'T *KNOW* THAT!
WHOOSH
IF YOU START WORRYING ABOUT FAILING AGAIN, YOU'LL NEVER DO ANYTHING!
REGRETS ARE FOR *AFTER* SOMETHING HAPPENS!!
SO…

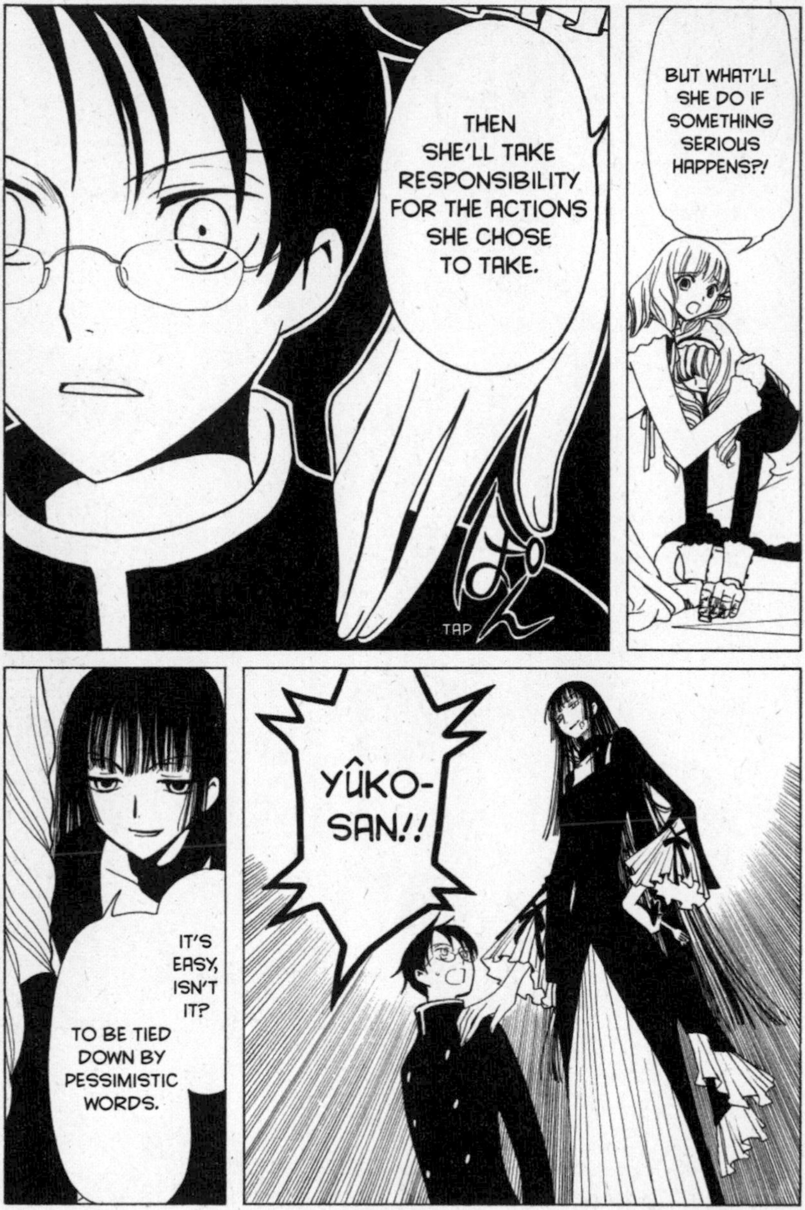
BUT WHAT'LL SHE DO IF SOMETHING SERIOUS HAPPENS?!
THEN SHE'LL TAKE RESPONSIBILITY FOR THE ACTIONS SHE CHOSE TO TAKE.
TAP
YÛKO-SAN!!
IT'S EASY, ISN'T IT?
TO BE TIED DOWN BY PESSIMISTIC WORDS.

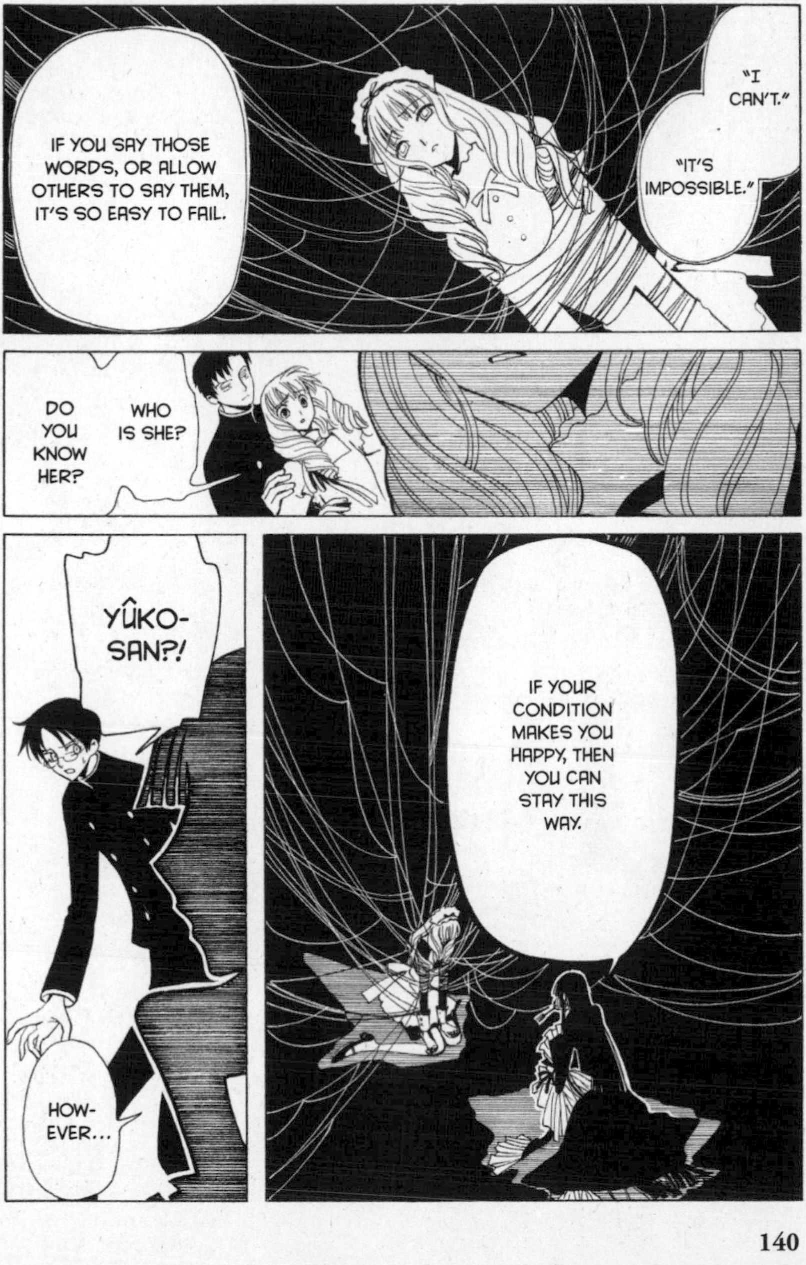
"I CAN'T."
"IT'S IMPOSSIBLE."
IF YOU SAY THOSE WORDS, OR ALLOW OTHERS TO SAY THEM, IT'S SO EASY TO FAIL.
WHO IS SHE?
DO YOU KNOW HER?
IF YOUR CONDITION MAKES YOU HAPPY, THEN YOU CAN STAY THIS WAY.
YÛKO-SAN?!
HOW-EVER...

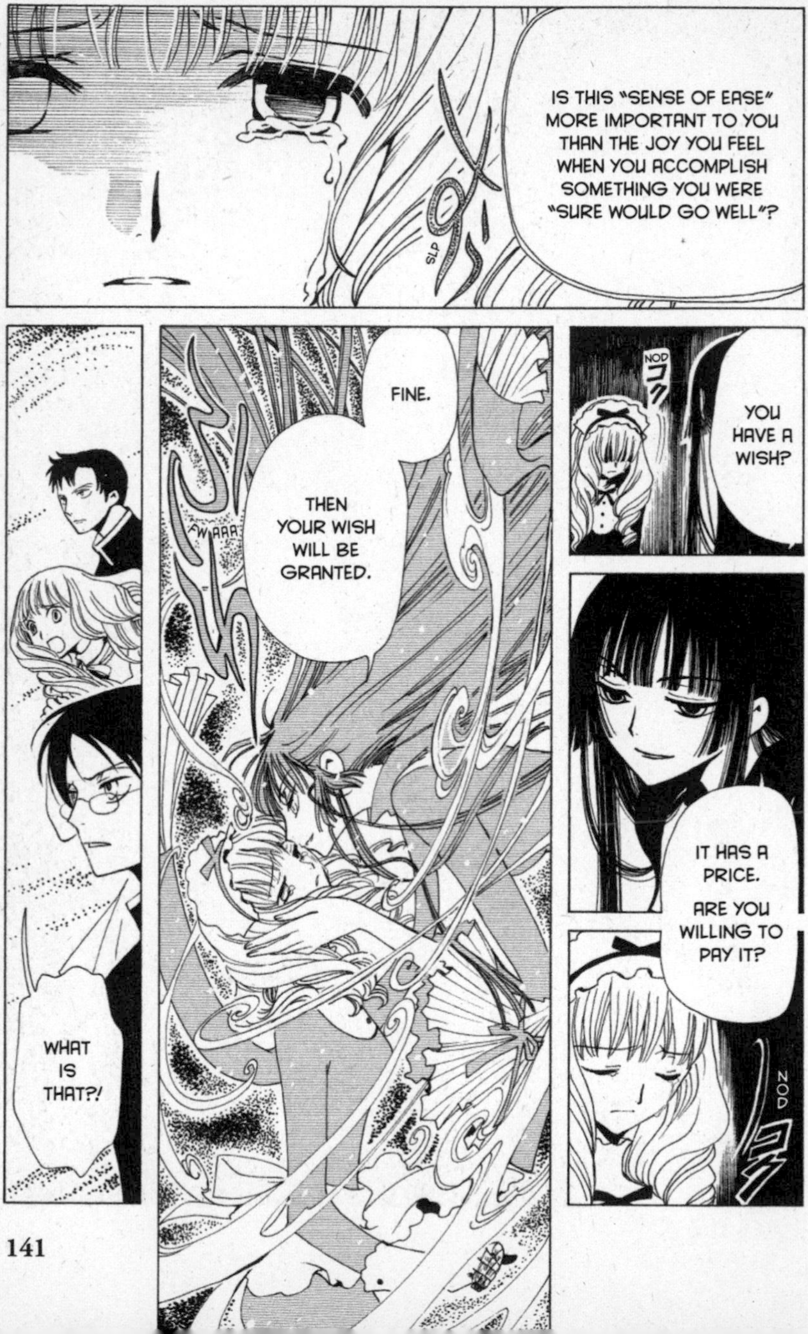

IS THIS "SENSE OF EASE" MORE IMPORTANT TO YOU THAN THE JOY YOU FEEL WHEN YOU ACCOMPLISH SOMETHING YOU WERE "SURE WOULD GO WELL"?
SLP
NOD
YOU HAVE A WISH?
IT HAS A PRICE.
ARE YOU WILLING TO PAY IT?
NOD
FINE.
THEN YOUR WISH WILL BE GRANTED.
FWAAA
WHAT IS THAT?!

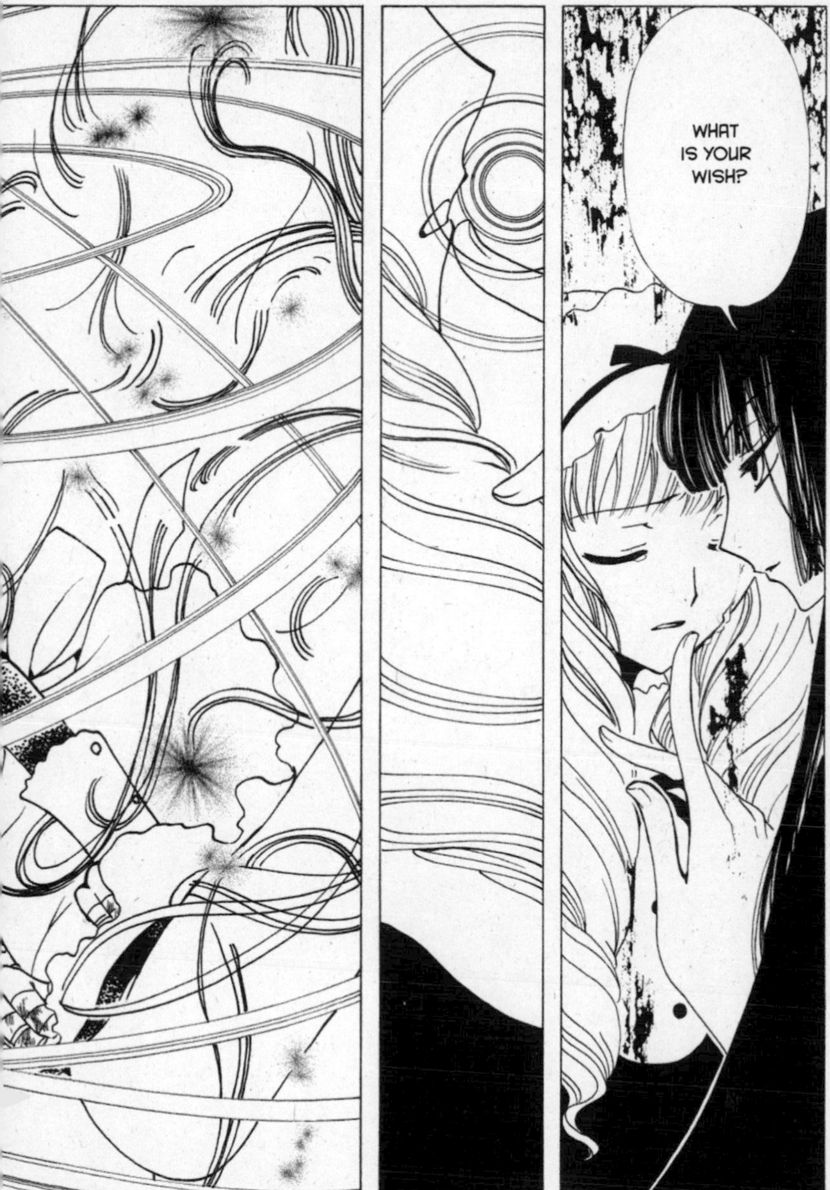
WHAT IS YOUR WISH?

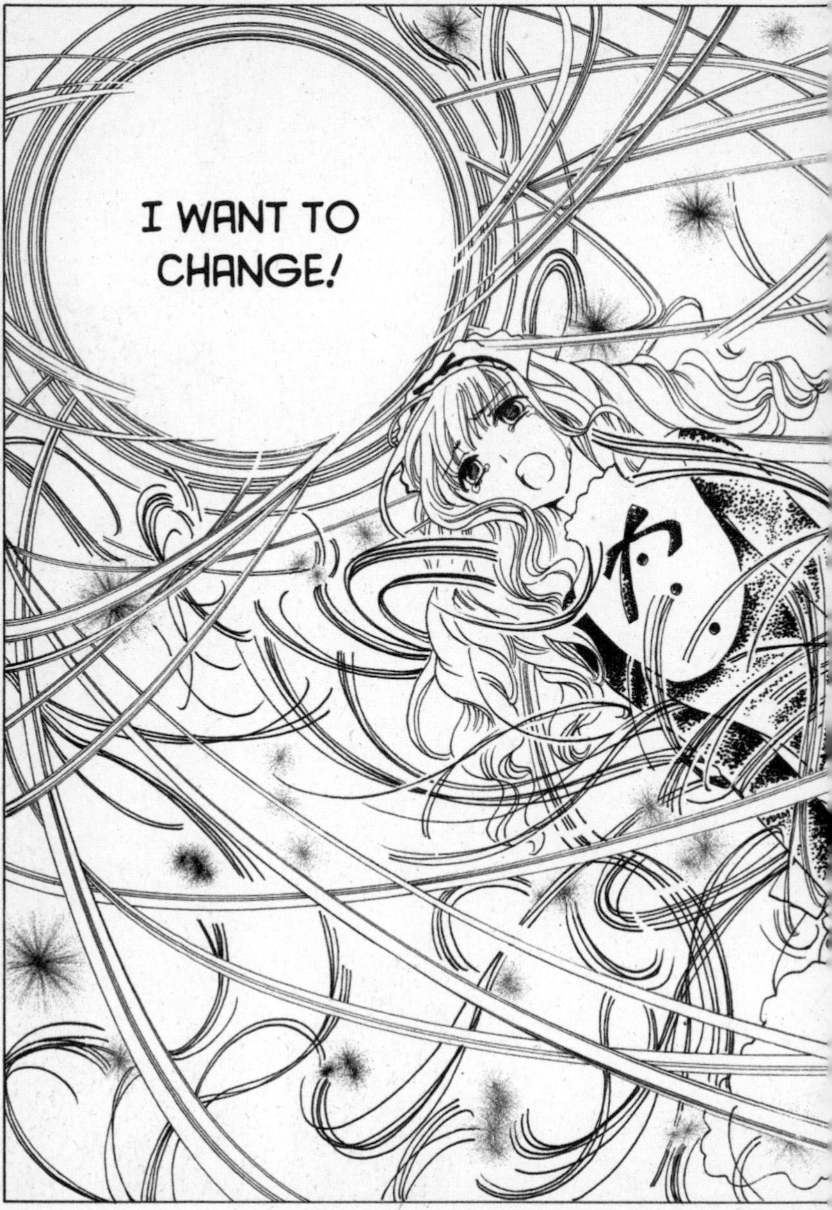
I WANT TO CHANGE!

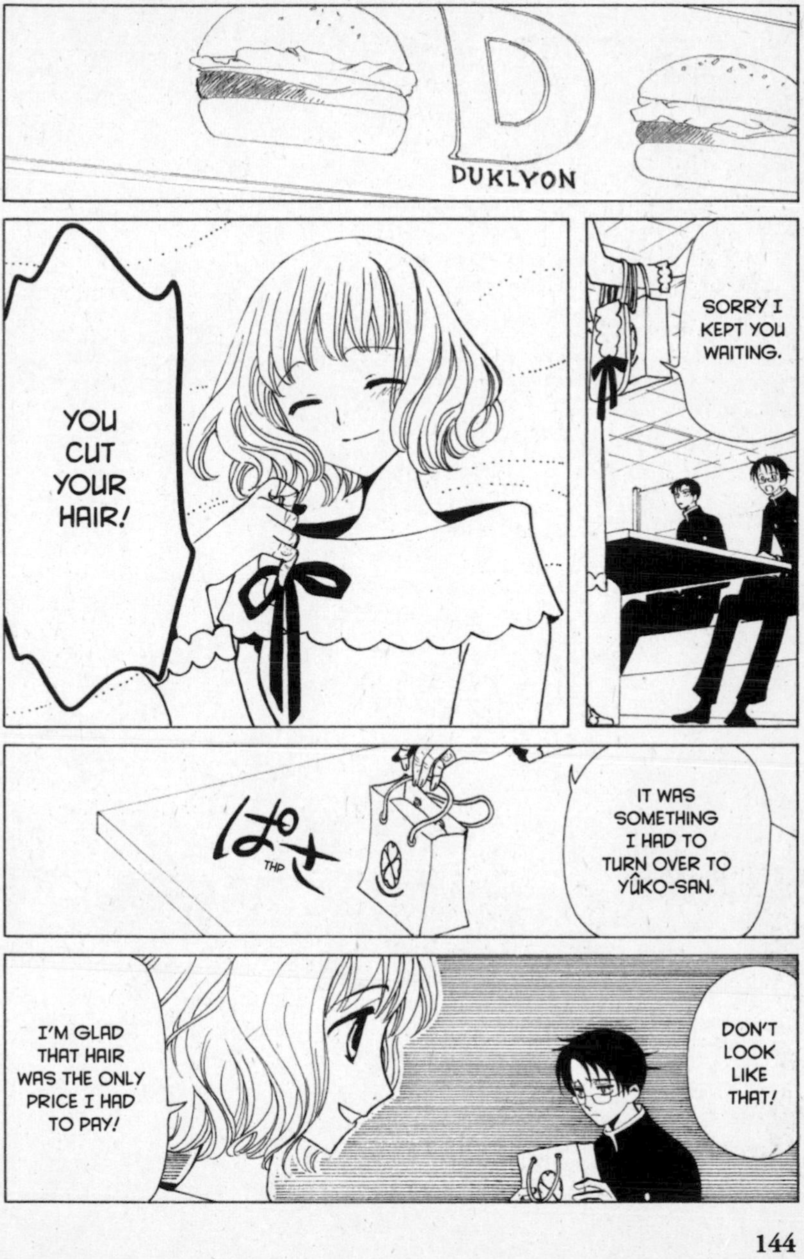
DUKLYON
SORRY I KEPT YOU WAITING.
YOU CUT YOUR HAIR!
IT WAS SOMETHING I HAD TO TURN OVER TO YÛKO-SAN.
ぱさ
THP
DON'T LOOK LIKE THAT!
I'M GLAD THAT HAIR WAS THE ONLY PRICE I HAD TO PAY!

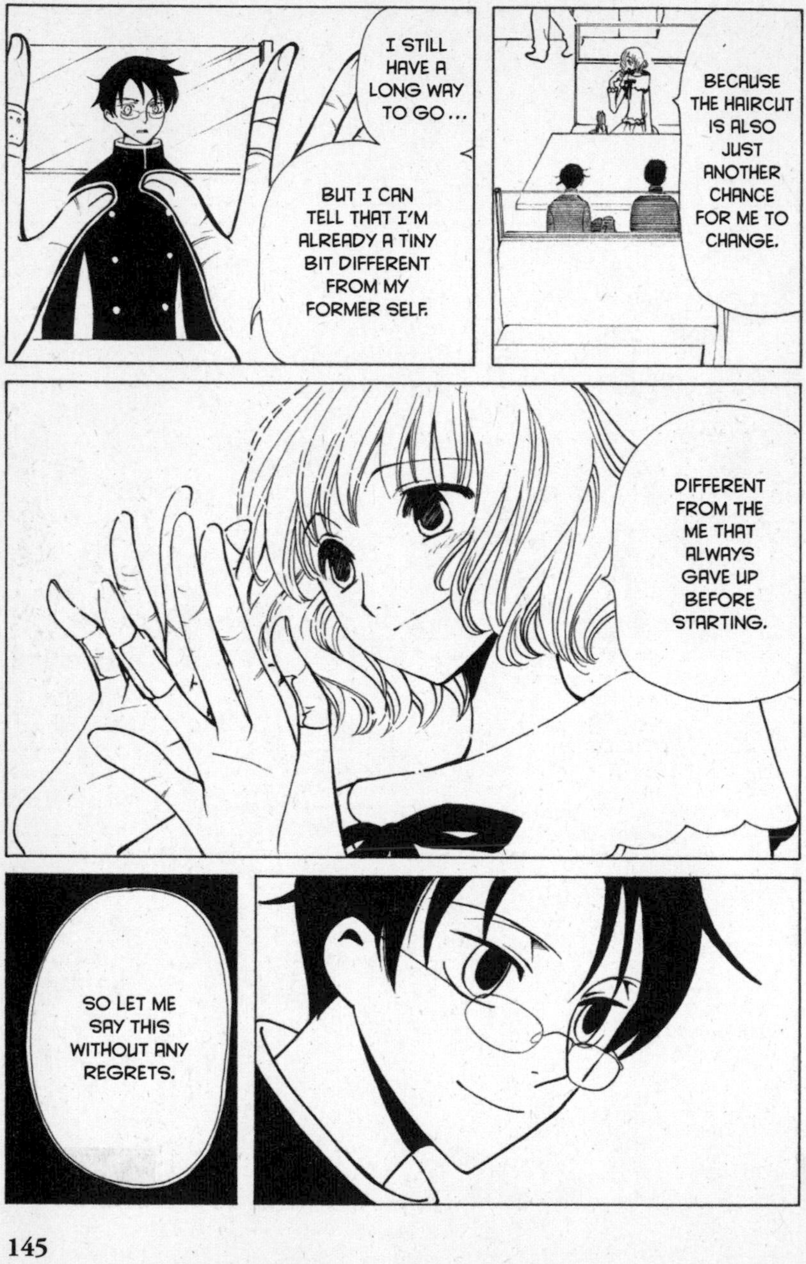
BECAUSE THE HAIRCUT IS ALSO JUST ANOTHER CHANCE FOR ME TO CHANGE.
I STILL HAVE A LONG WAY TO GO...
BUT I CAN TELL THAT I'M ALREADY A TINY BIT DIFFERENT FROM MY FORMER SELF.
DIFFERENT FROM THE ME THAT ALWAYS GAVE UP BEFORE STARTING.
SO LET ME SAY THIS WITHOUT ANY REGRETS.

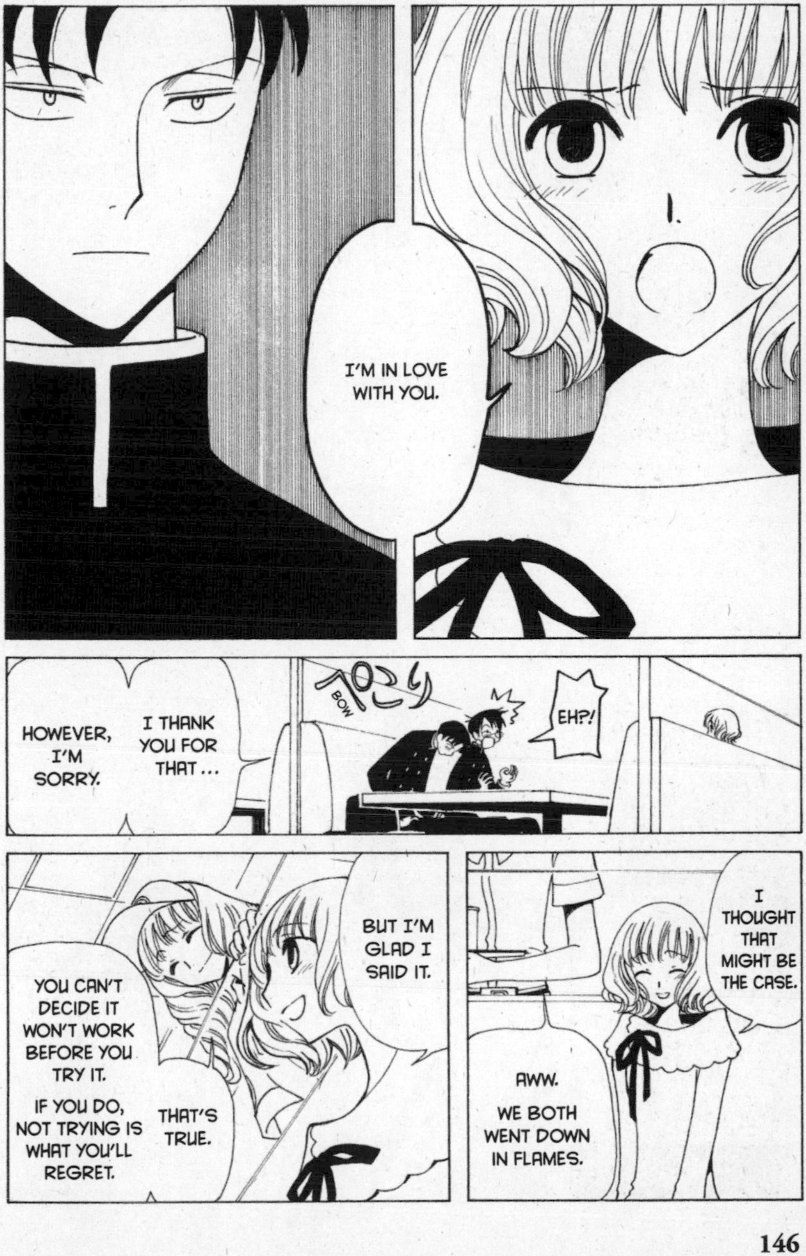
I'M IN LOVE WITH YOU.
EH?!
BOW
I THANK YOU FOR THAT ...
HOWEVER, I'M SORRY.
I THOUGHT THAT MIGHT BE THE CASE.
AWW.
WE BOTH WENT DOWN IN FLAMES.
BUT I'M GLAD I SAID IT.
THAT'S TRUE.
YOU CAN'T DECIDE IT WON'T WORK BEFORE YOU TRY IT.
IF YOU DO, NOT TRYING IS WHAT YOU'LL REGRET.

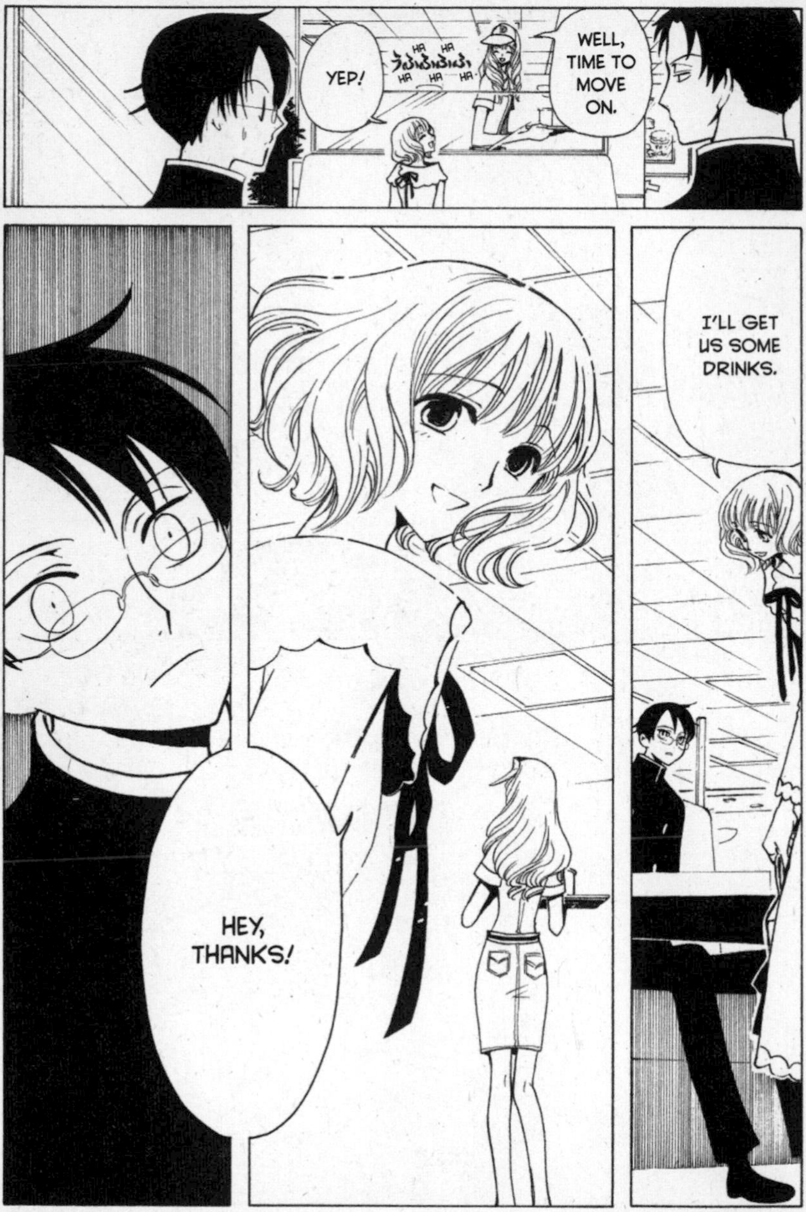
WELL, TIME TO MOVE ON.
YEP!
HA HA HA HA HA
I'LL GET US SOME DRINKS.
HEY, THANKS!

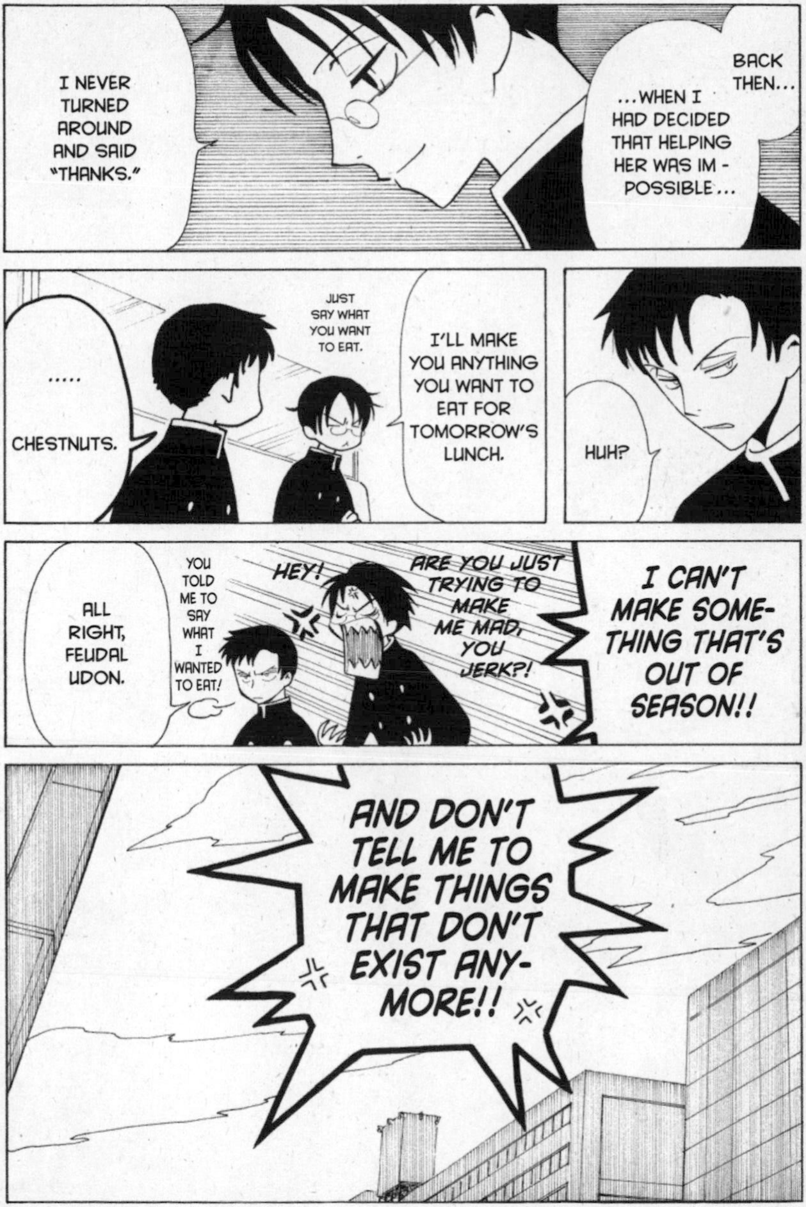
BACK THEN... ...WHEN I HAD DECIDED THAT HELPING HER WAS IM-POSSIBLE...
I NEVER TURNED AROUND AND SAID "THANKS."
HUH?
I'LL MAKE YOU ANYTHING YOU WANT TO EAT FOR TOMORROW'S LUNCH.
JUST SAY WHAT YOU WANT TO EAT.
.....
CHESTNUTS.
I CAN'T MAKE SOME-THING THAT'S OUT OF SEASON!!
ARE YOU JUST TRYING TO MAKE ME MAD, YOU JERK?!
HEY!
YOU TOLD ME TO SAY WHAT I WANTED TO EAT!
ALL RIGHT, FEUDAL UDON.
AND DON'T TELL ME TO MAKE THINGS THAT DON'T EXIST ANY-MORE!!

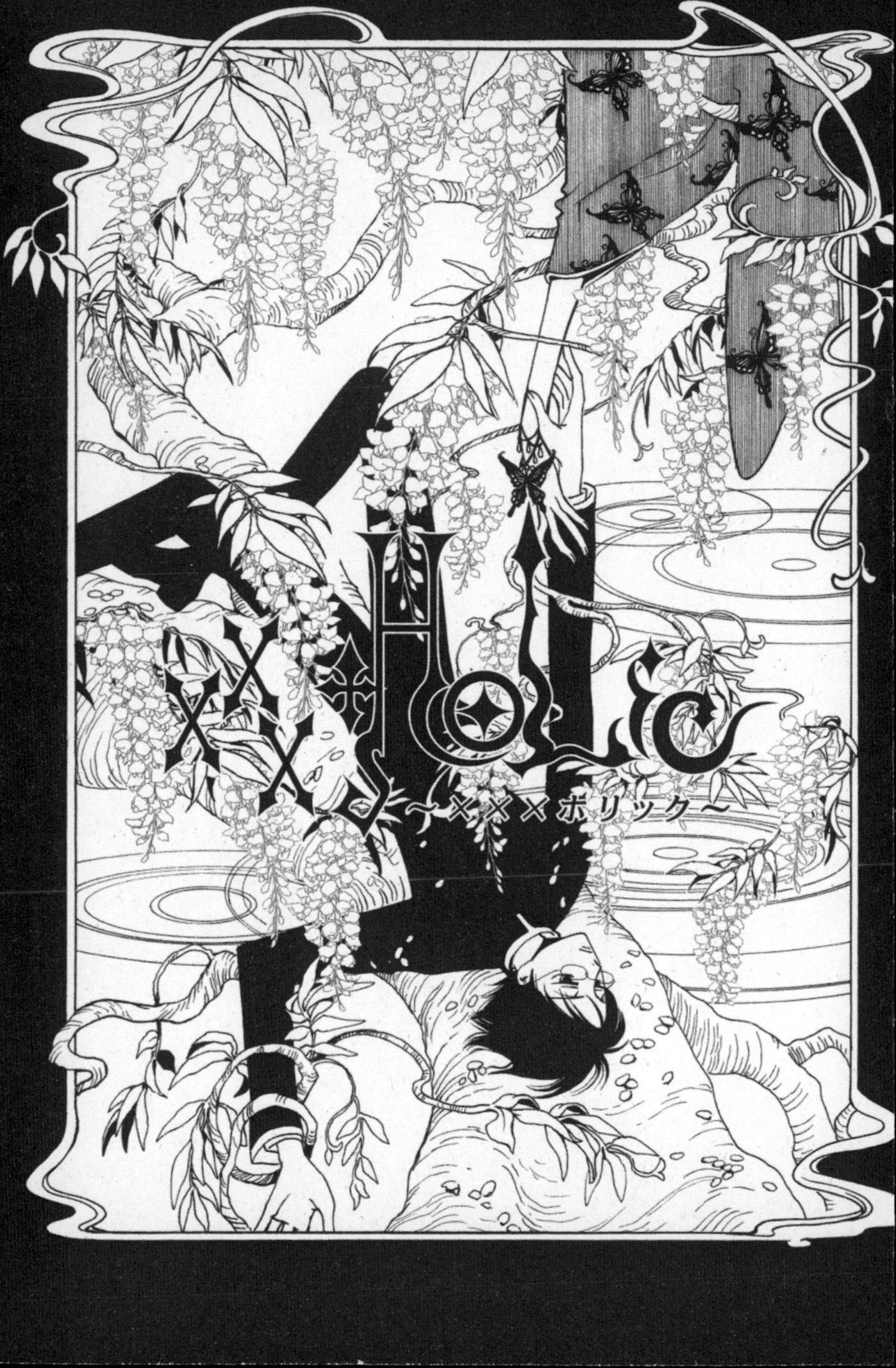
xxxHOLiC
～×××ホリック～

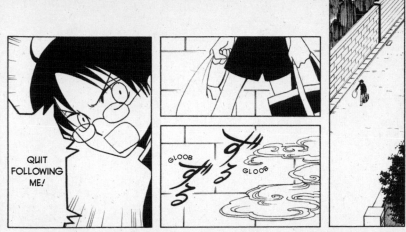

QUIT
FOLLOWING
ME!

GLOOB

GLOOB

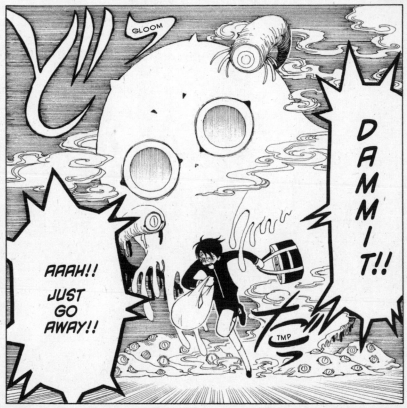

GLOOM

DAMMIT!!

AAAH!!
JUST
GO
AWAY!!

TMP

150

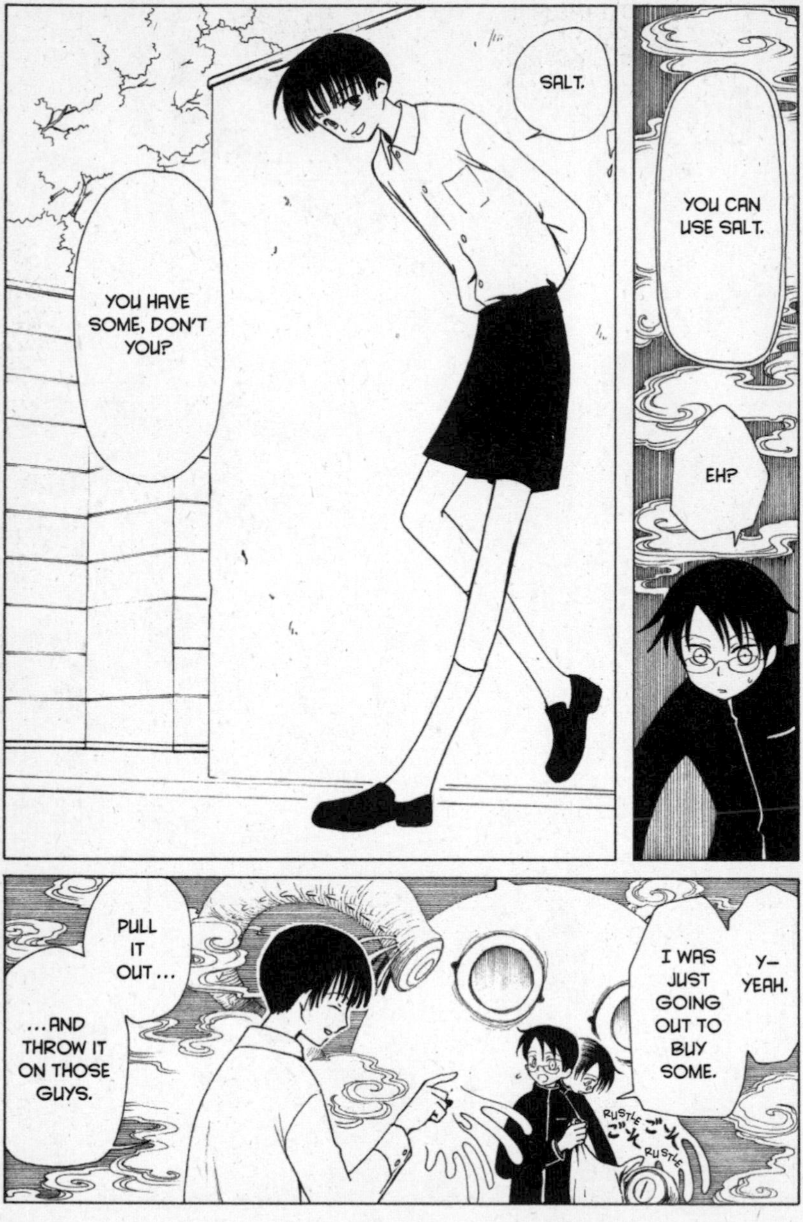
YOU CAN USE SALT.
EH?
SALT.
YOU HAVE SOME, DON'T YOU?
Y— YEAH.
I WAS JUST GOING OUT TO BUY SOME.
RUSTLE ごそ ごそ RUSTLE
PULL IT OUT...
...AND THROW IT ON THOSE GUYS.

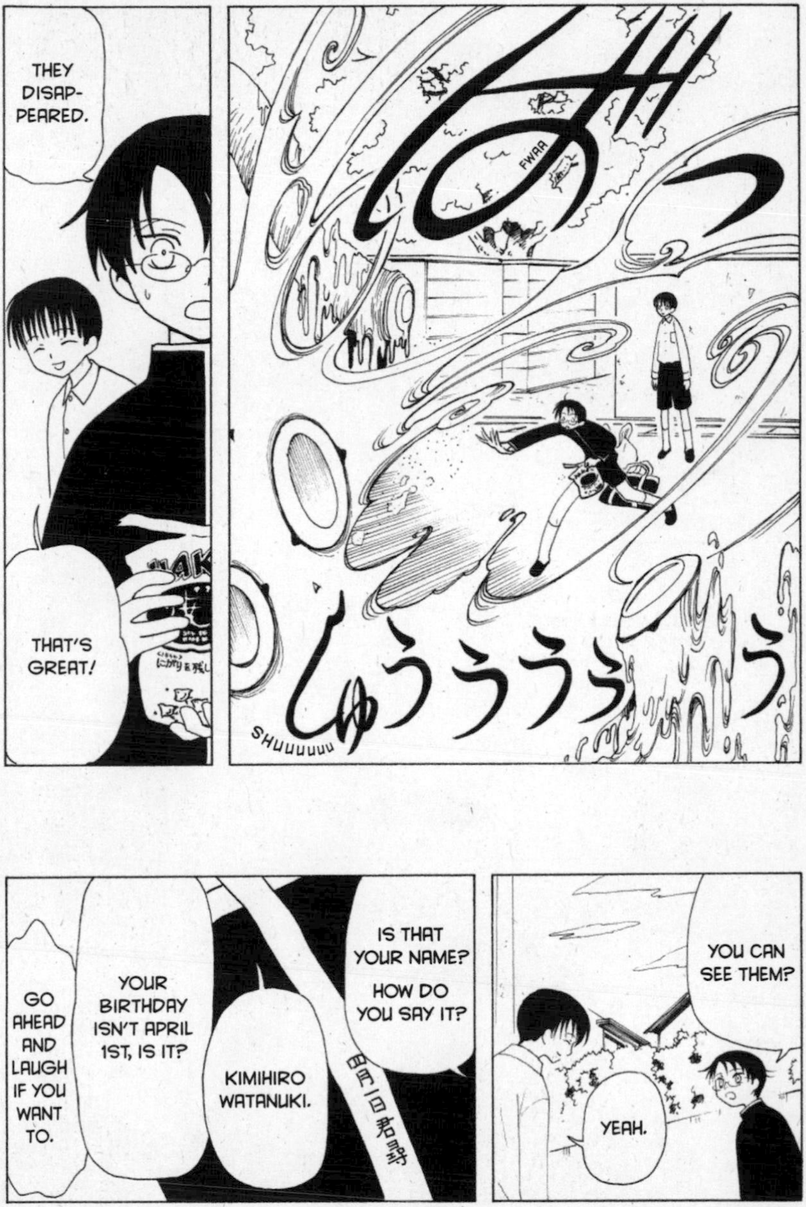
FWAA
SHUUUUUU
THEY DISAP-PEARED.
THAT'S GREAT!
YOU CAN SEE THEM?
YEAH.
IS THAT YOUR NAME? HOW DO YOU SAY IT?
四月一日君尋
KIMIHIRO WATANUKI.
YOUR BIRTHDAY ISN'T APRIL 1ST, IS IT?
GO AHEAD AND LAUGH IF YOU WANT TO.

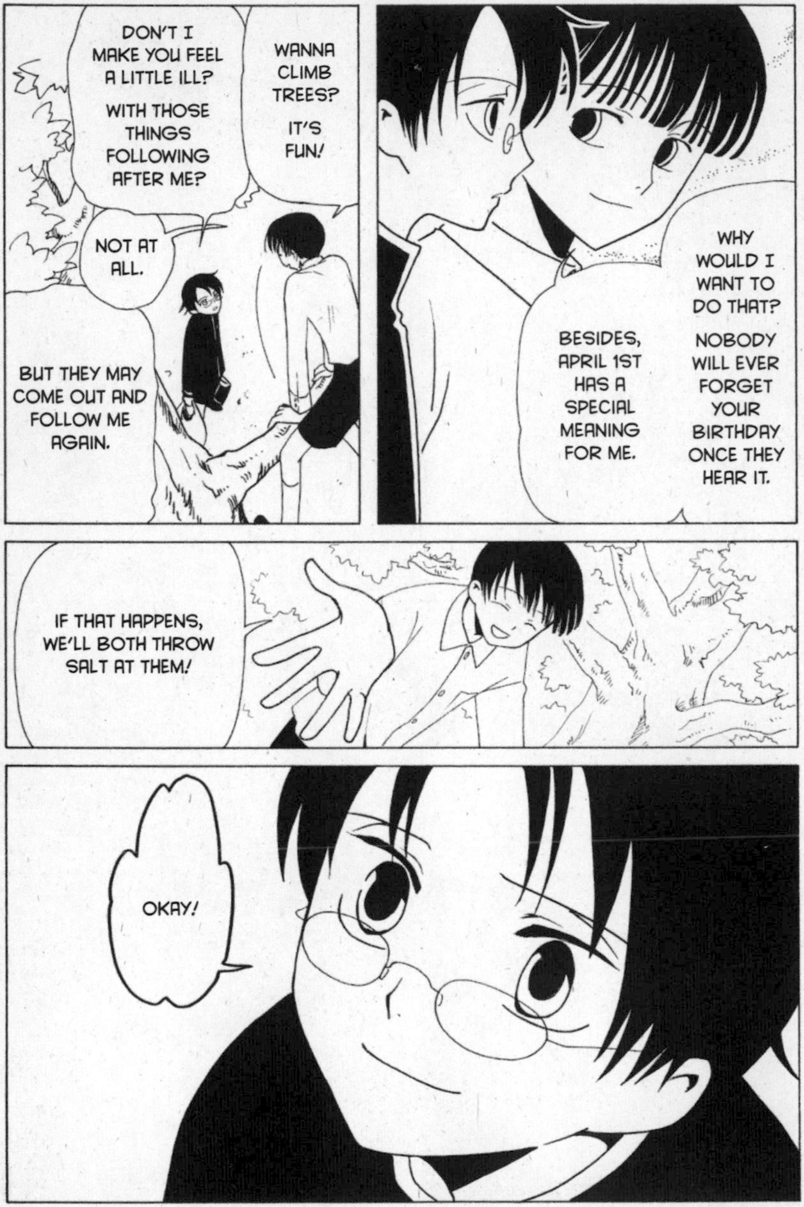
WHY WOULD I WANT TO DO THAT? NOBODY WILL EVER FORGET YOUR BIRTHDAY ONCE THEY HEAR IT.
BESIDES, APRIL 1ST HAS A SPECIAL MEANING FOR ME.
WANNA CLIMB TREES? IT'S FUN!
DON'T I MAKE YOU FEEL A LITTLE ILL? WITH THOSE THINGS FOLLOWING AFTER ME?
NOT AT ALL.
BUT THEY MAY COME OUT AND FOLLOW ME AGAIN.
IF THAT HAPPENS, WE'LL BOTH THROW SALT AT THEM!
OKAY!

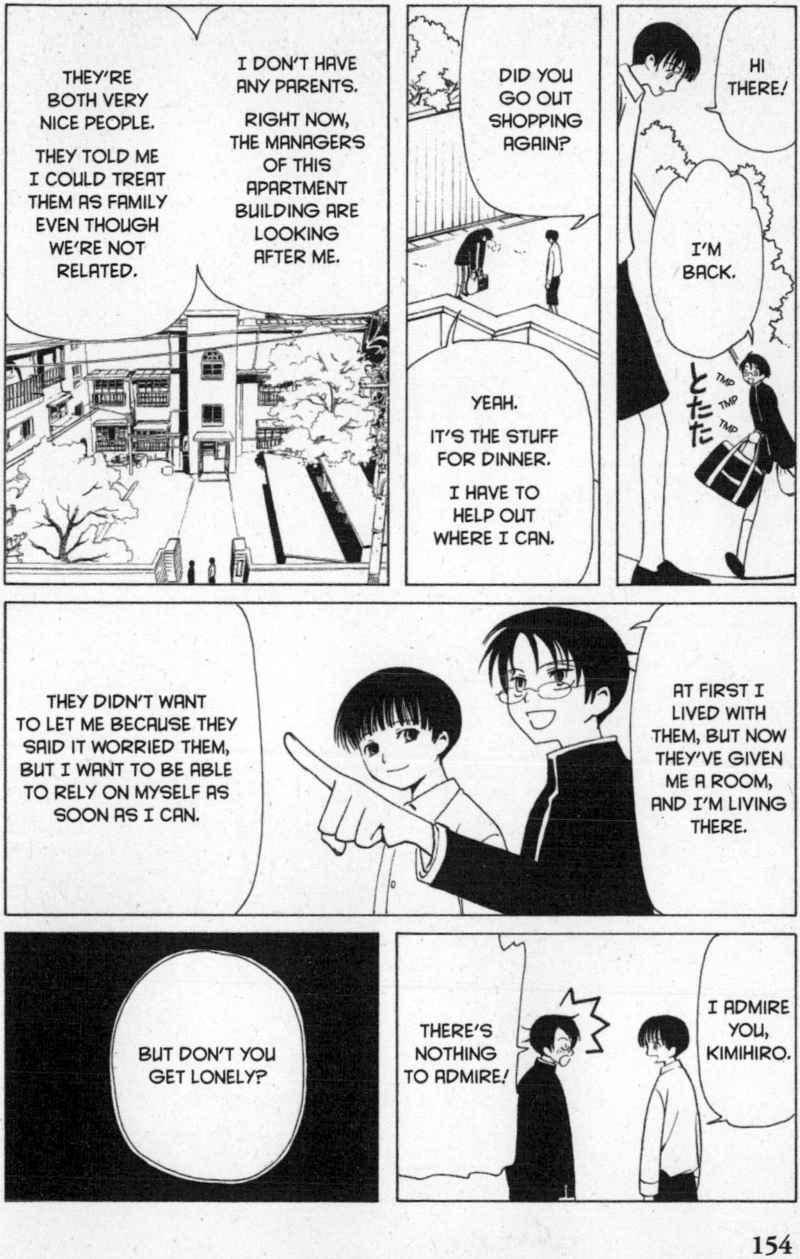
HI THERE!
I'M BACK.
とたた
TMP TMP TMP
DID YOU GO OUT SHOPPING AGAIN?
YEAH.
IT'S THE STUFF FOR DINNER.
I HAVE TO HELP OUT WHERE I CAN.
I DON'T HAVE ANY PARENTS.
RIGHT NOW, THE MANAGERS OF THIS APARTMENT BUILDING ARE LOOKING AFTER ME.
THEY'RE BOTH VERY NICE PEOPLE.
THEY TOLD ME I COULD TREAT THEM AS FAMILY EVEN THOUGH WE'RE NOT RELATED.
AT FIRST I LIVED WITH THEM, BUT NOW THEY'VE GIVEN ME A ROOM, AND I'M LIVING THERE.
THEY DIDN'T WANT TO LET ME BECAUSE THEY SAID IT WORRIED THEM, BUT I WANT TO BE ABLE TO RELY ON MYSELF AS SOON AS I CAN.
I ADMIRE YOU, KIMIHIRO.
THERE'S NOTHING TO ADMIRE!
BUT DON'T YOU GET LONELY?

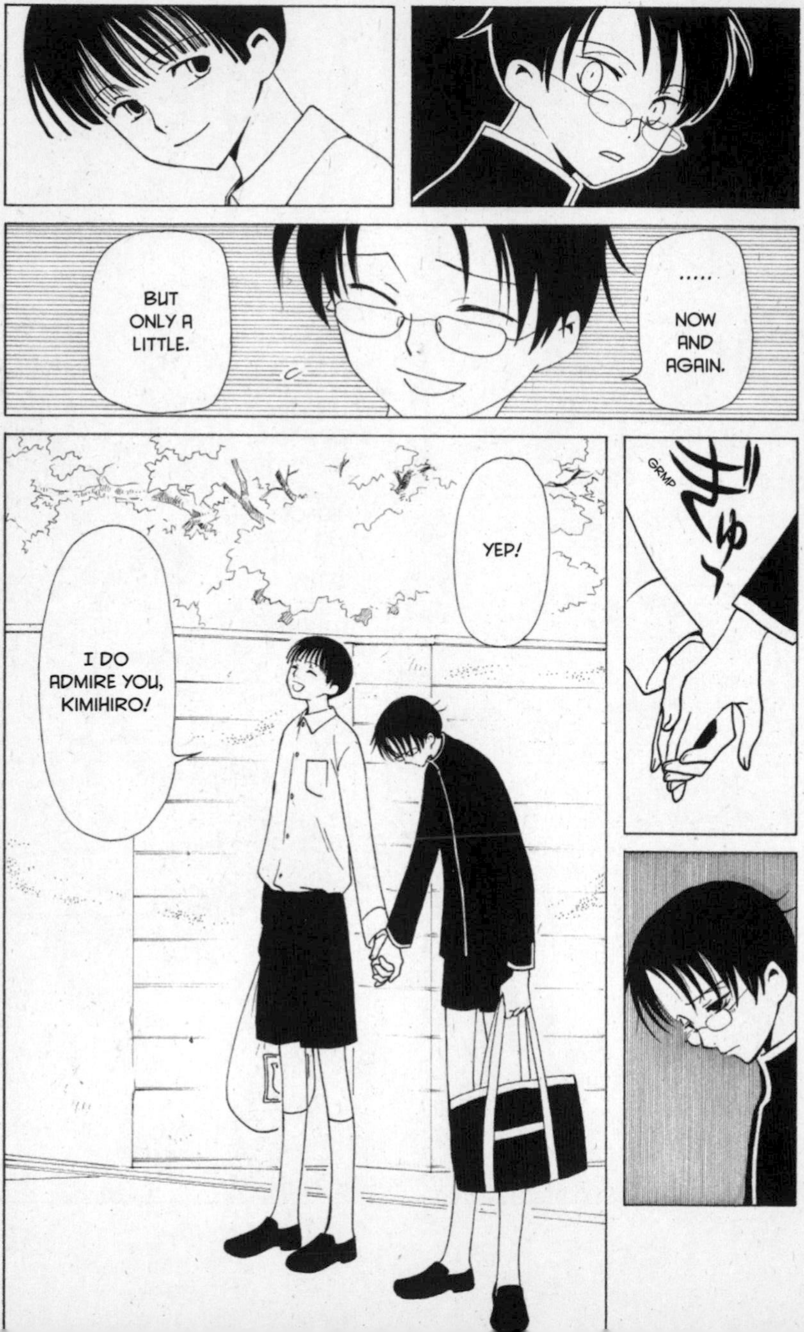
......
NOW AND AGAIN.
BUT ONLY A LITTLE.
GRMP
YEP!
I DO ADMIRE YOU, KIMIHIRO!

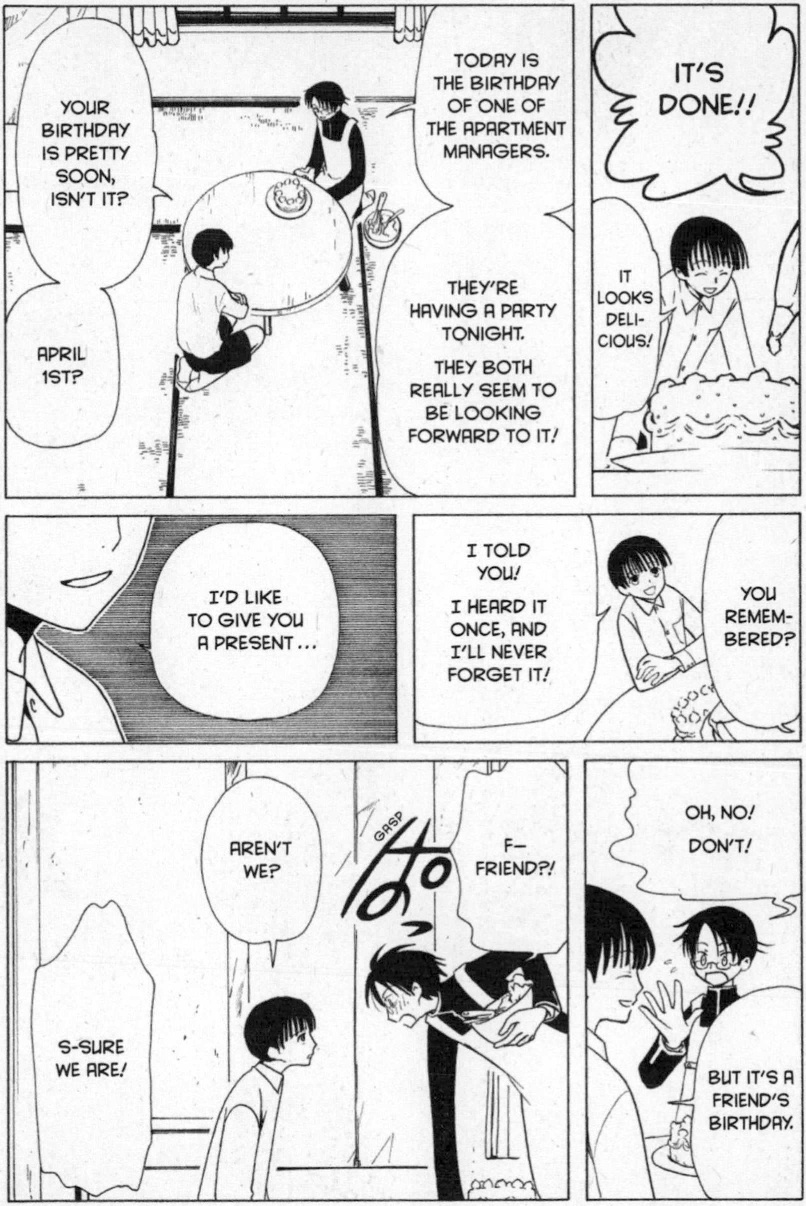
IT'S DONE!!
IT LOOKS DELI-CIOUS!
TODAY IS THE BIRTHDAY OF ONE OF THE APARTMENT MANAGERS.
THEY'RE HAVING A PARTY TONIGHT.
THEY BOTH REALLY SEEM TO BE LOOKING FORWARD TO IT!
YOUR BIRTHDAY IS PRETTY SOON, ISN'T IT?
APRIL 1ST?
YOU REMEM-BERED?
I TOLD YOU!
I HEARD IT ONCE, AND I'LL NEVER FORGET IT!
I'D LIKE TO GIVE YOU A PRESENT...
OH, NO! DON'T!
BUT IT'S A FRIEND'S BIRTHDAY.
F— FRIEND?!
GASP
はっ
AREN'T WE?
S-SURE WE ARE!

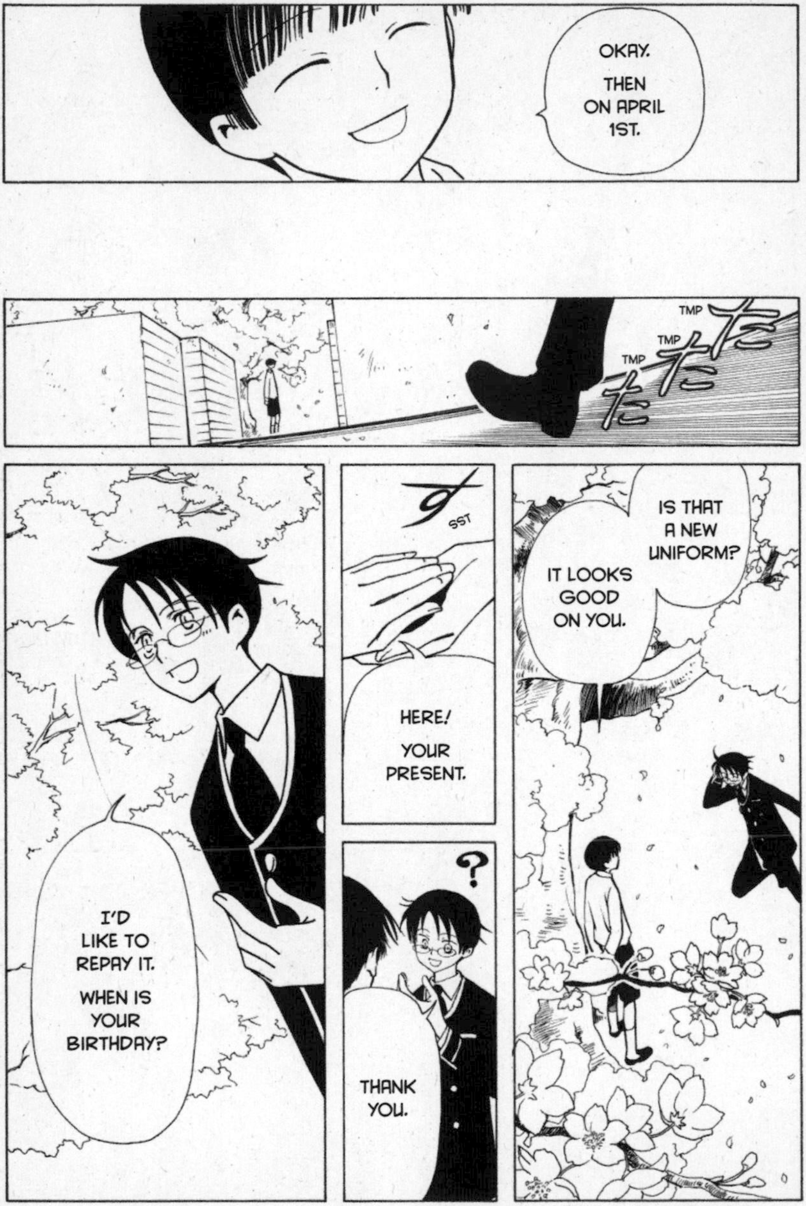
OKAY. THEN ON APRIL 1ST.
たたた
TMP TMP TMP
IS THAT A NEW UNIFORM?
IT LOOKS GOOD ON YOU.
SST
HERE! YOUR PRESENT.
?
THANK YOU.
I'D LIKE TO REPAY IT. WHEN IS YOUR BIRTHDAY?

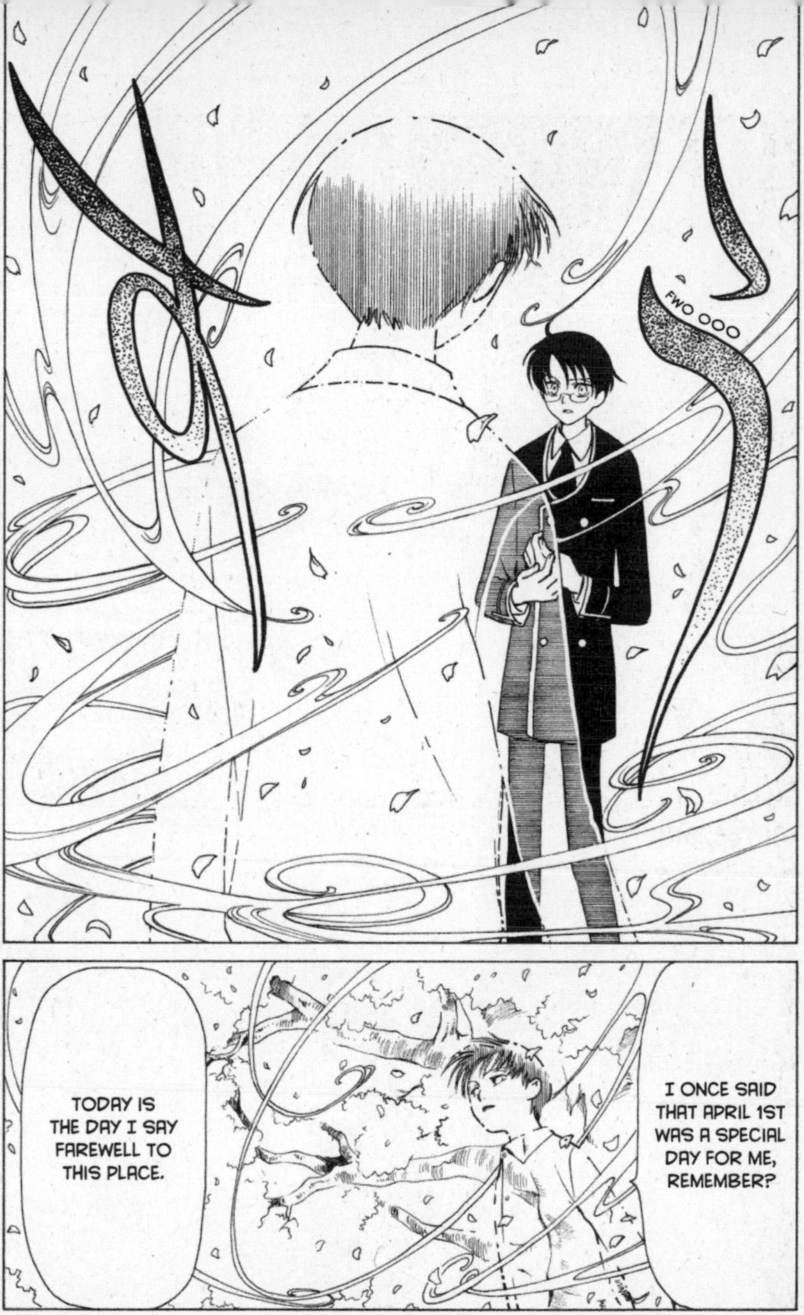
FWO OOO
I ONCE SAID THAT APRIL 1ST WAS A SPECIAL DAY FOR ME, REMEMBER?
TODAY IS THE DAY I SAY FAREWELL TO THIS PLACE.

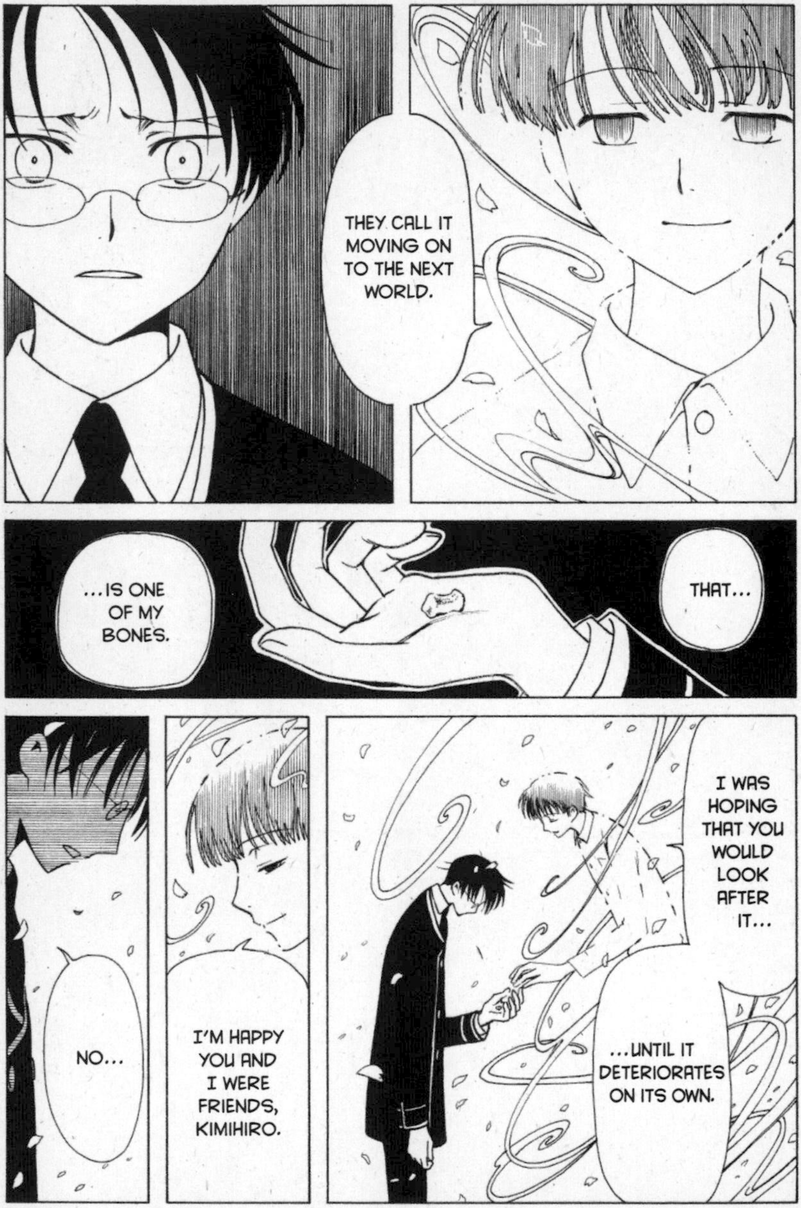
THEY CALL IT MOVING ON TO THE NEXT WORLD.
THAT...
...IS ONE OF MY BONES.
I WAS HOPING THAT YOU WOULD LOOK AFTER IT...
...UNTIL IT DETERIORATES ON ITS OWN.
I'M HAPPY YOU AND I WERE FRIENDS, KIMIHIRO.
NO...

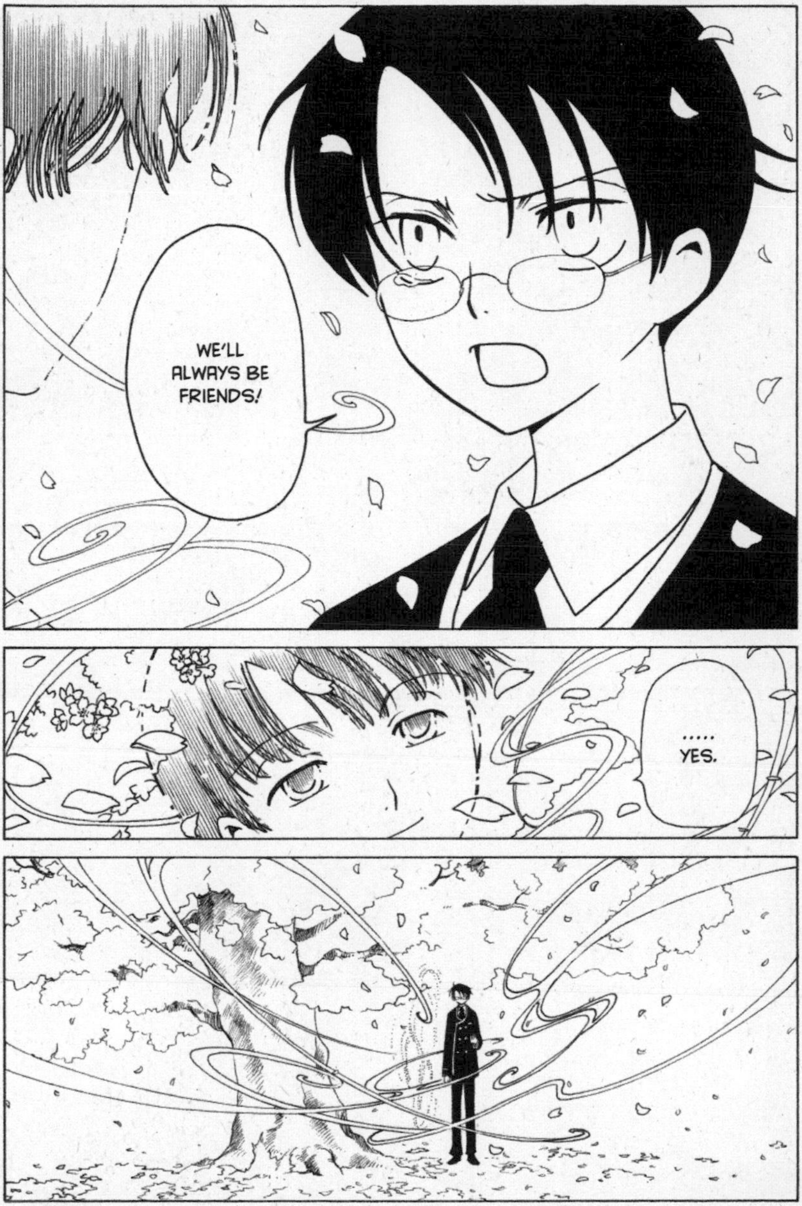
WE'LL ALWAYS BE FRIENDS!
..... YES.

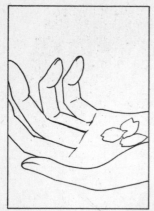

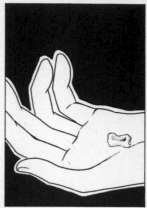

DURING THAT TIME, I WAS HOUNDED BY THE SPIRITS, AND THE ONLY WAY I GOT THROUGH IT ALL RIGHT...
...WAS ALL THANKS TO YOU.
FWFF
THANK YOU!

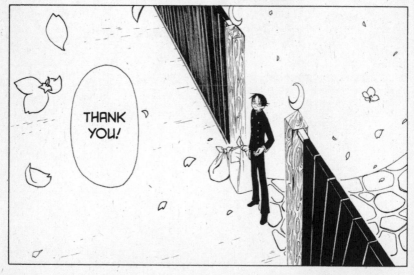

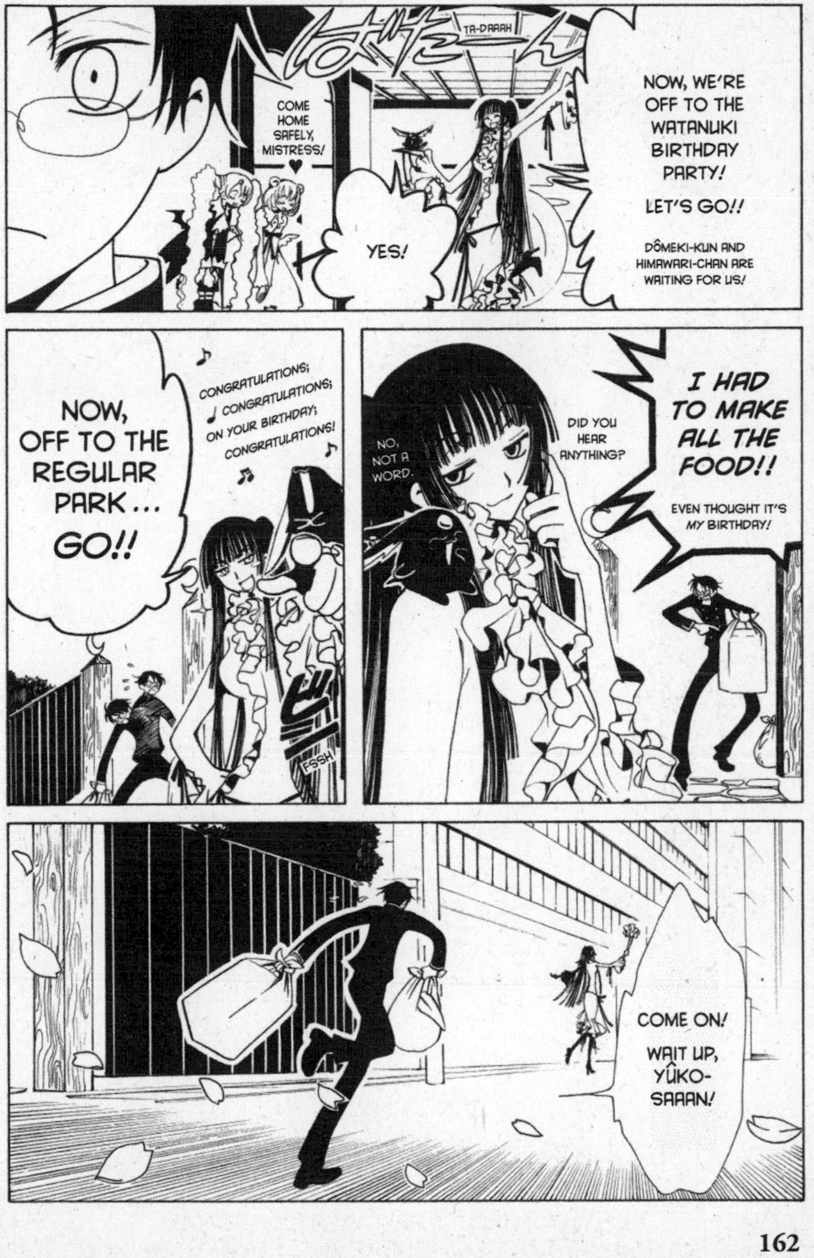
TA-DAAAH
NOW, WE'RE OFF TO THE WATANUKI BIRTHDAY PARTY!
LET'S GO!!
DÔMEKI-KUN AND HIMAWARI-CHAN ARE WAITING FOR US!
YES!
COME HOME SAFELY, MISTRESS! ♥
I HAD TO MAKE ALL THE FOOD!!
EVEN THOUGHT IT'S MY BIRTHDAY!
DID YOU HEAR ANYTHING?
NO, NOT A WORD.
CONGRATULATIONS; ♩ CONGRATULATIONS; ON YOUR BIRTHDAY; CONGRATULATIONS!
NOW, OFF TO THE REGULAR PARK... GO!!
FSSH
COME ON!
WAIT UP, YÛKO-SAAAN!

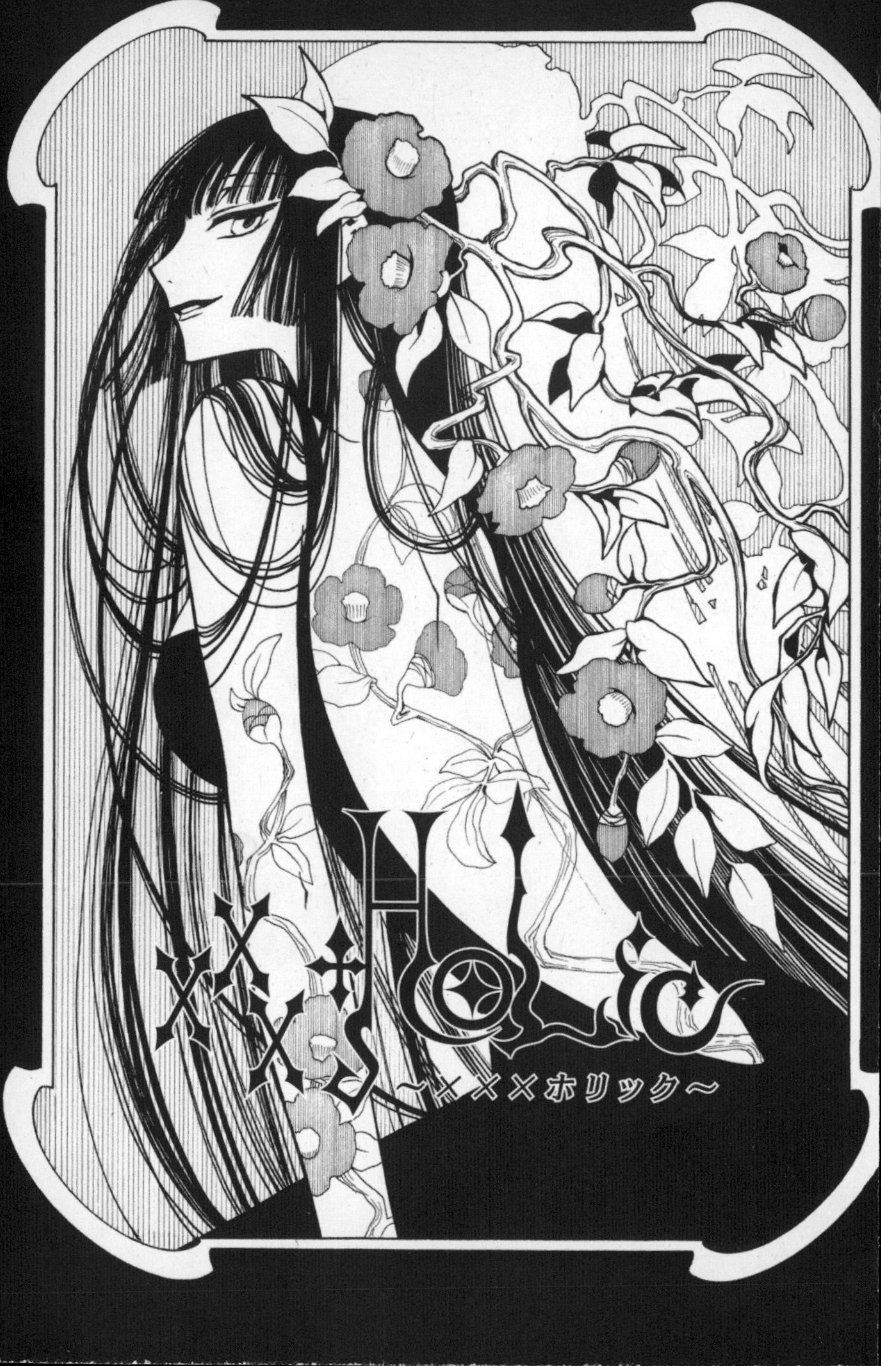
xxxHOLiC
~×××ホリック~

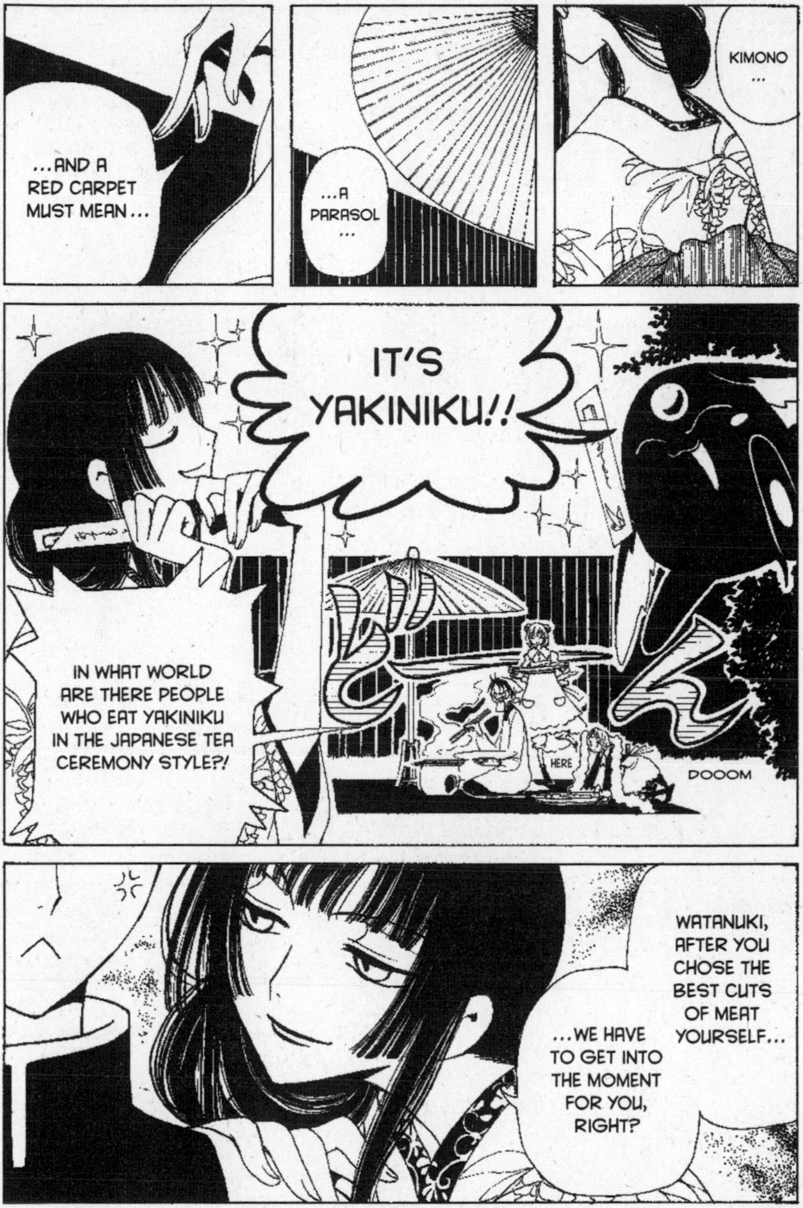
KIMONO ...
...A PARASOL ...
...AND A RED CARPET MUST MEAN...
IT'S YAKINIKU!!
IN WHAT WORLD ARE THERE PEOPLE WHO EAT YAKINIKU IN THE JAPANESE TEA CEREMONY STYLE?!
HERE
DOOOM
WATANUKI, AFTER YOU CHOSE THE BEST CUTS OF MEAT YOURSELF...
...WE HAVE TO GET INTO THE MOMENT FOR YOU, RIGHT?

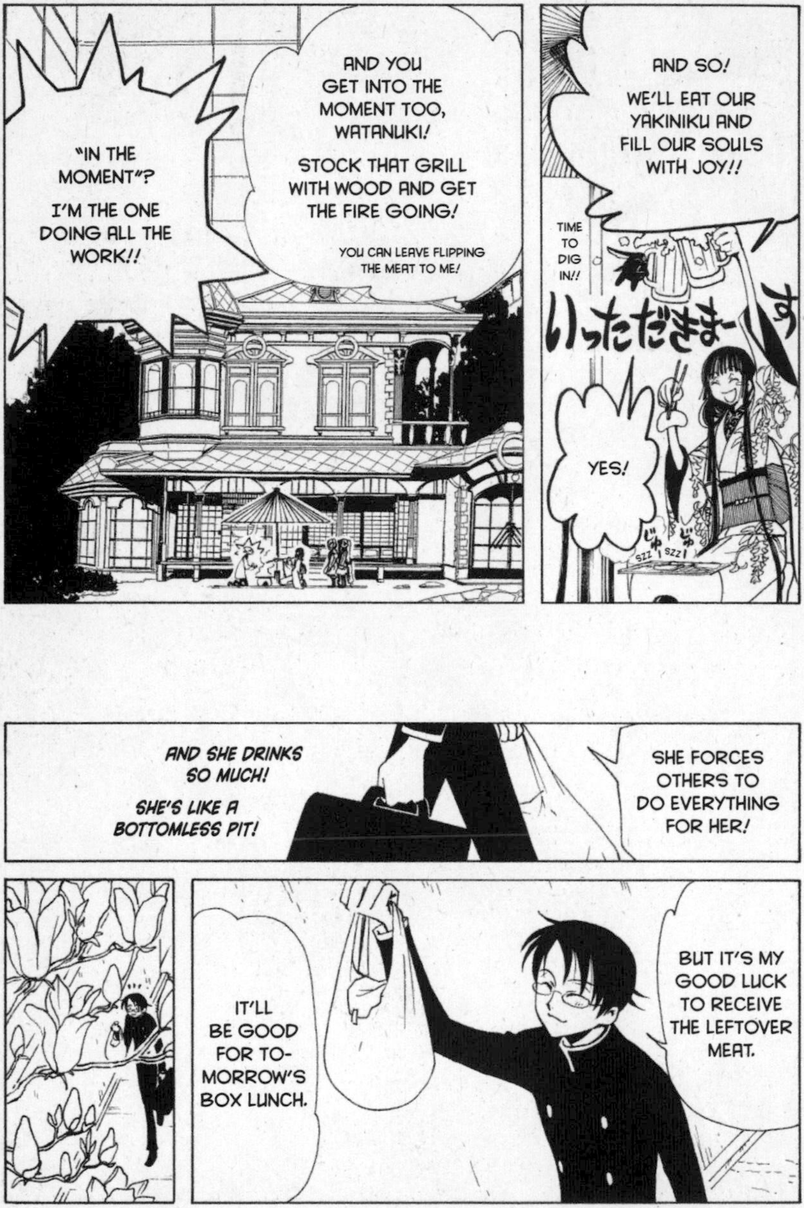
AND SO! WE'LL EAT OUR YAKINIKU AND FILL OUR SOULS WITH JOY!!
TIME TO DIG IN!!
いっただきまーす
YES!
じゅ じゅ
SZZ SZZ
AND YOU GET INTO THE MOMENT TOO, WATANUKI! STOCK THAT GRILL WITH WOOD AND GET THE FIRE GOING!
YOU CAN LEAVE FLIPPING THE MEAT TO ME!
"IN THE MOMENT"? I'M THE ONE DOING ALL THE WORK!!
SHE FORCES OTHERS TO DO EVERYTHING FOR HER!
AND SHE DRINKS SO MUCH! SHE'S LIKE A BOTTOMLESS PIT!
BUT IT'S MY GOOD LUCK TO RECEIVE THE LEFTOVER MEAT.
IT'LL BE GOOD FOR TO-MORROW'S BOX LUNCH.

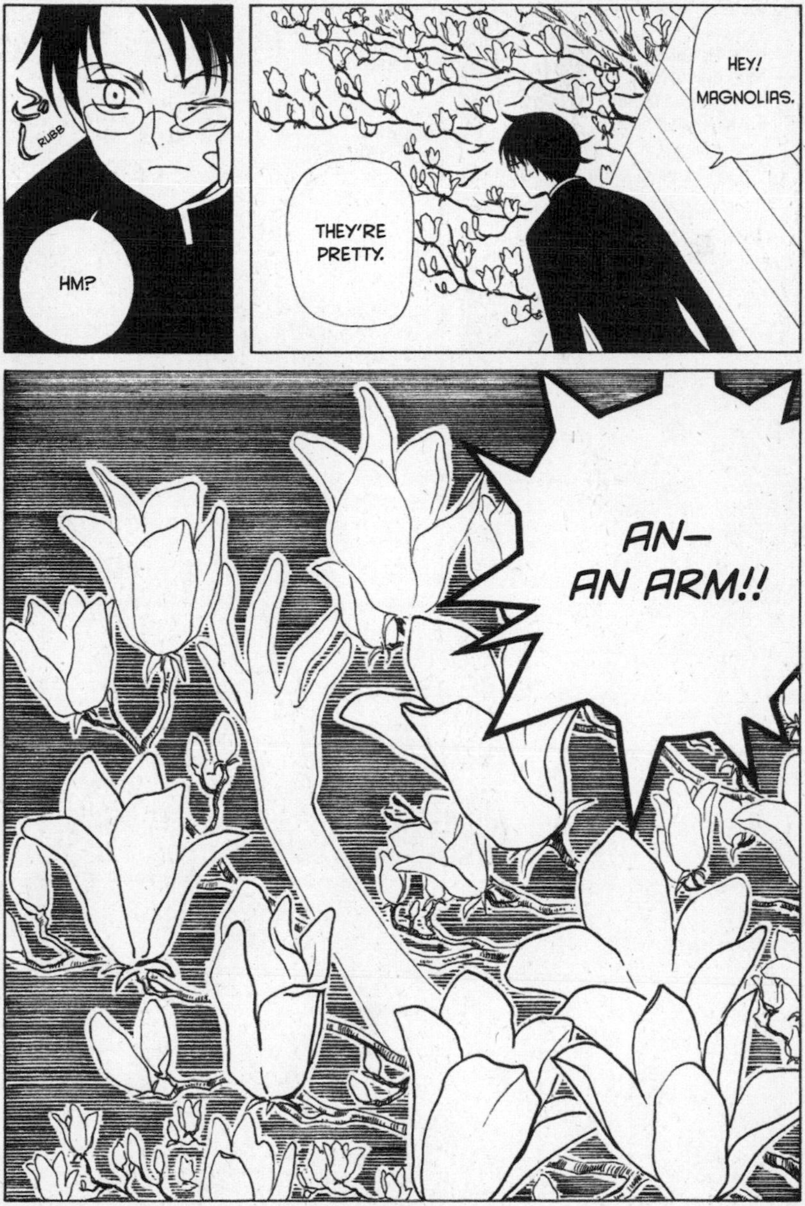
HEY! MAGNOLIAS.
THEY'RE PRETTY.
RUBB
HM?
AN—
AN ARM!!

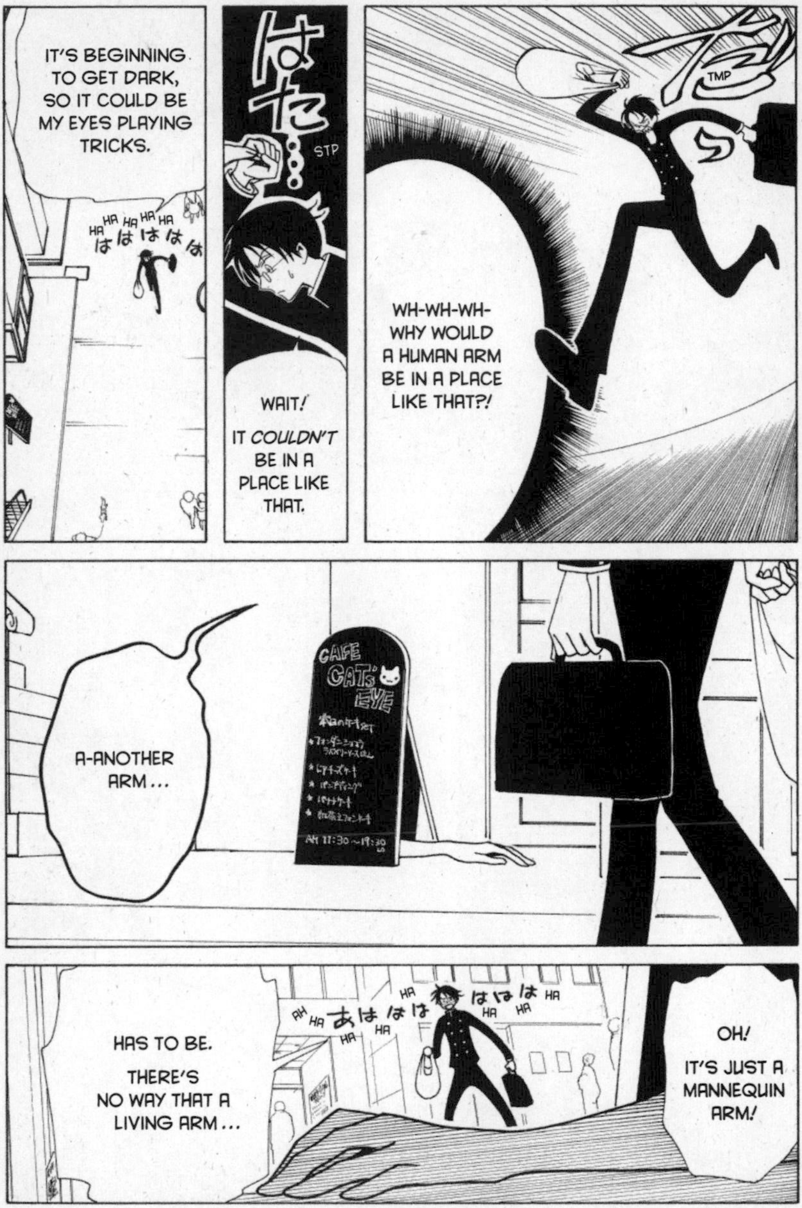
たっ
TMP
WH-WH-WH- WHY WOULD A HUMAN ARM BE IN A PLACE LIKE THAT?!
はた…
STP
WAIT!
IT *COULDN'T* BE IN A PLACE LIKE THAT.
IT'S BEGINNING TO GET DARK, SO IT COULD BE MY EYES PLAYING TRICKS.
HA HA HA HA HA
ははははは
A-ANOTHER ARM…
CAFE CAT's EYE
OH!
IT'S JUST A MANNEQUIN ARM!
HA HA HA
あはははははは
AH HA HA HA HA HA HA
HAS TO BE.
THERE'S NO WAY THAT A LIVING ARM…

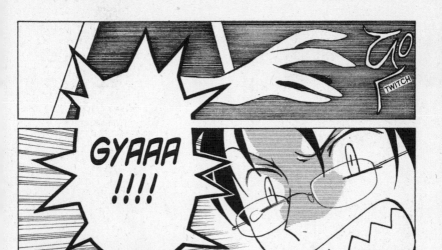

TWITCH
GYAAA !!!!
IT MOVED!
IT MOVED!!
TMP
HUFF
W-WAIT A SECOND!
IT'S A TRICK!
IT'S GOTTA BE SOME KIND OF TRICK!
THAT HAS TO BE IT!
SOMEBODY IS PLAYING A PRACTICAL JOKE.
MAYBE SOME PUBLICITY STUNT ...

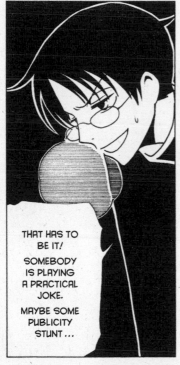

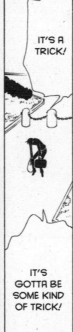

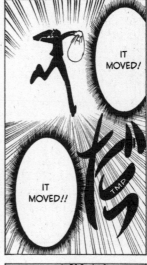

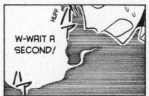

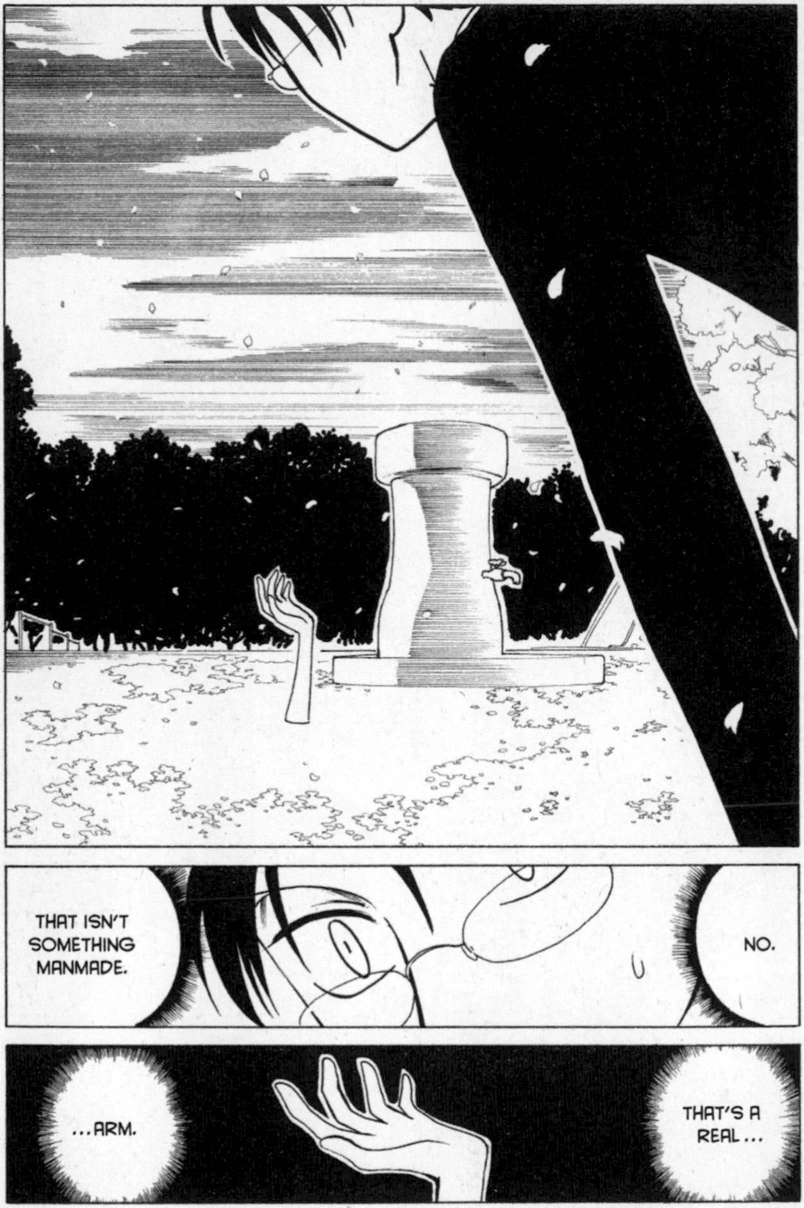
NO.
THAT ISN'T SOMETHING MANMADE.
THAT'S A REAL...
...ARM.

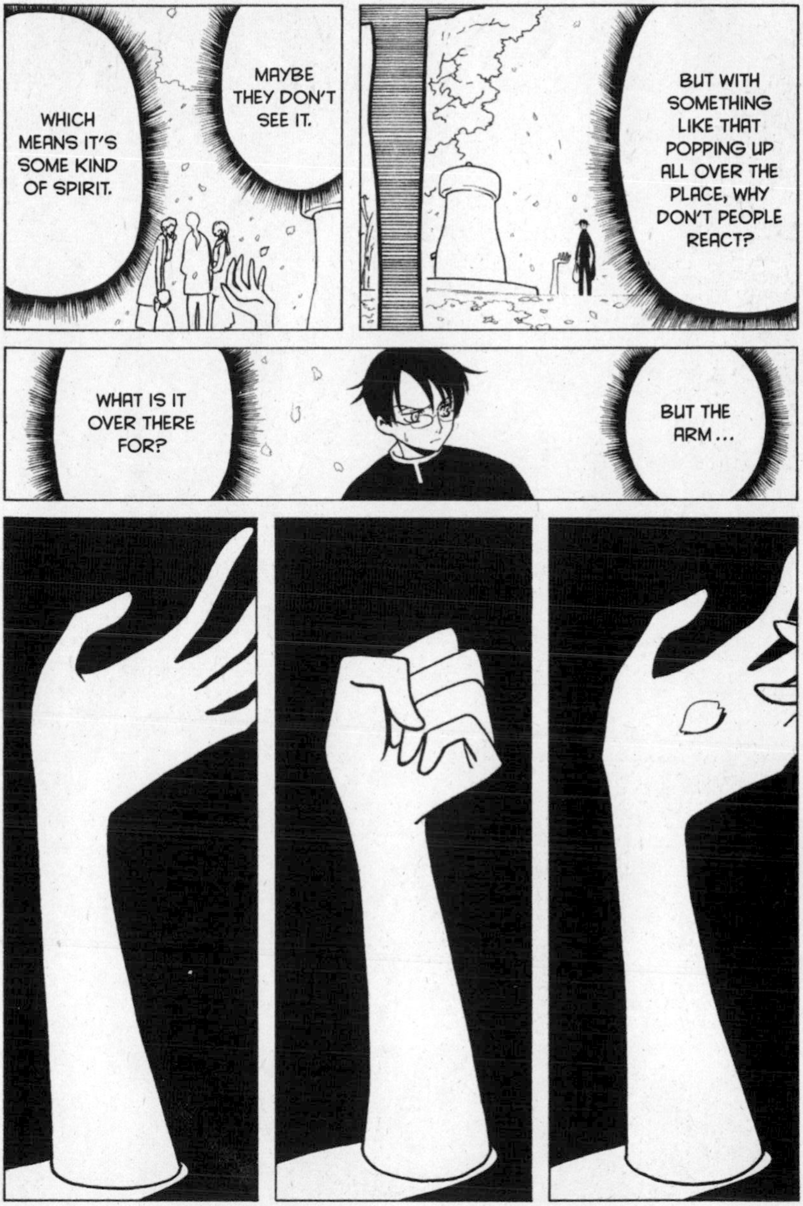
BUT WITH SOMETHING LIKE THAT POPPING UP ALL OVER THE PLACE, WHY DON'T PEOPLE REACT?
MAYBE THEY DON'T SEE IT.
WHICH MEANS IT'S SOME KIND OF SPIRIT.
BUT THE ARM...
WHAT IS IT OVER THERE FOR?

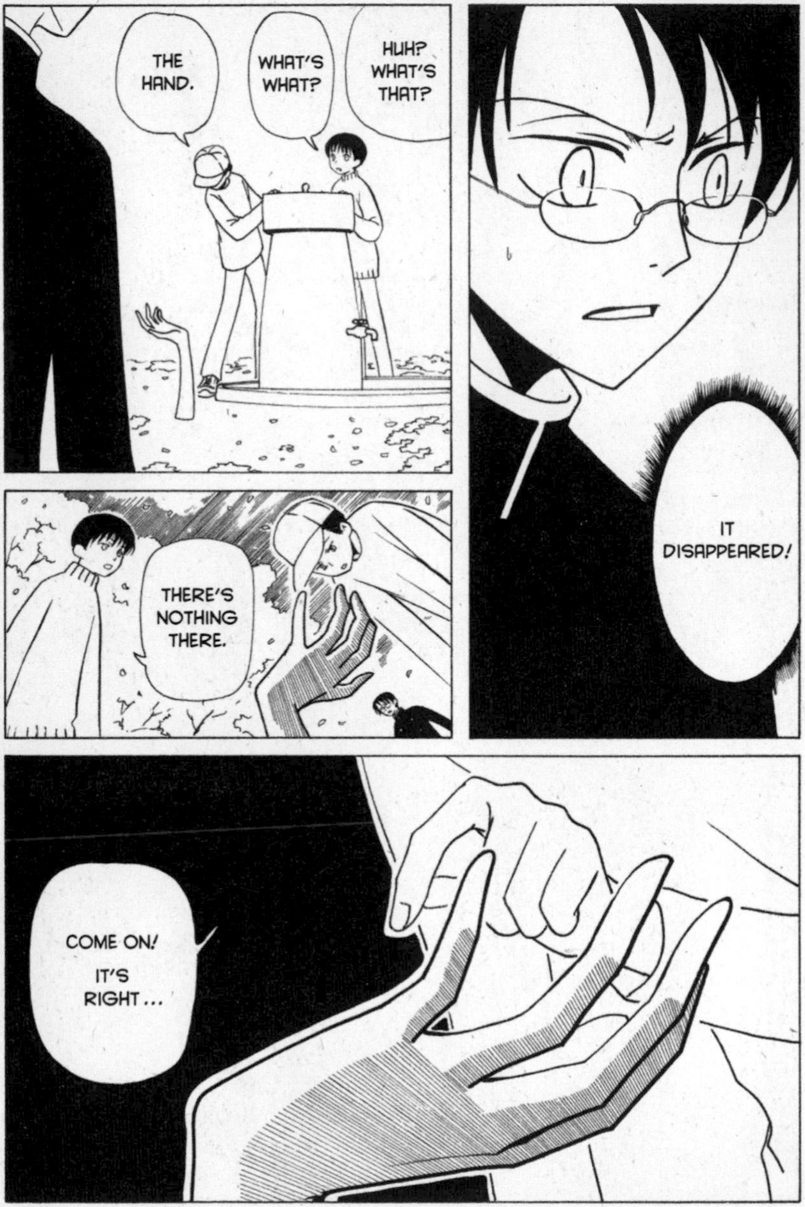
IT DISAPPEARED!
HUH? WHAT'S THAT?
WHAT'S WHAT?
THE HAND.
THERE'S NOTHING THERE.
COME ON! IT'S RIGHT ...

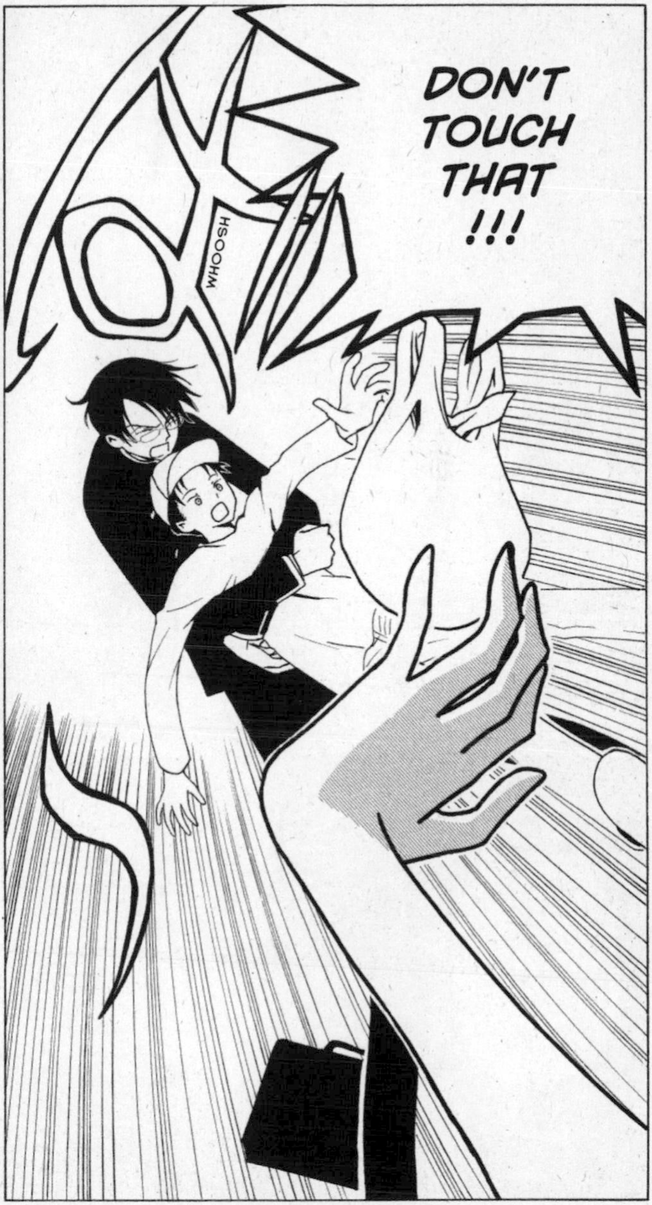
DON'T TOUCH THAT !!!
WHOOSH

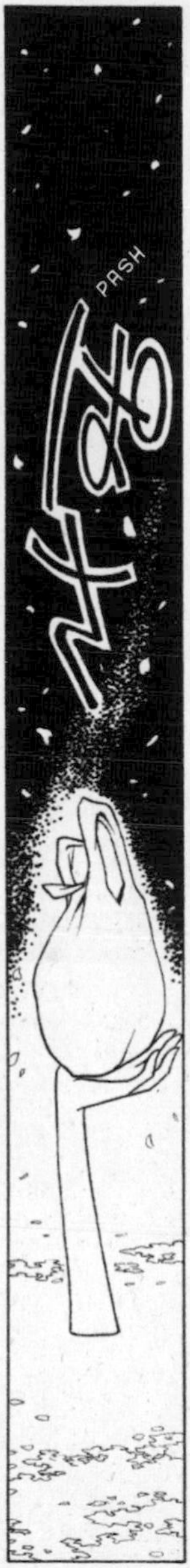
PASH

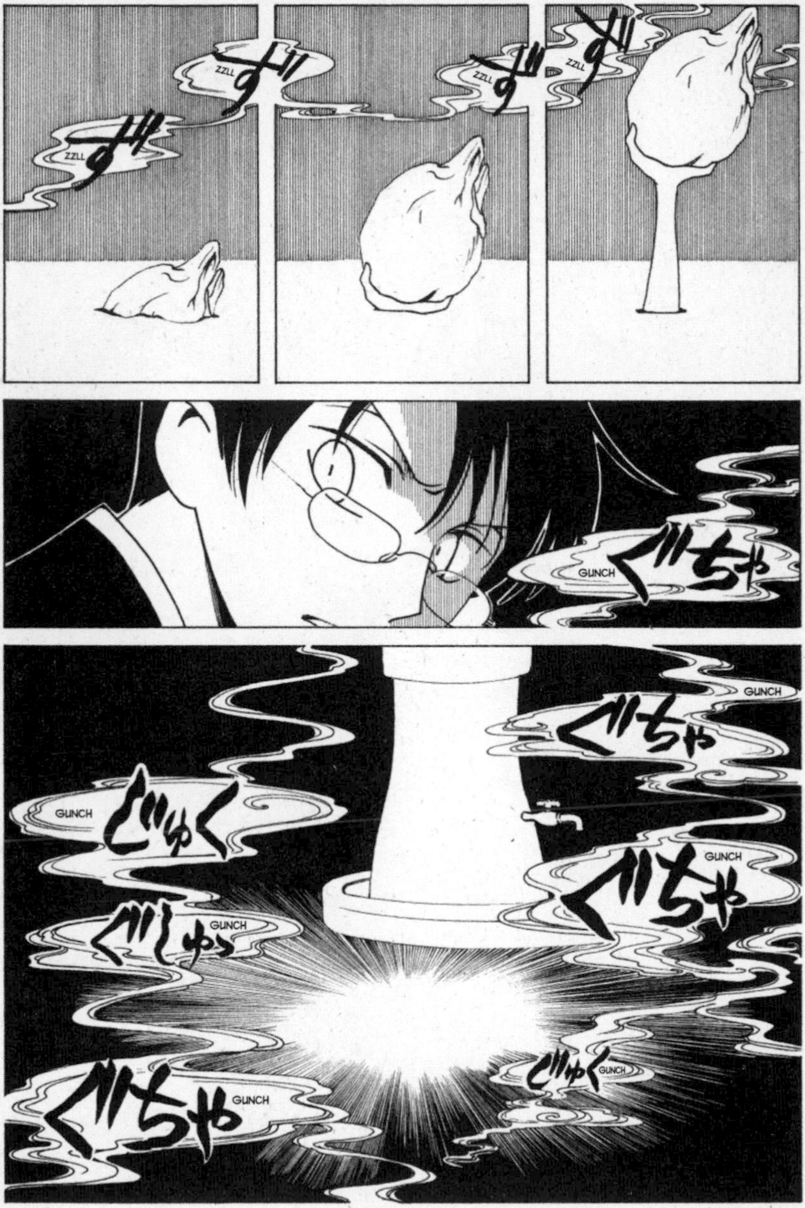
ず ZZLL
ず ZZLL
ず ZZLL
ず ZZLL
ぐちゃ GUNCH
ぐちゃ GUNCH
ぐちゃ GUNCH
ぐじゅく GUNCH
ぐしゅっ GUNCH
ぐじゅく GUNCH
ぐちゃ GUNCH

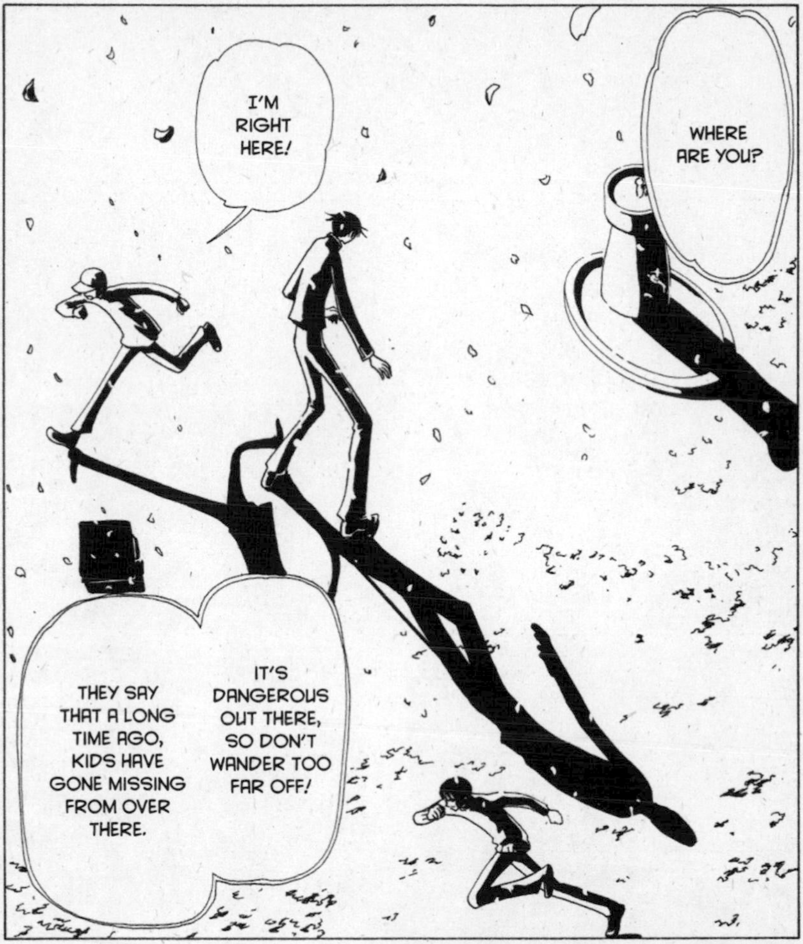
WHERE ARE YOU?
I'M RIGHT HERE!
IT'S DANGEROUS OUT THERE, SO DON'T WANDER TOO FAR OFF!
THEY SAY THAT A LONG TIME AGO, KIDS HAVE GONE MISSING FROM OVER THERE.

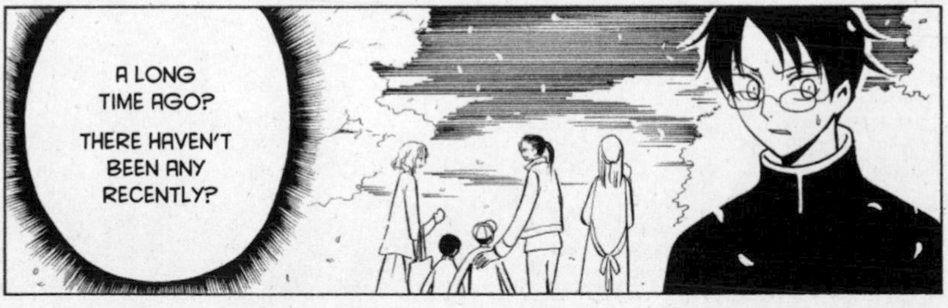
A LONG TIME AGO?
THERE HAVEN'T BEEN ANY RECENTLY?

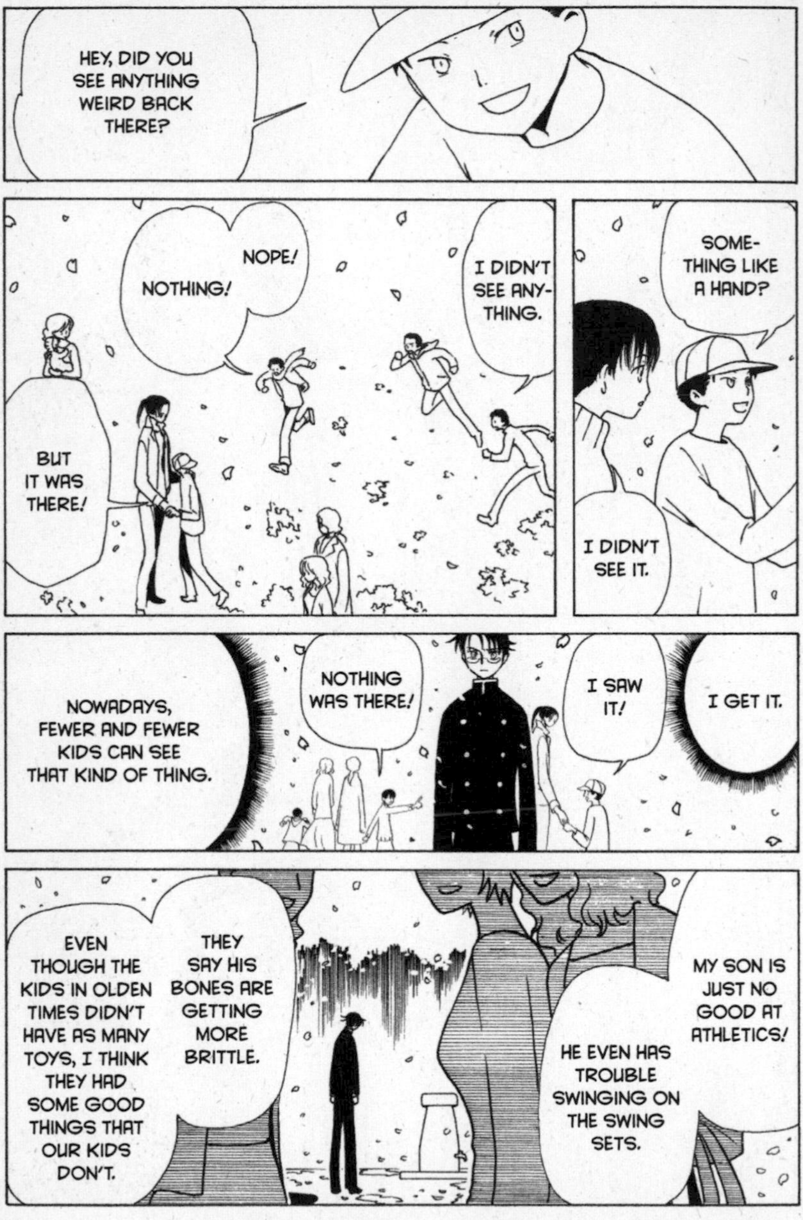
HEY, DID YOU SEE ANYTHING WEIRD BACK THERE?
SOME-THING LIKE A HAND?
I DIDN'T SEE IT.
I DIDN'T SEE ANY-THING.
NOPE!
NOTHING!
BUT IT WAS THERE!
I GET IT.
I SAW IT!
NOTHING WAS THERE!
NOWADAYS, FEWER AND FEWER KIDS CAN SEE THAT KIND OF THING.
MY SON IS JUST NO GOOD AT ATHLETICS!
HE EVEN HAS TROUBLE SWINGING ON THE SWING SETS.
THEY SAY HIS BONES ARE GETTING MORE BRITTLE.
EVEN THOUGH THE KIDS IN OLDEN TIMES DIDN'T HAVE AS MANY TOYS, I THINK THEY HAD SOME GOOD THINGS THAT OUR KIDS DON'T.

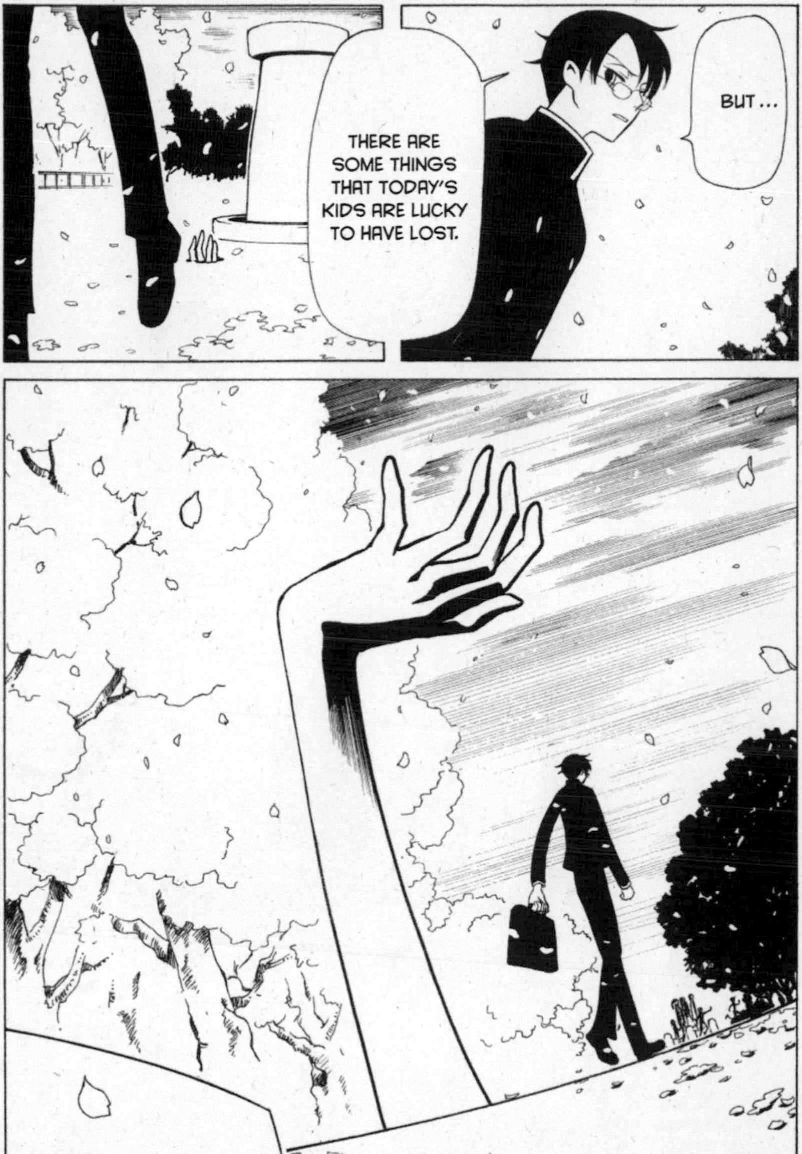
BUT...
THERE ARE SOME THINGS THAT TODAY'S KIDS ARE LUCKY TO HAVE LOST.

Continued

in *xxxHOLiC* Volume 5

About the Creators

CLAMP is a group of four women who have become the most popular manga artists in America—Satsuki Igarashi, Tsubaki Nekoi, Mokona, and Ageha Ohkawa. They started out as doujinshi (fan comics) creators, but their skill and craft brought them to the attention of publishers very quickly. Their first work from a major publisher was *RG Veda*, but their first mass success was with *Magic Knight Rayearth*. From there, they went on to write many series, including *Cardcaptor Sakura* and *Chobits*, two of the most popular manga in the United States. Like many Japanese manga artists, they prefer to avoid the spotlight, and little is known about them personally.

CLAMP is currently publishing three series in Japan: *Tsubasa* and *xxxHOLiC* with Kodansha and *Gohou Drug* with Kadokawa.

Past Works by CLAMP

Miyuki-chan in Wonderland

Miyuki is late getting started for school one morning. As she races for class, she sees a beautiful woman in a sexy leotard and bunny ears riding a skateboard. Distracted, Miyuki falls down a hole in the street and into Wonderland, a place that seems to be full of nothing but beautiful women who are all determined to either seduce Miyuki or just confuse her terribly.

CLAMP's very own version of Lewis Carroll's famous storybook heroine, Miyuki has parody adventures based on both *Alice in Wonderland* and *Through the Looking Glass*, retitled *Miyuki-chan in Wonderland* and *Miyuki-chan in Looking Glass Land*. In the *Wonderland* story, Miyuki meets sexy female versions of the White Rabbit (the skateboard-riding bunny woman), the twins Tweedledee and Tweedledum (here renamed To Lee and Cho Lee, two women in Chinese dresses who practice martial arts), the Mad Hatter, the March Hare, the Dormouse, the Cheshire Cat, and the Red Queen. In the *Looking Glass* story, Miyuki meets Humpty Dumpty, plus a mirror-image version of herself, who is much less shy than Miyuki is about taking off her clothes.

Miyuki's travels also include a trip into "TV Land," where she enters the world of the '6os sci-fi movie *Barbarella*, and "Part-Time Job Land," where a part-time waitress job results in Miyuki re-enacting a fighting contest from a popular video game. There are also crossovers to CLAMP's own universes in Miyuki's story, such as in "Video Game Land," where Miyuki becomes a *Rayearth*-like armored heroine, and "X Land," in which she goes to see the *X* animated movie, is pulled into the events of the film, and ends up filling in for both Kamui and Kotori.

Originally published in 1995 as a single-volume manga in the "100% Newtype Comics Extra" oversize format, *Miyuki-chan in Wonderland* was adapted into a thirty-minute animated video and also an audio CD.

Miyuki-chan also makes a cameo appearance as a background character in every world visited by Syaoran and his friends in *Tsubasa*. She may not be easy to find, but she's always there somewhere . . .

Translation Notes

For your edification and reading pleasure, here are notes to help you understand some of the cultural and story references from our translation of *xxxHOLiC*.

Page 4, Valentine's Day in Japan
There are very few holidays as associated with a particular product as Valentine's Day is with chocolate in Japan. Sure, the West has its chocolate hearts and gifts of assorted chocolate candies, but in

Japan, it has taken on a special significance—it has become the "Sadie Hawkins" day of relationships, where girls are encouraged to "confess their love" to their sweethearts. The gift of chocolate, and the acceptance of the gift, means that the guy is forced to at least consider the girl as a potential girlfriend. So

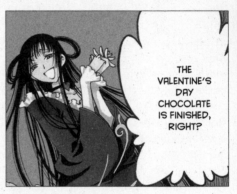

THE VALENTINE'S DAY CHOCOLATE IS FINISHED, RIGHT?

as it turns out, Valentine's chocolates are (to the joy of all males) specifically for women to give to men. But guys, don't get too excited, there are obligatory gifts of chocolates, too, that have no more meaning of love than an annual birthday card. For those gifts that do have romantic overtones, there is a particular day when the guy can respond, and that day is White Day (see later entry).

Page 9, White Day
With nearly half of the population giving chocolate on Valentine's Day (see previous entry) to the other half of the population, the chocolate manufacturers looked at this arrangement and let out a collective sigh. "Why can't it be the *entire* population giving chocolate to each other?" So the sweets manufacturers invented a

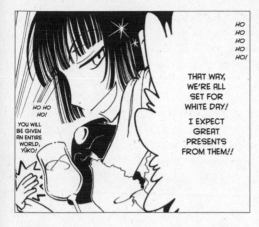

HO
HO
HO
HO
HO!

THAT WAY, WE'RE ALL SET FOR WHITE DAY!

I EXPECT GREAT PRESENTS FROM THEM!!

HO HO HO!

YOU WILL BE GIVEN AN ENTIRE WORLD, YÛKO!

holiday, exactly one month after Valentine's Day, for the men to give back to the women. They called it White Day, and suggested that the men return the gift of dark chocolate with a gift of white chocolate. They should have named it White Chocolate Day because there are a lot of white things that can run through a guy's dirty little mind. As the holiday wormed its way into the Japanese culture, sales of white panties boomed in the days before March 14th. In any case, the tradition has it that the guy who has just learned the girl's feelings on Valentine's Day must make his answer on White Day with a gift of something white. But obligation rears its head again, and like the way Yûko uses Fondant au Chocolat to force men to give back to her, a girl's receipt of a white gift on that day doesn't necessarily mean that they've been pledged a guy's undying love.

Page 46, *Zashiki-Warashi*

As told in folklore handed down from the Tohoku region of Japan (the northern part of the main island of Honshu), *Zashiki-Warashi* are ghosts or guardian spirits of a house that take the form of children. According to legend, if the *Zashiki-Warashi* leaves a house, sorrow will befall it. Recently the legend has taken on a "*Poltergeist*" feel with evil *Zashiki-Warashi* taking over traditional Japanese houses and terrorizing the residents.

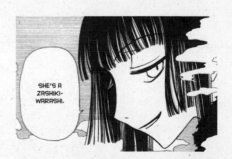

SHE'S A ZASHIKI-WARASHI.

Page 47, *Karasu Tengu*

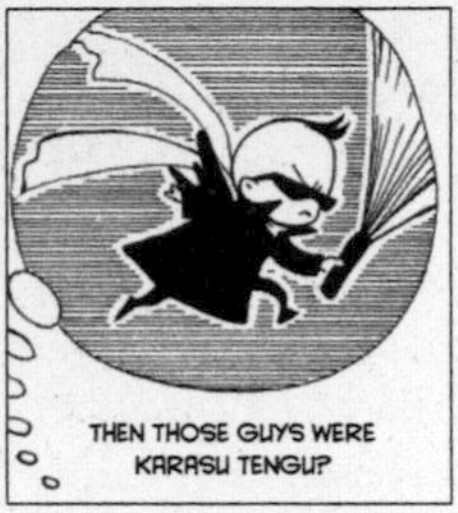
THEN THOSE GUYS WERE KARASU TENGU?

There are several *Tengu* types: *Daitengu* are the red-faced, long-nosed goblins that one may see in prints and wooden sculptures. *Kurama Tengu* are master swordsmen and tricksters associated with Kurama Yama (Horse-saddle Mountain) and the Buddhist temple there. And *Karasu Tengu* (Crow *Tengu*) are servants to magical masters. The *Karasu Tengu* usually are depicted as short creatures with crows' wings and heads, but wearing traditional Japanese garments and wooden *geta* sandals.

Page 59, *Yakitori*

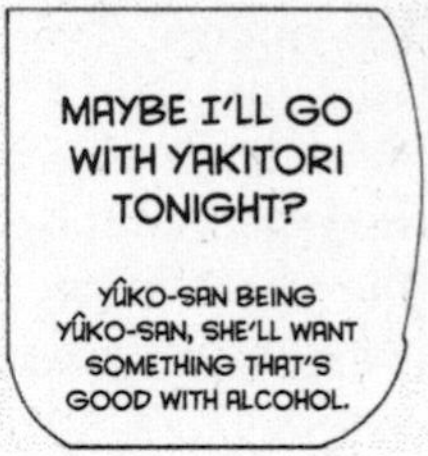
MAYBE I'LL GO WITH YAKITORI TONIGHT?
YŪKO-SAN BEING YŪKO-SAN, SHE'LL WANT SOMETHING THAT'S GOOD WITH ALCOHOL.

Marinated chicken and vegetables (usually leeks or onions) on wooden skewers and grilled over a charcoal frame. Other meats and vegetables can be used, but chicken is the main attraction. At the end of a long day, its aroma and inviting barbeque smoke surely does attract tired workers to the wooden *Yakitori* stands that line traditional Japanese streets. *Yakitori* can be eaten as a meal or a snack and is usually served with a tall, cold beer.

Page 62, *Teppan*

With the popularity of restaurants such as Benihana's, *Teppan*-style cooking has become as much a symbol of Japan in many North American towns as Teriyaki. Raw ingredients—meat and vegetables—are cooked on a hot, flat, iron griddle, flavored at the cook's discretion, and served up to be eaten immediately (although making *Teppan*-style food in the kitchen is perfectly acceptable for home consumption).

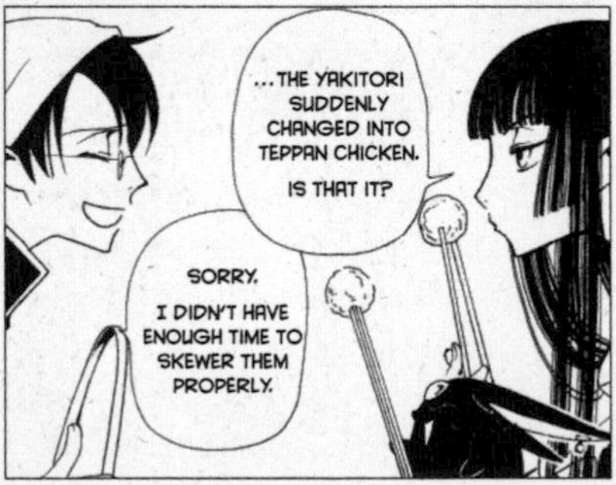
...THE YAKITORI SUDDENLY CHANGED INTO TEPPAN CHICKEN. IS THAT IT?
SORRY. I DIDN'T HAVE ENOUGH TIME TO SKEWER THEM PROPERLY.

Page 80, Cat's Eye

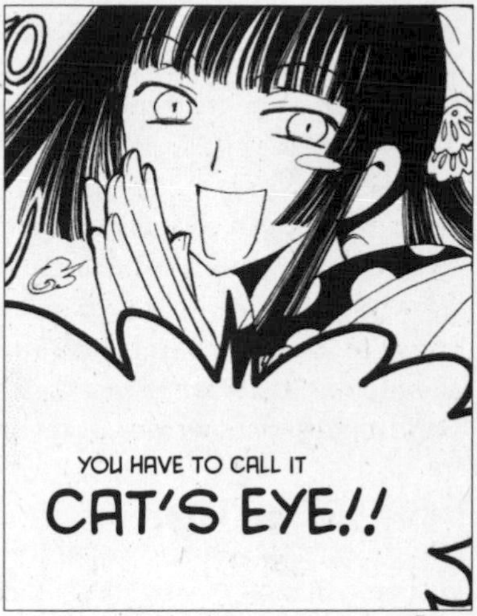
YOU HAVE TO CALL IT
CAT'S EYE!!

Their father missing and his collection of priceless paintings stolen, three sisters—sexy, twenty-something Rui; beautiful, college-age Hitomi, and cute high-schooler Ai—are out to retrieve the paintings and solve the mystery of their father's disappearance. So they take the guise of three cat burglars (in sexy, skin-tight outfits) that go by the name of Cat's Eye, stealing back their family's paintings from the scum that stole them in the first place. But during the day they run a coffee shop named Cat's Eye that is frequented by Hitomi's boyfriend, the very policeman charged with stopping the serial burglaries of priceless art! *Cat's Eye* started as the first hit manga series by Tsukasa Hojo (*City Hunter, F-Compo*), and the TV anime series ran for season after season of thieving adventure. There were also some live-action adaptations, including a high-budget special-effects movie in the '90s.

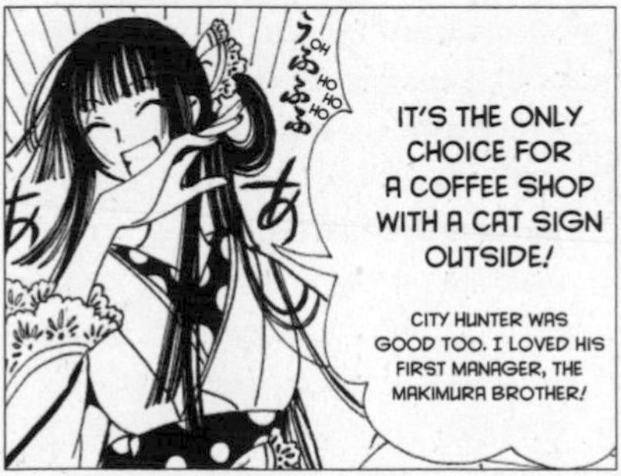
うふふふ
OH HO HO HO
あ
あ
IT'S THE ONLY CHOICE FOR A COFFEE SHOP WITH A CAT SIGN OUTSIDE!
CITY HUNTER WAS GOOD TOO. I LOVED HIS FIRST MANAGER, THE MAKIMURA BROTHER!

Page 80, *City Hunter*

The next big hit for Tsukasa Hojo, coming on the heels of his immensely popular manga series *Cat's Eye* (see previous entry). Ryo Saeba is so comfortable with guns and his own abilities that he has no problem either with pointing a pistol, or having one pointed at him. He runs a "protector for hire" business out of the bustling urban center of Shinjuku in Tokyo, Japan. All of his clients are beautiful

women between the ages of eighteen and thirty. . . . Why? Because Ryo Saeba is also the world's greatest lecher, and he limits himself to only those very customers. Every beautiful woman Ryo protects, Ryo also wants to seduce. Fortunately he's as inept at seducing women as he is competent at protecting them. Makimura (Yûko's favorite character) is Ryo's long-suffering manager, who is eventually replaced by Makimura's tomboyish little sister, Kaori. *City Hunter* was at least as popular as *Cat's Eye*, spawning multiple seasons of the anime TV show, animated movies, and even a live-action movie starring Jackie Chan! The *City Hunter* manga is available in English, and Tsukasa Hojo is presently working on a sequel series, *Angel Heart*.

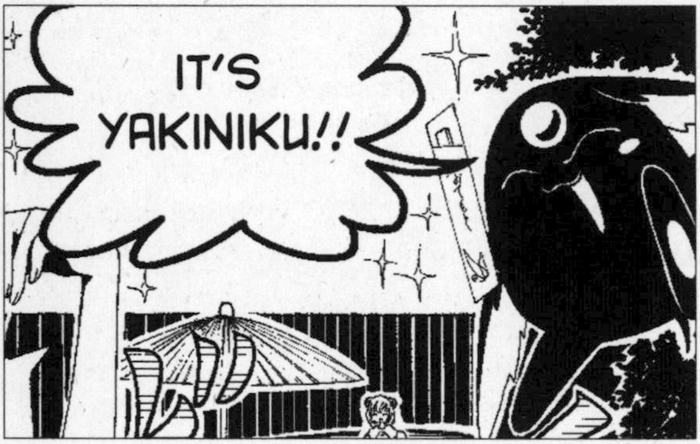
IT'S YAKINIKU!!

Page 164, *Yakiniku*

Not to be confused with *Yakitori* (see the earlier entry), *Yakiniku* is also known in North America as Korean barbecue. Marinated meats of all sorts are brought raw to the table where an open griddle (usually with a gas flame) is situated in the center. Then the customers cook the meat for themselves on the griddle. Vegetables are also a part of the process, but since *Yakiniku* means "fried meat," one can understand how the meat takes center stage of this delightful meal.

Preview of Volume 5

Here is an excerpt from Volume 5, on sale now in English.

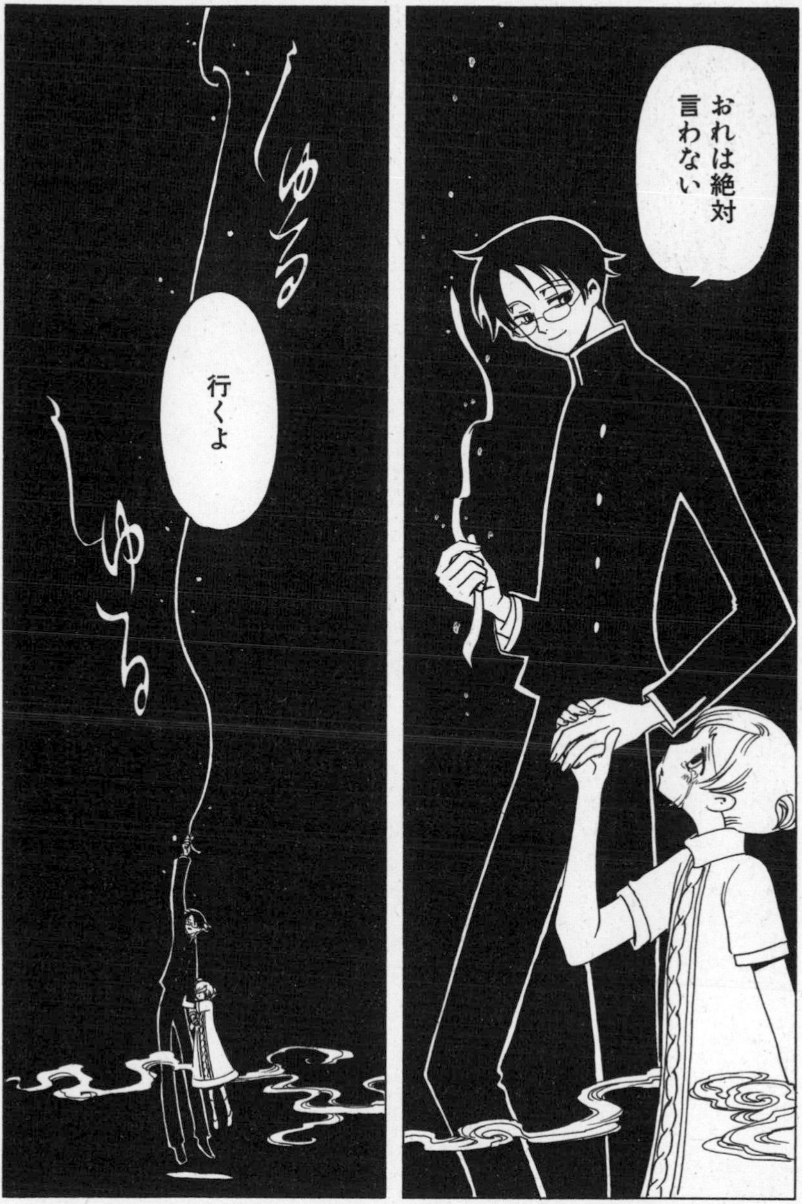
おれは絶対
言わない
しゅる
行くよ
しゅる

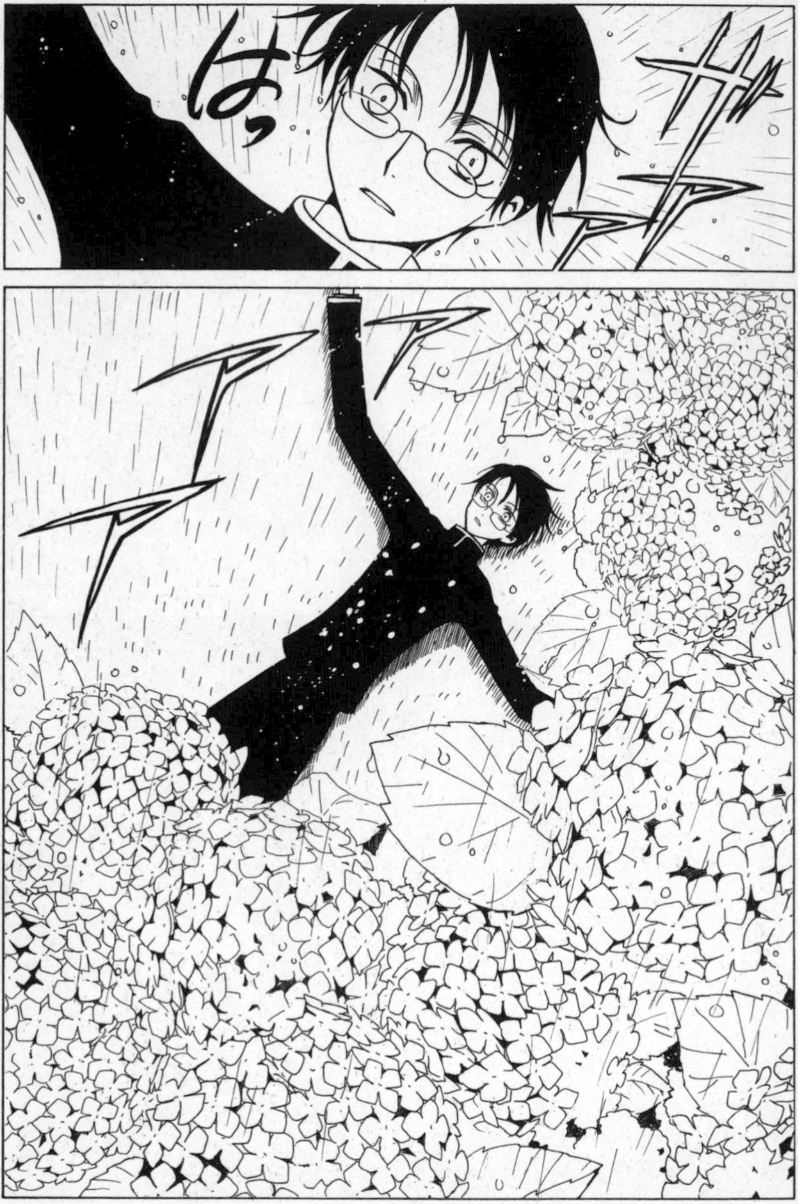
ザァア
はっ
アアア

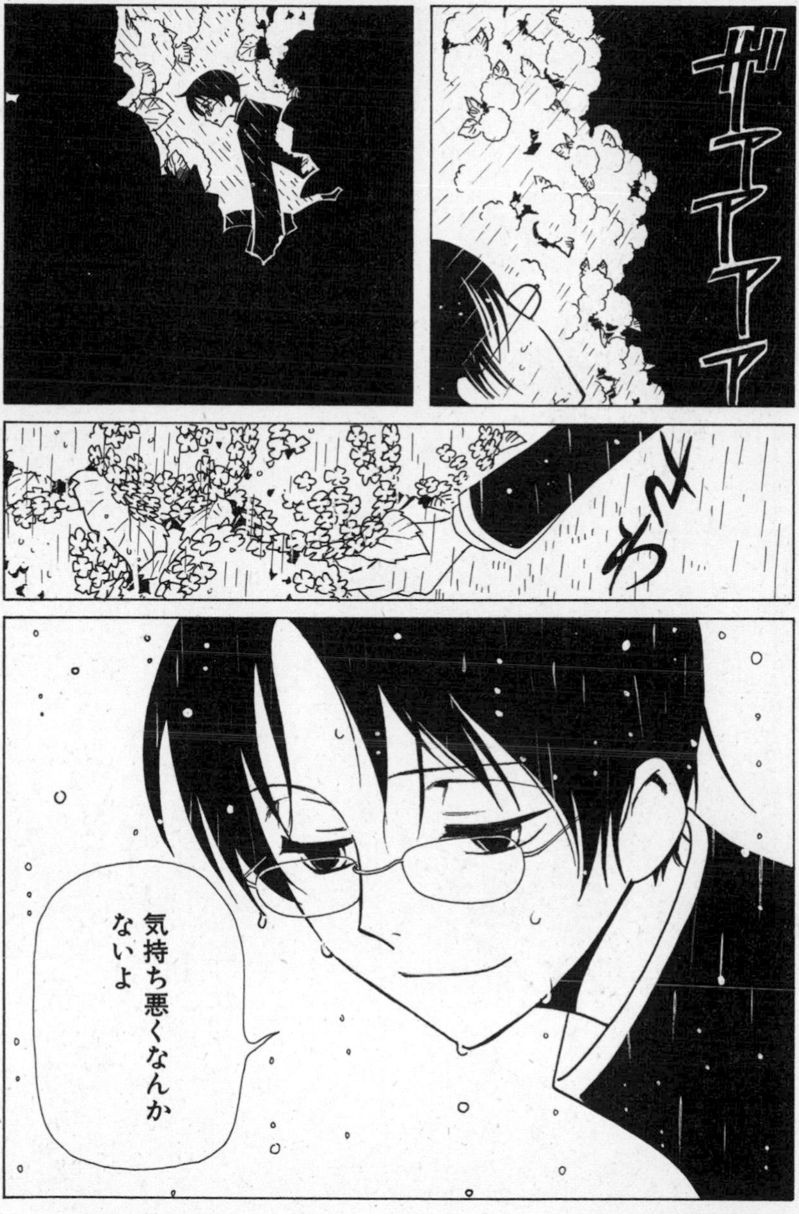
ザアアアア
さわ
気持ち悪くなんか
ないよ

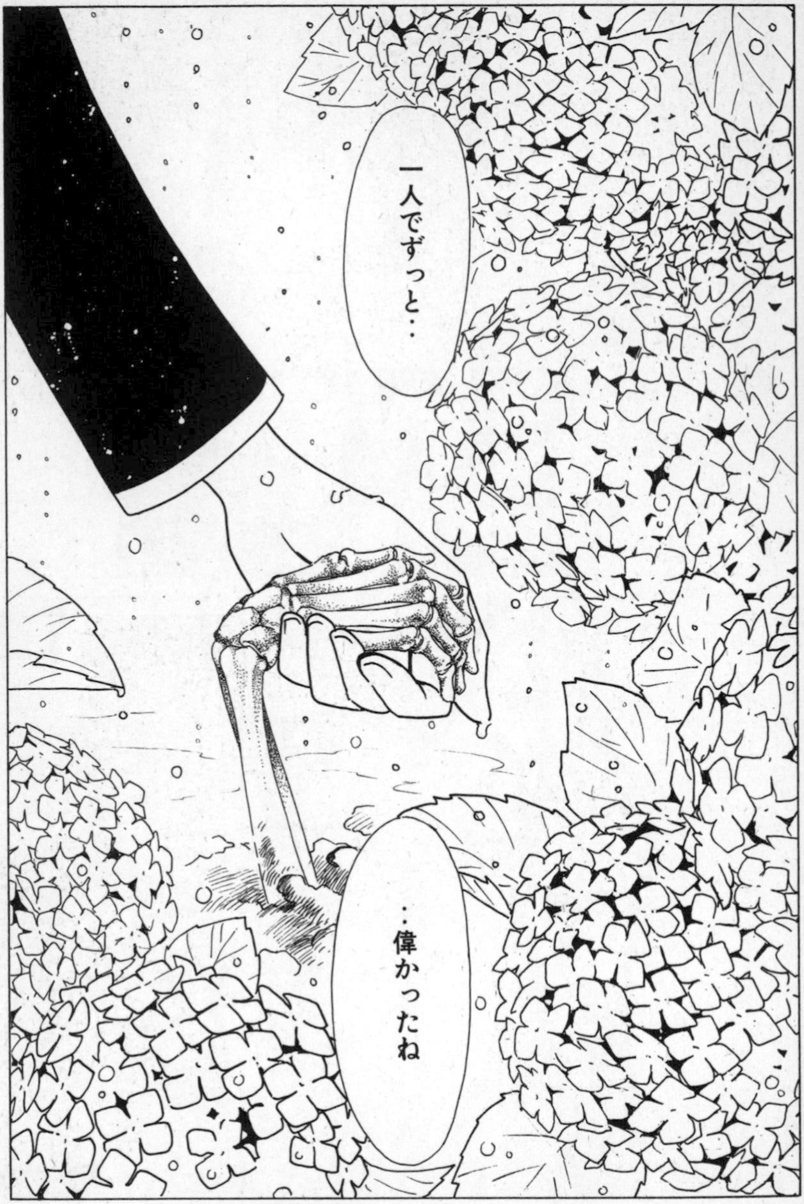
一人でずっと‥
‥偉かったね

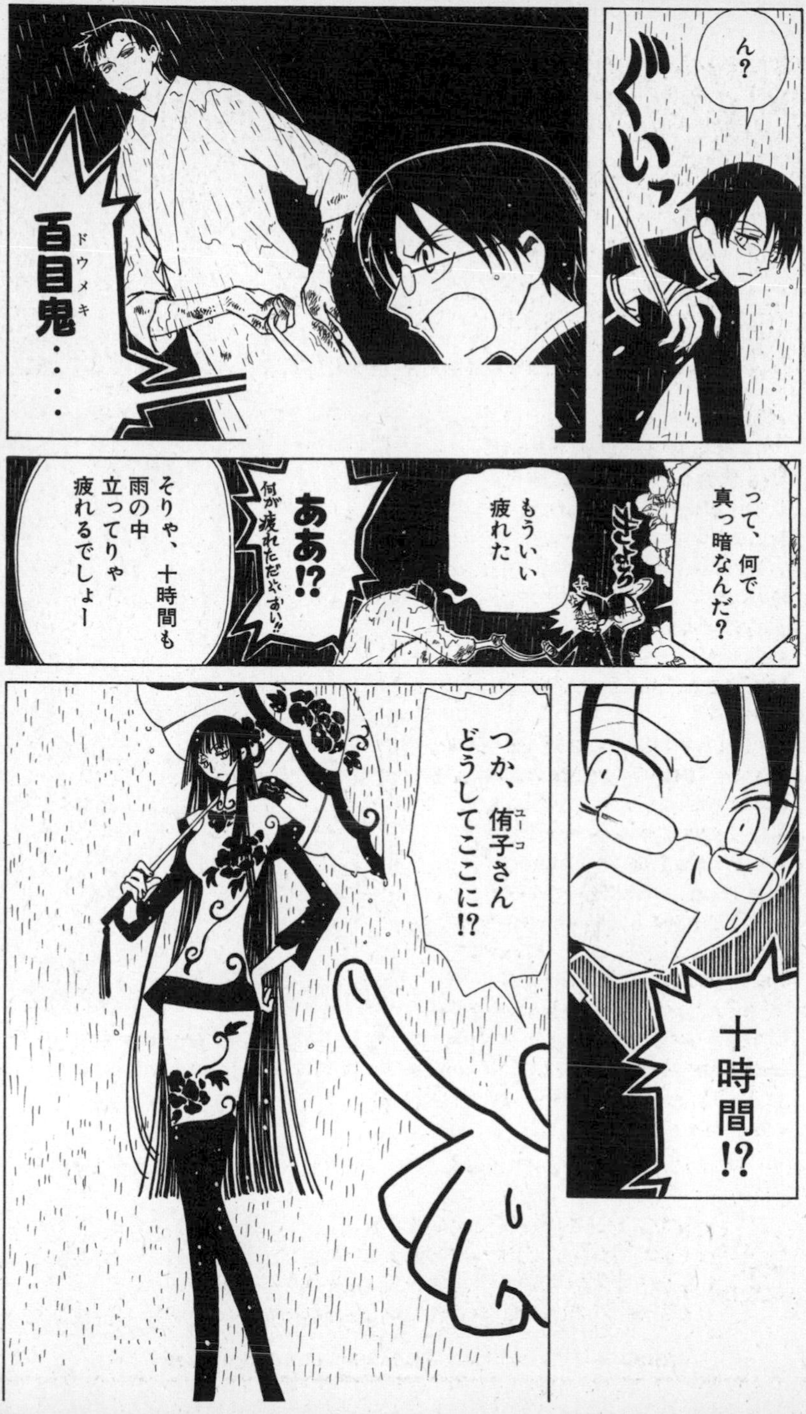
ん?
ぐいっ
百目鬼(ドウメキ)・・・・
って、何で真っ暗なんだ?
きょろ
もういい疲れた
ああ!?
何が疲れただ、おい!!
そりゃ、十時間も雨の中立ってりゃ疲れるでしょー
十時間!?
つか、侑子(ユーコ)さんどうしてここに!?

RESERVoir CHRoNiCLE

TSUBASA

BY CLAMP

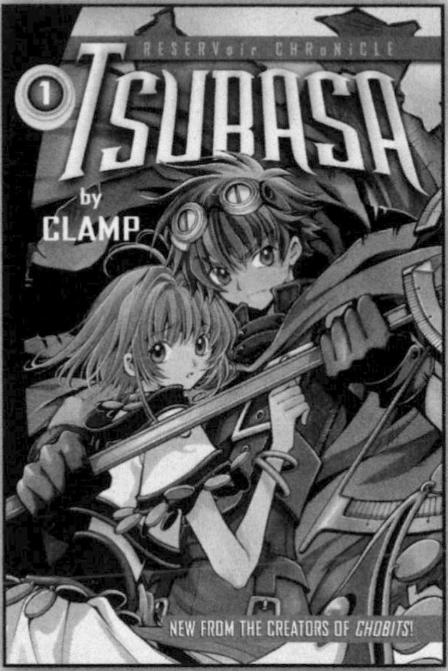
RESERVoir CHRoNiCLE
1
TSUBASA
by
CLAMP
NEW FROM THE CREATORS OF CHOBITS!

Sakura is the princess of Clow. Syaoran is her childhood friend, and leader of the archaeological dig that cost him his father. Fans of Cardcaptor Sakura will recognize the names and the faces, but these aren't the people you know. This is an alternate reality where everything is familiar and strange at the same time.

Sakura has a mysterious power, a power that no one understands, a power that can change the world. On the day she goes to the dig to declare her love for Syaoran, a mysterious symbol is uncovered that will have vast repercussions for Sakura and Syaoran. It marks the beginning of a quest that will take Syaoran and his friends through worlds that will be familiar to any CLAMP fan, as our heroes encounter places and characters from X, Chobits, Magic Knight Rayearth, xxxHOLiC, and many more! But all that matters to Syaoran is his goal: saving Sakura.

Ages: 13+

Special extras in each volume! Read them all!

DEL REY

VISIT WWW.DELREYMANGA.COM TO:
- View release date calendars for upcoming volumes
- Sign up for Del Rey's free manga e-newsletter
- Find out the latest about new Del Rey Manga series

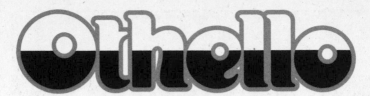

BY SATOMI IKEZAWA

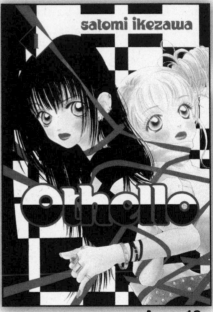

Yaya Higuchi has a rough life. Constantly teased and tormented by her classmates, she takes her solace in dressing up as a member of her favorite rock band, Juliet, on the weekends. Things begin to look up for Yaya when a cute classmate befriends her. Her devotion to Juliet, however, eventually just brings her more of the teasing and harassment she gets at school. Unable to cope, Yaya . . . changes. Suddenly, Yaya is gone—and in the blink of an eye, a new personality emerges. She is now Nana and she is tough, confident, and in charge. Nana can do things that Yaya could never do—like beating up the boys and taking care of all of Yaya's problems. How will Yaya live with this new, super-confident alternate personality? Who will be the dominant one, and who is the REAL Yaya?

Ages: 16+

Special extras in each volume! Read them all!

THE wallflower

YAMATONADESHIKO SHICHIHENGE

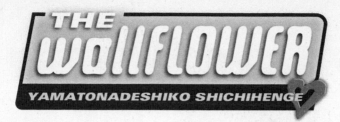

BY TOMOKO HAYAKAWA

It's a beautiful, expansive mansion, and four handsome, fifteen-year-old friends are allowed to live in it for free! But there is one condition—within three years the young men must take the owner's niece and transform her into a proper lady befitting the palace in which they all live! How hard can it be?

Enter Sunako Nakahara, the horror-movie-loving, pock-faced, frizzy-haired, fashion-illiterate hermit who has a tendency to break into explosive nosebleeds whenever she sees anyone attractive. This project is going to take far more than our four heroes ever expected; it needs a miracle!

1
THE wallflower
YAMATONADESHIKO SHICHIHENGE
TOMOKO HAYAKAWA

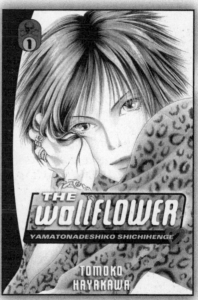

Ages: 16+

Special extras in each volume! Read them all!

DEL REY

VISIT WWW.DELREYMANGA.COM TO:
- View release date calendars for upcoming volumes
- Sign up for Del Rey's free manga e-newsletter
- Find out the latest about new Del Rey Manga series

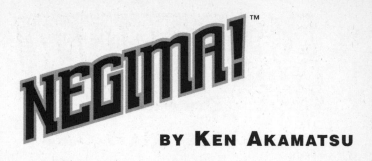

NEGIMA!™

BY KEN AKAMATSU

1
FOR MATURE AUDIENCES AGES 16+
NEGIMA!
MAGISTER NEGI MAGI
by
KEN AKAMATSU
CREATOR OF LOVE HINA!

Ages: 16+

Negi Springfield is a ten-year-old wizard teaching English at an all-girls Japanese school. He dreams of becoming a master wizard like his legendary father, the Thousand Master. At first his biggest concern was concealing his magic powers, because if he's ever caught using them publicly, he thinks he'll be turned into an ermine! But in a world that gets stranger every day, it turns out that the strangest people of all are Negi's students! From a librarian with a magic book to a centuries-old vampire, from a robot to a ninja, Negi will risk his own life to protect the girls in his care!

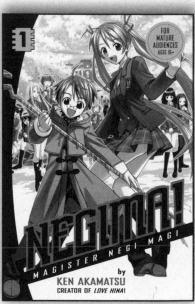

Special extras in each volume! Read them all!

DEL REY

VISIT WWW.DELREYMANGA.COM TO:
- **View release date calendars for upcoming volumes**
- **Sign up for Del Rey's free manga e-newsletter**
- **Find out the latest about new Del Rey Manga series**

Finished already?
Try these titles from
Del Rey!

THE SWORD OF SHANNARA
by Terry Brooks
A young boy who is the last of his bloodline is the only one
who can wield the mystical Sword of Shannara!

DRAGONFLIGHT
by Anne McCaffrey
On the planet called Pern, the magnificent flying dragons
and their human riders are the only protection from the
deadly rain called Thread. . . .

BLACK HORSES FOR THE KING
by Anne McCaffrey
Where did King Arthur get warhorses large enough to carry
his heavily armored knights? A fascinating and fast-moving
historical novel.

SECRET OF THE UNICORN QUEEN
by Josepha Sherman and Gwen Hansen
Sheila McCarthy accidentally falls through a portal into
another world—and finds herself part of a band of warrior-
women! Two complete novels in one book!

Published by Del Rey
www.delreybooks.com
Available wherever books are sold

More Del Rey titles
you will enjoy.

PAWN OF PROPHECY
by David Eddings
The Talisman keeping an evil god at bay has been
disturbed—and no one will be safe unless young Garion can
master the magic hidden within him.

TUNNEL IN THE SKY
by Robert A. Heinlein
For Rod Walker and his high school classmates, a simple test
has turned into a life-or-death nightmare.

HAVE SPACE SUIT—WILL TRAVEL
by Robert A. Heinlein
High school student Kip was willing to give up a lot to get
to the moon—but he never expected it to be his life!

ORPHAN STAR
by Alan Dean Foster
One man in the Universe holds the key to the mystery of
Flinx's past—and that man is trying to kill him!

Published by Del Rey
www.delreybooks.com
Available wherever books are sold

TOMARE!

[STOP!]

You're going the wrong way!

Manga is a completely different type of reading experience.

To start at the *beginning*,
go to the *end*!

That's right! Authentic manga is read the traditional Japanese way—from right to left. Exactly the *opposite* of how American books are read. It's easy to follow: Just go to the other end of the book, and read each page—and each panel—from right side to left side, starting at the top right. Now you're experiencing manga as it was meant to be!